Someday Rich

Published by John Wiley & Sons, Inc., Hoboken, New Jersey.
Published simultaneously in Canada.

For general information on our other products and services or for technical support, please contact our Customer Care Department within the United States at (800) 762-2974, outside the United States at (317) 572-3993 or fax (317) 572-4002.

Wiley also publishes its books in a variety of electronic formats. Some content that appears in print may not be available in electronic books. For more information about Wiley products, visit our website at www.wiley.com.

Library of Congress Cataloging-in-Publication Data:

Noonan, Timothy, 1963-
Someday rich: planning for sustainable tomorrows today / Timothy Noonan, Matt Smith.
    p. cm.—(Wiley Finance series)
  Includes index.
  ISBN 978-0-470-92000-8 (cloth); ISBN 978-1-118-16749-6 (ebk);
ISBN 978-1-118-16751-9 (ebk); ISBN 978-1-118-16752-6 (ebk)
1. Finance, Personal—United States.   2. Financial security—United States.   3. Financial planners—United States.   4. Portfolio management—United States.   5. Financial services industry—United States.   I. Smith, Matthew X., 1961-   II. Title.
  HG179.N57 2011
  332.02400973—dc23

2011029930

Printed in the United States of America.

10 9 8 7 6 5 4 3 2

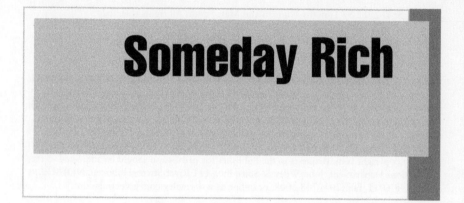

Someday Rich

Planning for Sustainable
Tomorrows Today

TIMOTHY NOONAN
MATT SMITH

WILEY

John Wiley & Sons, Inc.

For the remarkable Madeline and Genevieve Noonan,
the full realization of their potential in the world
is the object of my labor.
—Tim

To my parents Paul and Nancy Smith,
whose love and support made it possible
for me to follow my own path.
—Matt

Contents

Foreword

I would love to have written this book. But I wouldn't have done half as good a job.

The two authors are veterans, with many decades in the business of individual financial planning and helping wealth advisors in two ways: how to do more sensible things for their clients and how to run an efficient practice. And their experience shows, in the wisdom that this book contains.

It is written ostensibly for the advisor, but for many reasons it is of great appeal to me, the client.

If you are an advisor, they show you what are the characteristics of a successful practice, including how to get the market to find you. (Now there's unusual thinking—but it's how the market works. People are always asking, "How do I find a great advisor?") They tell you what makes advice valued by clients, and how to build a roadmap that systematically gets everything discussed and done. They have lots of examples and input from teachers and from successful advisors. They even include education in stand-alone chapters by other experts at the end, going into further detail. (And I'm delighted to find some of my own early, exploratory writing on longevity risk, the uncertainty about how long we'll live—how nice!)

All of that is far beyond my own experience. So I come at this from a different perspective. I'm not an advisor, I'm a client. Of course I want my advisor to be successful; the relationship won't last otherwise. But what that takes, I don't know. The authors do, and that's a big part of this book.

For my part, I start with some questions.

Am I rich? (I use "I" to mean my wife and me together: we're an indivisible unit.) I like the authors' definition of rich—it's not an absolute number, it just means that I'll have something to leave after I'm gone. If so, my assets will support my lifestyle for as long as I live. And that will be a huge relief to me, and a wonderful achievement. The whole book is based on that as its fundamental premise. Good!

The focal point of the authors' assessment of richness is based on a measure that technicians have long used in defined benefit pension plans: the funded status. First, calculate how much money, how large an asset base, it will take to support the client's lifestyle. (They show you how.)

What proportion of that amount do the client's actual assets represent? That's the funded status. Above 100 percent is rich, below 100 percent requires action. Well, above 100 percent also requires action, but there's a clear psychological dividing line between striving for security that you don't yet have, and buttressing security that already exists.

What's my role in all of this, as the client? I need to understand myself: my lifestyle, my goals, my psychological make-up, my decision-making quirks, how I am likely to react to good times and bad. I don't need to know as much as the advisor. I don't need to be able to create the advice myself; I do need to know enough to assess the advice I'm given, and challenge it. And then, when we agree on a plan and its implementation, I have to share responsibility for its acceptance. This is a partnership.

There's homework to be done. This book gives me the education and the tools, including fascinating insights into different human temperaments. I don't just want a good advisor; I also want to be a good client. As far as the relationship is concerned, I'm glad to find that my needs and goals are the focal point of the advisor's advice and actions. I don't want a conflict of interests. All of that becomes clear.

OK, now I'm ready. Talk to me, discuss with me, plan with me, advise me, implement my plan, monitor progress with me. As Dr. Frasier Crane used to say, "I'm listening."

DON EZRA
November 2011

Preface

The title of this book is *Someday Rich* because this is a book *about people* who are rich or who are becoming rich. It is written *for advisors* who serve them, and yet, as the central thesis of the book will detail, there is no good giving of advice without skillful receiving of it.

There is a tension with how-to books. Some are so technical that readers disengage. Others try to engage the reader through story telling or analogy, which runs the risk of not having enough practical advice so the reader has any chance of reaching a materially better outcome.

We want to strike the golden balance between those two approaches; to have enough engagement to allow the advisor to be a more effective conversation partner with his or her client, but also to have enough engineering to be able to link that conversation with real knowledge about the probability of success or failure.

If you want to read about engineering approaches to superior income distribution techniques there are better places to go for that information. We are not writing this book to push forward our own engineering progression of portfolio construction or asset allocation, although we appreciate the advances being made (indeed we are making some meaningful advances of our own) and support any efforts to make them more accessible. Nor are we pretending to be behavioral finance experts, although we acknowledge that without the psychological cooperation of the client there isn't sufficient engagement and receptiveness for them to do things differently than in the past. What this book is about is improving the conversation between an advisor and a client. To do this we must define two key terms at the outset: what is rich and what is financial security.

Rich means having more resources than you can consume in your lifetime. Once you have to think about who gets what's left over when you're gone you are someone we consider being rich. This book is written for advisors with clients who have the opportunity to be rich or who are already rich, and are preoccupied with remaining so. Why? Because that is the market of most interest to financial advisors.

Financial security means the ability to stay rich, a perpetual condition in which you can forecast having more than you can consume in a lifetime.

Many individuals see financial security through the lens of scarcity. For many clients, the only thing worse than not being rich is to have been rich once and to no longer be so. This is what engages the individual in a conversation about enjoying a sustainable lifestyle. The advisor who frames client conversations in terms of creating and sustaining a desired lifestyle will be more successful.

In this book we describe a strategy for sustaining financial security. It requires that you know how much your client needs to spend to support their desired lifestyle and whether their assets can be made to work hard enough to fund that lifestyle. Knowing these two amounts allows you also to know if they have more wealth than they need to annuitize. If they do, in most scenarios they are better off deferring annuitization as long as possible.

Financial security is the ability to always have enough assets to annuitize to meet essential needs. What an individual is doing when he entrusts his nest egg to an advisor is giving the advisor the responsibility to tell him if he can continue to maintain control over the retirement nest egg, that is, to avoid annuitization. The reason he desires to continue to avoid annuitization is to preserve options to do better with his assets. Once he buys the annuity he loses control and flexibility, he fixes the amount he will have to spend in the future, and subjects himself to greater fees in order to obtain the guarantee. In a way it's game over, and **no one wants the game to be over.**

This book is written at a time when mistrust of financial institutions and suspicion of financial advice is at an apex. However, one of the authors, Tim Noonan, began researching the subject of this book in the middle of July 2008, just two months before the great market collapse. He explains . . .

I was developing an interest in a framework to understand plans; the architecture of successful planning processes. A part of my thesis was that modern approaches—especially computer driven approaches to financial planning—were disastrously incomplete frameworks, bound to lead millions of investors and their advisors to destitution. In my lighter moments, I just considered them incomplete.

The longer I have been in the corporate world, the fewer original ideas I have. Even so, a habit I have developed over the past 20 years when I think that I have an important idea is to call my college classics professor, H. D. Cameron, a legendary Western Civilization professor at the University of Michigan. He still calls me "dear boy" despite my having just turned 45. I'm okay with that so long as he continues to take my calls,

"Help me qualify an idea," I began. I could visualize him sitting into his favorite leather lounger, stroking his goatee, perhaps wondering if he had time to quietly mix a martini before I arrived at the heart of the matter.

"I'm interested in the history of plans, the architecture of planning, and the evolution of planning strategy. How do plans get better in the sense that planners incorporate simultaneously more realism while incorporating more uncertainty, more scenarios, which, in the moment, seem bizarre and remote?"

There was silence on the other end of the line. This was of course his technique. He would let me spin, straining from the diameter of my orbit around a constellation of ideas before reorienting me on one key point.

And then he did it. He said the simple thing that confirmed that I had to write this book:

You're wasting your time looking forward. All you need to know about this can be learned by looking back. Way back. Planning may have become more complex as it would through modern times, as in the technology we have to measure time. Modern contributions, especially from the field of mathematics and probability, game theory, behavioral finance, and new quantum mechanics, provide a progression of refinements. But they do not alter the structure. The sun still rises and sets once every 24 hours. The greatest and most unresolved challenge of planning is found within the story of the first recorded plan in Western literature."

I was hooked. It was now me searching for the martini shaker—where are those olives?—listening through the phone so intensely I was afraid I would bump foreheads with my brilliant old classics teacher who once again patiently watched my crazy orbiting around 10 different ideas, only to order me back for splashdown in the cradle of civilization.

"The first recorded plan in Western literature is found in Homer's *Iliad*. It's Zeus's plan for the victory over the Greeks at Troy." The most important aspect of this plan is that it fails, if not in general outcome, certainly in its explicit strategy. To fully absorb the importance of this point, you must know that Zeus was not just any god; he was the head god, the boss-god, if you will, of all the other gods, each of whom was immensely powerful in his or her own right. Of importance is not simply the lesson that even a boss-god cannot predestine his will but rather the reason Zeus's plan failed. **It failed to foresee the competing plans of his god competitors, and, in doing so, he underestimated the challenges to his plan.**

The story about Zeus's failed plan is the great warning about planning. It connects a number of ideas that most people today know. The most obvious is the idea of uncertainty. Events will happen that are difficult or impossible to predict. As Yogi Berra said, "It's tough to make predictions, especially about the future." People know this but it doesn't mean that trying to understand and make plans for the future is a folly. We need to do that in order to organize our resources and priorities. However, at the same time we need to be mindful of the fact that those plans are imperfect and need constant surveillance, which is the second idea.

A plan is no good without vigilance attached to it. That's the reason advisors are paid ongoing fees. The fees pay for vigilance. What are they supposed to be vigilant about? First, whether their client continue to be financially secure (can they still be rich) and second, making sure their clients' resources work as smart as they can to preserve their options to secure financial security into the future. Clients are paying the advisors to help them create and maintain surpluses such that they have more than enough assets to buy annuities to meet their basic needs. As the surpluses grow, so do their feelings of affluence and security. Their options expand, and in the process so, too, expands their ability to cope with difficult-to-forecast scenarios.

The third idea is what can go wrong. Individuals who do not understand the plans and the carelessness of people around them have a problem. They must consider the plans of other people in their family, those who depend on them or who they depend on. It is important that their plans are accessible and are disclosed to the people around them so expectations can be created. Then there are the plans of those in government. The government's plan, or its ability to keep in place a previously promised plan such as entitlements, may affect the individual's future purchasing power. This has potential for huge impact on your clients' financial security because, for a significant part of the population, a large percentage of their future purchasing power is derived from Social Security and Medicare. The less affluent they are, the more concerned they should be about how those plans might change as they and their boomer peers live longer and longer in retirement.

This is the central conundrum of individual investors today: to be able to effectively plan in an uncertain world, to have the vigilance to adjust their plans when needed, and to have the awareness of how others' plans might affect their own. The advisors' reason for being in business is to help clients solve this conundrum.

Acknowledgments

Writing this book was truly a team effort. We were fortunate and even a bit amazed by how generous people were with their time and effort to help us make this book a reality. There are many more people who helped than we will name here (many of whom will join the team even after this is written). To all who supported us great or small with this project, thank you.

We have spent a good portion of our careers at Russell Investments. The mission espoused by George and Jane Russell, "to improve financial security for people" has served as our true north over the years: guiding us and influencing our work. We want to acknowledge Andrew Doman, Sandy Cavanaugh, and all the Russell associates who encouraged and supported this project.

The input and feedback from advisors who've dedicated their professional lives to helping individuals achieve and maintain financial security was invaluable to us during this project. We conducted many interviews with advisors, some of whom we are not allowed to thank by name. Those we can name include; Dan Baker, Bob Bishopp, Charlene Carter, Craig Cross, Ilene Davis, Russ Hill, Peter Rekstad, Marlene Shalton, Andrea Shenocca, Syd Walker, Jim Warren, Tom Weilert. Thank you all for your generosity of time and insight.

Much of the content for this book was influenced by the expert insights of our contributors including; Albert Bandura (Stanford University), Dr. Laura Carstensen (Stanford University), Don Ezra, Yuan-An Fan, Richard Fullmer, Grant Gardner, Randy Lert, Steve Moore, Sam Pittman, Meir Statman (Santa Clara University). We would like to thank these contributors for allowing us to incorporate their ideas and writings into this book.

While not a direct contributor to this project, we want to acknowledge the influence of Moshe Milevsky's work on this book. We think of Moshe as one of the foundational sources of progressive thinking in the area of retirement income and security. There are many common roots between his work and the concepts we discuss here.

Besides being a dear friend, Steve Moore taught us a great deal about working with financial advisors and how to help advisors build more valuable practices. Steve taught us that all the portfolio construction insight in the world is useless without an engaged client. And, that real client engagement is the key to establishing advisor/client trust.

Don Ezra was an original partner in this project and his influence can be found throughout this final version. This book would not have been completed without Don's input and encouragement. Don's brilliance extends beyond investments and actuarial science. He is a teacher, making concepts real by using his own life as an example in his speeches and writings. That is a rare kind of generosity and we thank Don for his tutelage over the decades we've known him.

Sam Pittman's work is core to the central theme of this book. Sam was able to accomplish one of the most difficult tasks we face in our profession, taking complex concepts and demonstrating their usefulness in the form of practical examples. Thank you Sam for playing such a key role in this project.

Randy Lert provided key insights and original thinking related to the Personal Asset Liability Model. Like Sam, Randy went beyond the conceptual by helping us articulate how the model can be practically applied to investor scenarios. Like many of the other contributors to this book, Randy's contributions came at the expense of his personal time. Thanks, Randy.

In our search for more effective ways to work with financial advisors and end investors, two firms, Mathew Greenwald & Associates, Inc. and maslansky luntz + partners, conducted research for Russell Investments that was especially helpful to us. We would like to thank the respective principals of these firms Matt Greenwald and Michael Maslansky for their work. A summary of their research is provided in the appendices of this book.

We want to thank Dallas Salisbury and the staff at the Employee Benefit Research Institute for providing us with research data and review comments. Dallas in particular gave us very thorough and thoughtful review comments that we very much appreciate.

We also want to thank the folks at John Wiley & Sons, especially Bill Falloon, for supporting this project and being patient with us throughout. In addition, Jen MacDonald, our development editor at Wiley, was very helpful during the writing of the manuscript. Jen's encouragement and guidance got us through the tougher moments.

Finally, the authors want to acknowledge each other, for the energy and delight they brought to each other in this project, which stands as a great reminder that you "get by with a little help from your friends."

Someday Rich

Introduction

The audience for this book is financial advisors who want to build more valuable relationships with their clients. If you are one of them, welcome. Thank you for taking time to read what we have to say.

Valuable should have a common definition for you and your client. For your client it should mean that, by working with you, they have a clearer vision of the lifestyle they want to live and of the plan for sustaining that lifestyle. For you it should mean that you are more effective at helping your clients clarify their vision, build a plan to achieve it, and manage that plan so your clients stay on track.

Combined, we have over five decades of experience working in the financial services industry. We have worked together for most of the past decade, long enough to ride the markets up and down together (a couple of times). Our experience spans many vectors: from individuals to institutions, advisors to advisor networks and platforms, United States to international, and products to processes. We have given speeches, written articles and books, and been interviewed by the media countless times. The one thing all our experience has in common is that, in some way, it has involved helping people achieve financial security. Our goal in writing this book is to bring to bear our experience in that pursuit.

This book marks a place in time in our development of helping advisors build more valuable practices. We are sure the ideas and processes we talk about in this book will continue to evolve and improve over time. We encourage you to take what you can from this book to improve your practice. Use the processes and information we provide where they make the most sense for you and your clients. It would be cliché for us to say, "If you get one good idea from this book or we help you improve the outcome of a single client, then it is worth your time reading this book." We don't believe that. One idea is not enough; neither is improving the outcome for a single client. Our goal is to start you on a path that leads to revolutionizing the way you provide advise to clients. If you are already on that path we hope this book furthers your progress.

Much of the content in this book is focused on helping advisors manage their client's wealth in a way that gives them a higher probability of living the lifestyle they desire in the future. This advice is most relevant for individuals who are close to having enough wealth (maybe a bit more, maybe a bit less) to sustain their desired lifestyle, so this is where we spend much of our time. This does not mean we believe the only value an advisor can bring to their client is managing their portfolio or that these are the only clients that need an advisor. Wealth management is about more than ensuring your client has enough money to pay their bills. As our friend Steve Moore said, "People are designed to have an impact on the world. The advisor's role is to maximize their client's impact on the world during and after their life."

We were fortunate to have many talented contributors to this book. There are clearly marked sections in this book that were written by contributors (authors other than Tim and Matt). In those sections, our comments are set apart in a different font to distinguish them from the contributors' text.

HOW THE BOOK IS ORGANIZED

The first nine chapters provide the context, description, and implementation suggestions for the personal asset liability model. As we explain in Chapter 4, the concepts that form the foundation of the personal asset liability model are derived from research papers written by our colleagues. We provide these pieces of research at the back of the book as chapters for those who wish to take a deeper look at the details. Therefore, Chapters 10–14 are single-topic essays that can be read as stand-alone pieces.

Many pieces contributed to this book were written by different authors at different times. In some cases the examples they use to illustrate their concepts require assumptions such as expected equity and bond returns, expected volatility, asset class correlations, yield curves, etc. Because these research pieces were written at different times the assumptions used may differ. The point of providing this research and their examples is not to suggest the appropriateness of a particular assumption value rather it is to demonstrate the methodology. Therefore, if you wish to use any of the formulas provided in this book you should reconsider the required assumption values and adjust accordingly.

Here we provide a short summary of each chapter.

Chapter 1: Time for a Real Conversation

One of the most important lessons we've learned through our careers is that the effectiveness of advice is in direct proportion to the degree of receptiveness of the recipient. The recent global financial crisis has created an opportunity for financial advisors; individuals are now more receptive than ever to having real conversations about their financial security. What will you say to them? The real conversation is not about investment returns or market volatility; it is about sustainability—the sustainability of the individual's financial security and the sustainability of the advisor/client relationship.

A small number of advisors are reshaping the wealth management industry. We've been fortunate to be associated with some of them, and we hope we've played a small part in nudging the industry toward a more effective way for advisors and individuals to work together. The model of advice we offer is adaptive to how individuals regard their future financial security, the realities of the capital markets, and advisors' practical limitations in providing advice.

This model of advice is most effective when provided to individuals with enough wealth (or the ability to accumulate enough wealth) to have a real chance of funding their desired lifestyle, and who have the willingness to engage with an advisor in a meaningful way. These individuals are more likely to consolidate their wealth with one advisor. The surviving advisor of the future will be the one who is able to help their clients answer three key questions: How much income do I need to fund my desired lifestyle? Will my money last as long as I do? Am I doing everything I can to ensure my financial security? The methods we describe in this book help advisors answer those questions in a masterful way with the potential for meaningful follow-through from their clients.

The foundation of this advice model is in measuring success differently than in the past. The single most important metric we want to focus advisors on is the clients' funded status, that is, whether they have enough wealth to fund their future liabilities. Matching assets to liabilities is a lesson we've learned from consulting for some of the largest pensions in the world. The model is based on a process, not on a magical product. Products obviously have their place in implementing an individual's financial plan, but they should be a means to a destination not the destination.

Chapter 2: How We Got Here

Both advisors and their clients are preoccupied with the question, "How many of my assumptions about financial security are no longer solid?" That question takes many forms, from the most basic—"Should I regard my primary residence as a device to build up wealth, after all, the government incents me to do so through mortgage interest credits?"—to more subtle questions about asset allocation and optimization.

The global financial crisis accelerated the obsolescence of many assumptions: More people are retiring at the same time and they have little savings, longevity is increasing, health-care costs are rising faster than inflation and concentrating at the end of life when people can least afford it, savings rates are at historic lows, people are working fewer hours in their lifetime, Social Security is at risk of insolvency, fewer people are covered by an employer-provided pension, and capital markets continue to be volatile.

These conditions are leading to increased concerns about financial scarcity (or at the very least the possibility of increased scarcity). More people have barely enough to sustain their financial security. It's this scarcity that requires the prudent advisor to be more precise in their planning processes and more attentive to their clients. Precision is required because the margin for error has become smaller; for many individuals the difference between achieving sustainable financial security or not is the precision of their financial plan. Attentiveness is required because each individual's desired lifestyle is unique, and individuals now expect personalization in all aspects of their lives. **Precision and attentiveness are now the joint standards of quality advice.**

Chapter 3: The Right Clients

There is a wide distribution of wealth among individuals, more than ever before. When creating a plan for sustainable financial security, those with more wealth have more options. However, absolute wealth is not the only factor that must be considered when evaluating an individual's options. An individual's wealth *relative to his desired lifestyle* defines his alternatives. Using this perspective, we categorize individuals into one of three conditions: Those who have more wealth than they need, those who have just enough (or close to enough), and those who do not have enough to meet their future needs.

Today, advisors commonly segment clients by asset size; by itself this is often an incomplete heuristic for the desirability of a client. Asset size does not, in our experience, correlate directly to profitability of the client relationship *or* solvability of the client's goals. This must shift: We encourage advisors to segment clients according to their clients' potential to reach their goals. In order to be effective in the client's eyes, advisors need to be skillful at three different conversations based on their client's condition. For individuals who have more than enough wealth, the conversation is about maintaining surplus wealth. For those who clearly do not have enough to meet their future needs, the conversation is not just about investments but also about behavior modification and adjusting expectations (saving more before retirement, working longer, and reducing spending expectations in retirement). It's for everyone else—the group in the middle—for whom the conversation may have the most meaningful impact. These individuals (by definition) have enough that, *if they make the right decisions,* they will be able to sustain their desired lifestyle in the future, but they do not have so much wealth that just any plan will work.

Our model for advice, the personal asset liability model described in Chapters 5 and 6, is both a means for uncovering which conversation you should have with your client and a process for creating a plan that matches their situation.

Chapter 4: Connecting the Dots

There has been a progression of people, events, and ideas that influenced the personal asset liability model we describe in the Chapters 5 and 6. The ideas that inform the model come from the diverse disciplines of investments, actuarial science, financial planning, communications, psychology, and linguistics. Our job has been to pluck promising ideas from each of these perspectives, as they apply to helping individuals create sustainable financial security, and connect them in an advice model that is both practical and effective.

Chapters 5 and 6: Personal Asset Liability Model

In Chapter 1 we talk about the three key questions that individuals must answer: How much income do I need to fund my desired lifestyle? Will my money last as long as I will? Am I doing everything I can to allocate my assets to improve my chances for sustainable financial security?

There is, in fact, a way to answer these questions, and the methods for doing so have been around for a long time (matching assets to liabilities). What we propose as new is twofold. First, that these three questions will become the central focus of the financial-planning process (replacing other questions such as, "Did my portfolio beat its benchmark last quarter?"). Second, that the idea of matching assets to liabilities for individuals will become the new convention for advisors and individuals to answer these fundamental financial security questions.

For a vast majority of advisors, the methods in the personal asset liability model have not been accessible in a practical way to use with a large number of clients. Our framework not only brings together the technical methods to answer these questions in a way that is feasible, but also includes the communication and language strategies that we hope can make the delivery of the advice model effective and engaging. The framework also includes a way to keep the client's focus on the single most important metric—their funded status—through the use of goals-based reporting.

Our research shows that many advisors and investors intuitively accept that the strategies that work for accumulating wealth may not be ideal when it comes to decumulation. This chapter provides a context for advisors in setting asset allocation for their clients to better solve their retirement income problem. The framework translates client preferences and constraints into portfolio-construction guidelines, and offers guidance for assessing appropriate investment strategies (which may include both investments and annuities).

Chapter 7: Making a Good Business of Giving Good Advice

Good advice is inseparable from the trustworthiness of the organization from which the advice originates. Building a quality advisory practice requires a unity of vision among the leaders of the practice, mastery of regional economy, efficient use of resources, and a passion for measuring the right business metrics. It also requires quality control of the advice including suitability, the ability to implement, and a systematic attentiveness to clients. External factors can also help or hurt the practice including economic climate, regional conditions, and the technical expertise of the team members in the advisory practice. All these factors are discussed in Chapter 7. Our motive is to share with you not simply a technical vision, but our experience about what is required for that technical vision to translate into increasing the enterprise value of your advisory practice.

Finally, the successful advisor must be able to deliver quality advice in both a personalized and scalable way. The Client Engagement Roadmap is a business process advisors can use to coordinate and harmonize all the tasks associated with the personal asset liability model and delivering wealth management to their clients. We adapt this model so its central focus is the surveillance of your client's funded status.

Chapter 8: Investor Archetypes

Technology developments have brought us to a point where consumers expect high levels of personalization in most aspects of their lives. Each individual has a vivid and unique image of what constitutes financial well-being. That has always been true, but in most cases it has not been either practical or necessary for the advisor to deal with that individual image in the way it is now. The financial crisis has increased the degree to which individuals withhold their trust until they feel they're being treated in a personalized way, until they feel seen. These realities leave you with a difficult challenge. How do you develop client trust and deliver personalized service when you have so many clients?

One way is to adapt your communication using your client's personality temperament as a guide. We describe a method developed by Professor Meir Statman of Santa Clara University for achieving personalized communication in a time efficient manner. This method saves time and is research based. The method uses psychological profiles to help you adapt your communication. Underneath these profiles is real information about how different personality temperaments process decisions.

Chapter 9: Tripping Over the Finish Line

All the good work of planning for financial security can come undone by financial accidents. The core of this book addresses the major risks in retirement such as savings, spending, investment, and longevity. However, there are other contingency risks that need to be considered. Chapter 9 discusses the challenges facing the Social Security system and the potential impact of possible changes to the system on your client's financial security. Also discussed are life, health, disability, and long-term care risks; each of which can be insured. Finally we talk about age-related cognitive decline, its prevalence, the forms it takes, the warning signs, and how to manage the risk it poses to your client's decision making and, by extension, their financial security.

Chapter 10

Albert Bandura is the David Starr Jordan Professor of Social Science in Psychology at Stanford University and past president of the American Psychological Association. He is a world-renowned expert on self-efficacy; the belief in one's capabilities to organize and execute the actions required to produce desired results. Professor Bandura gave a speech to a group of our advisor clients during the peak of the financial crisis in 2008. His talk was so inspiring, and relative to the challenges advisors face, that we wanted to share it with you in its entirety.

The development of self-efficacy (confidence) is critical to the success of your advisory practice as well as the success of your client's financial plans. We believe that excellent advisors are made, not born, and that **learning to give excellent advice is an acquirable skill.** The self-efficacy you cultivate for the skill to give excellent advice is vital to your success as an advisor.

Chapter 11

In August 2006, Grant W. Gardner, PhD and Yuan-An Fan, PhD authored a white paper on the design of target-date funds. We've provided in this chapter the entire text of that paper. Grant and Yuan-An's framework relates to the challenge of managing your client's financial security by establishing two foundational ideas that are reflected in the personal asset liability model. First, it incorporates human capital into the asset allocation decisions for individuals accumulating wealth for retirement. Second, it uses for its definition of success a wealth target sufficient for the individual at retirement to purchase an annuity equal to their targeted replacement income. They create rules for an intelligent evaluation for individuals to balance the value of their human capital with a basket of financial assets throughout the course of their career.

Chapter 12

In this chapter, Don Ezra discusses the "Investment Aspects of Longevity Risk." According to Don,

> After retirement, wealth is no longer the yardstick (for success). Rather, income becomes the yardstick. The trade-off is now between higher expected income and higher uncertainty of income. But in retirement, unlike in pre-retirement, it is no longer acceptable to have an approximate time horizon for planning. The time horizon extends until one's death–and that is unpredictable.

Don evaluates the danger to individuals when they lose their ability to pool their longevity risk by no longer being a member of a pension plan. The individual's inability to pool their longevity risk is a key foundation of the personal asset liability model. It's our starting position to apply our knowledge and expertise from working with institutions to conceive of a model appropriate to an individual.

Chapters 13 and 14

Both of these chapters are reprinted white papers authored by Richard Fullmer, CFA. In Chapter 13, Fullmer discusses the mismeasurement of risk in financial planning. He explains,

> Financial planning is complex. Modeling tools have proliferated as a way to help wade through the complexity and facilitate sound

decision-making processes. The selection of the risk measure in these tools is all-important. Poor decisions can result if the risk measure is faulty or incomplete.

Fullmer argues the risk that should be focused on when planning for retirement income should be the risk of income shortfall rather than volatility of portfolio return. The total risk measurement he proposes is the product of the probability of shortfall times the magnitude of shortfall.

Chapter 14 is Fullmer's paper, titled "Modern Portfolio Decumulation." It is a logical extension of his mismeasurement of risk work from Chapter 13. It "describes a new framework for efficient portfolio construction in the 'decumulation' phase of the investment lifecycle, in which an investor who has accumulated assets over time wishes to use those assets to fund ongoing living expenses. It combines elements of both investment theory and actuarial science, introducing an effective way to manage longevity risk in the portfolio." Fullmer makes the argument that the conventional standard for accumulation of wealth is not optimal for decumulation. He outlines an alternative approach for investing in the decumulation phase, developing his thinking along lines of dynamic asset allocation models.

CHAPTER 1

Time for a Real Conversation

What this book is about and the reason we are writing it now are inseparably related. This book offers financial advisors and their clients an alternative roadmap for the way they engage with each other. This alternative might not be right for all advisors or their clients; we suspect it won't. But for some it will. You might guess we are motivated to write this book now because of the financial crisis and the severity of American retirement under funding. That's partly true.

> *This book offers financial advisors and their clients an alternative*
> *roadmap for the way they engage with each other.*

The reason we are writing this book now stems from the single most valuable lesson we've learned in our combined five decades working in the asset management business, namely that the effectiveness of the advice you give is in direct proportion to the degree of receptiveness of the recipient. Most professional consultants understand that knowing how to defer giving advice until their client is indeed ready to receive it is as important as the advice itself.

In a sense, the crash of 2008 was the catalyst for this project, although not for the obvious reasons (asset losses, systemic shocks, collapse of confidence in the financial system—pick one), but rather because it created, in our opinion, this rare harmonic convergence allowing financial advisors and their clients the mutual recognition that it was time to do things differently. Our research indicates (in hopeful ways) that advisors and their clients are at least momentarily interested in a new and different framework for wealth management.

Another outcome of the global financial meltdown was its trivialization of the differences between segments of financial advisors. Whatever the points of differentiation prior to the meltdown, they faded in importance because client needs became nearly homogenous. There is a single overwhelming client concern that advisors today must be prepared to address: Will their clients be able to fund their desired lifestyles for as long as they live? Many people believe that the only thing worse than being broke is going broke. Individuals want to have real conversations with their advisors about how they can sustain their desired lifestyle for as long as they might live.

At the heart of this concern about sustainable financial security are three questions. First, "How much is enough?" The individual must first have a no-nonsense estimate of how much money they will spend each year in order to live the lifestyle they desire. Second, "Will my money last?" Knowing what they will spend and how much they have (or will have) saved, they need to know which they will run out of first, time or money. Third, "What can I do?" They need to know what they can to do to sustain their lifestyle; whether it's to save more, spend less, work longer, or invest differently, they want to know what they can do to improve their outlook on success.

This is what we mean by real conversations. Real conversations involve tough questions; the client staring at you from across the table expects answers. The good news is that there is a way to answer these questions. We call the framework for answering these questions the personal asset liability model, although we don't expect (and, indeed, discourage) you to describe it in this way to your clients, for reasons we enumerate in this book. The model is built around what we believe is the single most important metric individuals (and their advisors) should focus on: their funded status, the likelihood that the lifestyle they envision is possible. The funded status (a concept used for decades in institutional pensions) tells the individual if they have enough money to fund their desired level of spending. The model is explained briefly at the end of this chapter and covered in detail in Chapters 5 and 6.

THE GREAT EQUALIZER

Leading up to 2008, having experienced the greatest bull market in the history of modern capitalism, the financial services industry became an increasingly significant portion of the global economy. This had a couple of mixed effects: it created a broad democratization of investing whereby individuals gained unprecedented access to the capital markets, and it led to a cycle of product development and financial innovation, giving individuals a blinding number of choices about how they might participate in investing, banking, and insurance products. Advisors came to be seen as guides into that world of exciting capital markets and product complexity. In the face of that, advisors began to specialize; to develop patterns of advice that were consistent with their views (and the views they perceived to be their clients'). This led to the way the financial services industry talks about the segmentation of advisors, in terms of specialization.

If someone were to talk about segments of financial advisors 30 years ago nobody would know what they were talking about, but today it seems very natural that there are segments of advisors. The initial way that the advisors were segmented was according to their institutional affiliation: brokers, bankers, insurance, and so forth. Then along came the independents, and they confounded the definition of specialization because they could be any or all of those.

The next step in the segmentation progression occurred when advisors were seen to be either investment advisors or money managers. The investment advisors made up the larger segment. Their specialty was finding the highest returns for their clients. They were the putative experts on markets and products, and their objective was to find the most exciting capital markets products (namely returns) for the clients. The money managers made up the smaller segment. They were essentially no different than institutional money managers except that they had private clients.

Finally, the category of wealth manager emerged. What made the wealth managers different was that they were willing to accept a broader definition of success for their client. They did not focus on just returns but whatever their client's total objective or outcome was that they wished to achieve. They took a comprehensive approach to managing their clients' financial needs by understanding their clients' entire financial ecosystems. The clients' portfolios were one of many things that they cared about. The portfolios were often the central vehicles for creating satisfaction for the clients yet, other times, their satisfaction related to financial planning, budgeting, taxes, estate planning, and so forth. The point here is that the clients' abilities to achieve their overall financial visions superseded the portfolios themselves in order of importance.

The chief difference between the first two segments, investment advisors and money managers, and wealth managers was that, in the first two segments, the object of the advisors' focus was on the returns the capital markets produced by way of the specialty of the advisors' affiliated firms. The wealth managers, in order to be true to their claim of this more holistic advocacy for their clients, needed to focus primarily on the client-facing activities, such as fact finding, estate planning, and so on. This caused them to outsource many aspects of the investment function so they would have time necessary for these client-facing activities.

Those different types of advisors operating in those different platforms—brokerage firms, banks, insurance, independents—they were all attempting to address different versions of investment success that they perceived their clients wanted, and they were correct in doing so. The crash of 2008 in a way acted as an equalizer, unifying large numbers of people around a similar concern about their financial security. The calamity of the financial crash and the consequences were so severe that it made all of those previous distinctions trivial. What emerged as a unifying characteristic of all of the investors, regardless of what kind of advisors they were using, was the question of sustainability: "Will I have enough?"

Now, after that crash, it is predictable that investment advisors, money managers, and wealth managers will all find their own answers to this question of sustainability. They will all do that in a way that's consistent with their experiences and their focuses. The advisors we are trying to cultivate are those who believe holistic planning is the future for them, and is the basis on which they intend to build their client relationships, not those depending on either the ingenuity of the financial services industry to create exciting new products or the beneficence of the capital markets to produce huge returns. Rather, they spend time with clients and dig into the question of what type of sustainability might be possible for them and having sober discussions of what trade-offs that might involve. Finally, once they understand what kind of financial security is sustainable for their clients, they make their assets work as intelligently as possible in support of that goal.

IN SEARCH OF A REAL CONVERSATION

Before 2008, most people were focused on accumulation in which family wealth was assumed to rise based on rising values of primary residences and investment returns on assets. Many financial advisors built their practices consistent with this thought. Because their services were largely about producing superior market returns rather than the impact of those returns on personalized plans, clients had difficulty differentiating one advisor from another. As a consequence, clients often rotated from one advisor to the other, in serial monogamy, or they employed several. Indeed, today over half of affluent Americans (defined as those with over $2 million of investable assets) report working with two or more financial advisors.[1] Over half of ultra-high-net-worth individuals (those with over $10 million of investable assets) report working with five or more advisors.[2]

One way to look at the advice we are offering in this book is that we are trying to help advisors become their clients' surviving advisor, the one to which the individual consolidates all their assets. The future as we see it moves to a one-advisor-per-client model. The question for you is, "How do you be that advisor?"

Things are different now. The events during and since 2008 have created deep mistrust among individuals. They don't want to return to the way they did things before the onset of the financial crisis: to financial markets that jarred them, to financial advisors whose advice they seem to think did not work, to guarantees of security that were empty, or to a system in which players' interests were (and maybe still are) conflicted. They have an accurate intuition that they should be doing something different but are unable to articulate what that different something should be.

Financial advisors are keenly aware of their clients' dissatisfactions, and they have their own anxieties. Yet some see this scenario not as a threat but as an opportunity. They know they need to retool their practices in order to absorb new information from their clients, and they need a sensible process for managing their clients' wealth based on this new information. Finally, they need a new way of communicating with their clients. Into this scenario in which the individual and the financial advisor want and need a new way to work together, this book provides a framework for that new way.

Prior to the financial meltdown, an idea took root that free-market capitalism was universally good and had only good effects. This merged, disastrously, into the argument that markets were perfectly omniscient, and, therefore, market prices could never be wrong. There were no victims or at least no victims that didn't deserve it, and there was no need to regulate markets. Indeed, it was argued, doing so would impede their efficiency. The markets were so intelligent and efficient that the self-interest of the market participants would regulate themselves. However, taking the fact that the market is truly hard to beat and concluding that that means the market is always right is a whale of an error!

Yale University economist Robert Shiller had this to say in 1984—nearly 25 years before the crash: "This argument for the efficient markets hypothesis represents one of the most remarkable errors in the history of economic thought. It is remarkable in the immediacy of its logical error and in the sweep and implication of its conclusion."* Despite the dissenting opinions, this environment not only encouraged speculation to cataclysmic levels but also obscured a more fundamental thought that the purpose of modern capital markets was to maximize the value of assets.

In the modern world, financial assets have become among the most significant forms of private property: indeed, they are what human capital is exchanged for over the course of the modern lifetime. The idea that private property needs to be stewarded rather than exploited was a sacred tenet in the formation of America. It goes back to John

Locke's idea that private property (as opposed to property held in common) should come about from the result of one's labor. And, no one should take more than that which can be combined with his own labor, lest it spoil from disuse. Locke also believed that no one should accumulate so much that it prevents others from having a share. This doesn't mean there shouldn't be winners and losers, but winning or losing should be the result of one's labor (or lack thereof) rather than randomness. If you choose not to work, your rewards should be commensurate. However, **speculation alone is not work, by itself it creates no value.**

By 2008, Locke's ideal was seemingly appropriated by a "grab as much as you can and screw everyone else" mentality. Unfortunately, or fortunately depending on how you look at it, this later mentality was a catalyst in the financial meltdown. As society reconsiders what are the appropriate levels of leverage, speculation, and regulation, it will be interesting to see if we move back toward that ideal. There are important champions wearing the white hats in the Fourth Estate; Gretchen Morgenson comes to mind. In government, Alistair Darling in the U.K. and Elizabeth Warren (President Obama's advisor to the Consumer Financial Protection Bureau) come to mind. Let us hope their points of view prevail.

*Robert J. Shiller, "Stock Prices and Social Dynamics," *Brookings Papers on Economic Activity* 1984(2), 457–510.

SUSTAINABILITY

The message of this book is profoundly simple. When a person's most precious asset was considered to be his soul, we knelt to the priests. As time progressed and a man's productivity became his badge to win bread, the physician usurped the priests. As time further progressed and people became capable of amassing more property than they could exhaust in their lifetimes, lawyers took the high priest role, as they were instrumental to the orderly transfer of property. Today financial advisors have the calling to take this place in the pantheon, but they must earn that place, as their predecessors have, by rising to the emergent dilemma. The dilemma facing financial advisors today is how to manipulate financial assets long after employment has ended in order to secure their clients' most central and emotionally vital goal: **to make their assets last longer than they do.**

The remedy to this dilemma, however, is not to be found in a miracle product. There are no magic beans to grow a stalk to the heavens. The remedy is not to be found in the likelihood that the market will produce returns so spectacular that they will cure all ills, because it may or may not. The remedy might, however, be found in a different approach for the advisor and client to work together, a different mutual recognition of their challenge. This should absorb their joint attention. That problem is how to be sure they can sustain the desired lifestyle for as long as the client lives: the achievement of sustainable financial security.

The object of this new approach for working together is not to enrich investment bankers, proprietary trading desks, and other generators of financial innovations. We need more of those products like we need a second belly button. The effect of those products all too often has been to surreptitiously shift risk from the innovator to the consumer of these exotic instruments. No, the purpose of this new approach is to put the focus where it always should have been, on sustainability—the sustainability of the client's financial security, the sustainability of the advisor's practice, and sustainability of the client/advisor relationship.

People today are universally concerned about sustainability. The specific edge that they bring to this concern in the domain of retirement planning is simply one form of a more pervasive question of whether X will outlast Y. Consider the possibility that the question, "Will my money outlast me?" is one avatar of a more dominant question that is a focus of central concern and source of significant public anxiety.

Will the ozone last long enough to shield me (and my grandchildren)? Will clean water hold out? Will the enormous budget deficits capsize the American dream? These questions are anchored in anxiety about what's happening to us, the answers to which require some insight into the future, forecasts. Although forecasting is credited with enabling western civilization to move beyond the dark ages by transforming "the perception of risk from chance of *loss* into opportunity for *gain* . . . and from helplessness to choice"[3] it fails us at times. When conventional assumptions about "reasonable" forecasts spectacularly fail, it engenders a doubt about forecasts in general. This partly explains the fascination with black swans and hundred-year floods. Our point is that the very first step on the path to working together to build sustainable spending plans (which are the essence of your clients' lifestyles) is noticing that the emotional intensity (anxiety) brought to the exercise may not be directly related to the task at hand, but attached to a more general fear about the future and doubt about the reliability of forecasts concerning it. A good question to ask clients that acknowledges this condition is simply "What keeps you up at night?"

Although this is far from irrational, it is not rational—strictly speaking. Recalling the insight provided earlier by Professor Shiller, difficulty in forecasting the future is not a legitimate excuse for tossing in the towel on the effort overall. That's like saying "curing cancer is tough, and most attempts fail, so let's quit and go have lunch." The fact that we cannot exactly forecast which event will be the catalyst for a next cycle of global economic expansion should not be confused with doubting there will be a next stage of global economic expansion. Moreover, as in the adage "my life might not be great, but consider the alternative" we need to make assumptions about the future as a fundamental means to discriminate between plausible expectations (and corresponding courses of actions to reach them) and implausible ones.

Nothing is worse than fearing the future; it is the one thing certain to unfold in front of you every moment of your consciousness. However, to begin an effective dialogue about sustainable financial security we might have to out the Jungian dragon of cosmic doom and put a lance in its fire-breathing mouth before we can advance to a more prosaic topic of budget estimates. How else can you refocus on a client's aspirations, unless you first allow room for their doubts?

THREE QUESTIONS

If you have any doubts about the level of anxiety people have over the sustainability of their lifestyle, you won't after learning this statistic. A survey by Allianz Life Insurance Company of North America released in 2010 found that 61 percent of those surveyed said they were more afraid of outliving their assets than they were of death.[4] This was a shocking statistic for us to learn considering (we presume) people are still very much afraid of dying. The first step to getting at a solution for their sustainability concern is to break it into its elemental parts. There are three questions that we believe are at the heart of an individual's financial security concerns.

How Much Do I Need?

So that we're clear, the long version of this question is, "How much money will I need to spend each month from now until I die to experience the lifestyle I desire?" Later we'll talk about how much wealth a person needs to fund their level of spending. In this book we refer to the client's budget as their spending plan.

Most people don't keep track of how much they spend during their working years, let alone know what they might spend after they stop working. Tim Noonan's advisor, Peter Rekstad, had this to say about people's ability to budget:

> ... *they have a steady amount coming in but many households are running deficits even though they know what their paycheck is going to be. They do things like take home equity loans and become highly indebted with credit cards and everything else, and spend future money without restraint. So, that is what people do during their working years when their semi monthly paycheck is known. Now they go into this retirement timeframe and they have to keep spending money. But, if they couldn't understand how much they could spend when they had a $4,500 deposit twice a month into their bank account, how are they ever going to understand how much they can spend when they are staring at an IRA account worth $1.6 million that has to last them the rest of their lives?*

Will My Money Last?

Individuals need to know if they will be able to keep spending at their desired rate for as long as they might live. Our previous comment that the only thing worse than being broke is going broke hints at the fear behind this question. People don't want to find out that after years of living at a certain standard they will have to make huge cutbacks because they lived longer than they thought they would or because the markets decided to misbehave at the worst possible time for them.

What Can I Do?

There are a few key variables that determine a client's chances of success (financially) in retirement: how much they save, how much they spend, how long they work, and how they invest their wealth. (We recognize that there are other important factors such as protecting against loss of income due to disability and or the expense of long-term care. We discuss these topics in Chapter 9.) It is the combination of all these factors that determines people's funded status. Your answer to their questions should be guided by their funded status, because, we assert, it is the most concise way to encapsulate all the information available that can answer the client's question: "Am I on track?"

There are a few key variables that determine a client's chances of success (financially) in retirement: how much they save, how much they spend, how long they work, and how they invest their wealth.

THREE ANSWERS: THE PERSONAL ASSET LIABILITY MODEL

We propose the personal asset liability model as your new framework for answering these three questions. Your clients may not always like the answers, but you will be able to give them real answers based on sound principals on which they can plan their future. The model was, in part, a product of our experience with and understanding of how institutional investors solve conceptually equivalent financial problems. Not all of their methods apply directly to individuals managing their own retirement. We have taken what is useful from the institutional space and incorporated it into our model. See the sidebar "The Advantage of Pensions."

The Advantage of Pensions—Pensions have several advantages that individuals don't have when dealing with the challenge of providing income in retirement. Understanding how pensions work, how they are different, and what we can borrow from them to help the individual has informed the personal asset liability model we propose in this book.

One advantage pensions have is that they can pool longevity risk. Pensions promise to pay their members for as long as they live (and in some cases for as long as the surviving spouse lives). In this way, pensions take on the longevity risk of their members. However, pensions also *only* pay their members for as long as they live. Some members die earlier than average. The actuarial credit the plan experiences from some members dying early helps pay the benefits of those who live longer than average. This is called longevity pooling and it reduces the overall cost of longevity risk to the plan by spreading it over many members. By themselves, individuals are not able to pool longevity risk. The individual's inability to pool longevity risk is a key reason they need a process like the personal asset liability model. The process looks at the cost of purchasing an annuity to meet the individual's spending needs in the future—annuities are a form of private longevity pooling—and sets that amount as the target wealth below which we do not want the individual's assets to fall.

Another advantage pensions have is they are able to assume they will be in existence for a very long time. In human terms they can be considered to be unending. This assumption provides them with two advantages: They are able to invest assuming a consistent and long-time horizon and they can assume they will have a perpetual source of funding from their sponsoring organization. Both of these assumptions form the central advantage allowing pensions to weather the most turbulent market conditions. They are able to keep their asset allocation focused on the long term rather than reacting to the gyrations of the market. Individuals cannot assume an endless time horizon or source of funding. This is why the personal asset liability model recommends an adaptable asset allocation methodology for those who are close to having just enough assets to meet their future spending needs.

Finally, in the United States, federal statute (ERISA) dictates that fiduciaries of pension plans sponsored by corporations operate under a standard of prudence. This is an advantage because it ensures (conceptually) that pensions will be managed in a skillful manner. There is an old saying that, "prudence is process." Individuals are not held to a standard of prudence nor are they required to follow any particular process for managing their wealth. However, there is nothing that says they can't adopt some of the best practices used by pensions to adopt a more procedural approach to the management of their wealth.

The basics of prudence for plan fiduciaries are to establish and follow rules, determine what information is relevant and gather the information, analyze the information and understand the implications (risks), maintain records, discuss options and make decisions, document those decisions, and, most importantly, when it is clear they don't have the skill or knowledge needed to make a prudent decision, seek expert advice. These steps form the foundation of the personal asset liability model proposed in Chapters 5 and 6.

This framework may not be right for all your clients. After reading the descriptions and examples in this book and testing the model with select clients, you will be in a better position to determine for whom it best applies, including you, foremost. This framework does not work well for an individual who has their money spread across many advisors. Also, it relies on the individual not hiding things (assets, liabilities, objectives, motivations, and so forth) from their advisor. It requires trust.

Chapters 5 and 6 describe the model in its entirety. Here we give you a brief overview. The best way to do this is by explaining the steps of the model as they apply to the three questions we just discussed.

How Much Do I Need?

In part one of the model, we determine a person's funded status. The funded status is the result of dividing the present value of future liabilities by the present value of assets. (Later in the book we explain how to do this, provide an example, and give you the formulas so you can do it yourself.) The numerator of the funded status fraction, the present value of liabilities, is based on the individual's spending plan. This is central to the success of the model because without a solid valuation of future liabilities you cannot determine if your client is properly funded.

In some cases, your client will already know how much they will spend in retirement. In those situations you can help them check their assumptions and move on to the next step in the model. If you need to help them build their spending plan, we describe several ways to do this. You can start with their existing paycheck and, working from this reference point, determine how much they will need to replace it. You can build the plan from scratch using their current spending patterns and their description of their future lifestyle. Or, you can solve for their spending plan and investment plan simultaneously showing them the trade-offs between standard of living and certainty that each spending plan/investment plan combination yields.

Will My Money Last?

An individual's funded status is, in our view, the best indicator today of whether their money will last far into an unreliable future. We can answer this question with relative certainty because we use as our basis the amount it would take to purchase an annuity that would meet their spending needs for the rest of their life. We call this the *annuity hurdle*. We are not suggesting they buy the annuity, only that they use this amount as a persistent reference point for how much is enough. A 100 percent funded status means they have just enough.

However, there is a bit of a catch. Having enough to buy an annuity to cover their future spending is not the same as having enough to self-insure their longevity risk for the rest of their life. It simply means that if they wanted to completely offload their longevity risk they could (at that moment), because they have enough wealth to buy the annuity. (Keep in mind, they would be giving up control of their assets, subjecting themselves to counterparty risk, and likely be paying a high cost for the protection afforded by the annuity.) If the 100 percent funded individual decides not to buy the annuity (and, therefore, self-insures their longevity risk), then they must consider the risk associated with the withdrawal rate they plan on taking from their portfolio. (We define this risk as the product of the probability of success and the magnitude of failure. Success is defined as not running out of money before they die. Again, all this is explained in detail in Chapter 6.)

The catch is that individuals close to 100 percent funded may find that they are not comfortable with the risk of self-insuring but are also not comfortable giving up control of their assets by buying an annuity. This is where you come in. There are ways to help your client make these decisions and manage their wealth that give them the best compromise between their desire for spending and desire for certainty. It is for individuals who are close to 100 percent for whom you can deliver the greatest economic value in helping them reach and maintain their desired lifestyle. For people outside this range, we have other suggestions that are covered in Chapter 6, bearing in mind that fewer assets tend to result in fewer options.

What Should I Do?

For individuals who are well below 100 percent funded, they lack sufficient financial assets to rely on as the means to solve their problem, as it is currently framed. Assuming their frame is immovable, their best course of action involves obvious noninvestment-related adjustments such as save more, spend less, and work longer. If they cannott correct their situation with these adjustments, they may have to take on significant investment risks as their only recourse. By definition, they don't have enough to annuitize, and a conservative investment approach will not get them to 100 percent funded status. Helping clients avoid this condition is a noble objective in and of itself, but bringing clients into your practice already in this condition is inviting you and your team to participate in the chaos and confusion of their financial future.

Individuals who are well above 100 percent funded have better choices. Depending on how great their funded surplus they may well be able to adopt any reasonable investment approach and still have high certainty of meeting their spending needs. These individuals will make their investment decisions based more on their risk preference rather than their funded status (because their surplus creates the risk budget to do so).

It's the giant group in the middle, those slightly overfunded or underfunded, who need the most surveillance of their funded status, and need from you the higher level of precision in teaching them their trade-off truth or consequences. Their wealth needs near constant surveillance. We say these people are in the adaptive zone because their portfolio (in our opinion) is best managed adaptively. By adaptive we are not suggesting you attempt market-timing investment decisions based on what's happening in the capital markets. The adaptive process we are suggesting is that **as these people's funded status gets closer to 100 percent, you invest their portfolios more conservatively in order to defend their surplus.** If, instead, their funded status increases, then you might also elect to take more risk with their portfolios. This is what we mean by adaptive.

So, the answer to your clients' question about what they can do is conditioned on their funded status. For clients in each of the three categories—underfunded, overfunded, and everyone in between—you must be prepared to have a different conversation about what they can do. The model provides you with answers for all three conditions. In Chapter 3 we talk about client segmentation and suggestions for how to conduct those three different conversations.

FOCUSING ON THE RIGHT THING

There is some portion of the investor population that is disengaged and cynical about the future, including engaging in financial planning for a future they essentially dread. There is also a portion of the advisor population that is innately cynical. Obsessing over facts about the macroeconomic environment, such as housing prices, unemployment rates, the likelihood of interest rates going up, the pressure on the U.S. currency due to government debt, and so forth is causing people to further disengage. They are so focused on the negatives that are out of their control they are unable to imagine things happening in the future that may counteract these issues, and this is a problem.

The problem for you is that you are spending a lot of your time explaining to your clients why they shouldn't fear the future. For your clients, worrying about the future prevents them from being receptive to any message you have about managing their future. Now, what should you do about that? You should focus your clients' attention on one thing that bridges the present and the future: their funded status, and what they can do to improve or maintain it. In the end, this is the most abbreviated diagnostic of their potential for financial security—with or without you—and it encompasses decisions and behavior in their actual circle of influence, today.

Concerns about reductions of living standards or diminution of purchasing power in the future are rational, whether they are caused by insufficient wealth, the inability to control spending, the loss of purchasing power due to long-term inflationary effects, or probable reductions in both the certainty and absolute value of government sponsored benefits. What is irrational, given the amount of anxiety this engenders, is that these concerns have not brought about a more universal recognition for the need for precision approaches to matching assets to liabilities (hence personal asset liability model). In the next chapter, we make the case for the emerging retirement crisis in America and how it's causing a need for greater precision in managing individuals' funded status. Maybe this will become a new standard of prudence? We earnestly hope it will.

NOTES

1. Cogent Research, "Investor Brandscape 2010" study (copyright 2010); used with permission.
2. James R. Hood, "Wealthy Investors No Longer Content With a Single Financial Advisor," ConsumerAffairs.com, interview with Katharine Wolf, Cerulli Associates, March 24, 2011.
3. Peter Bernstein, *Against the Gods* (New York: John Wiley & Sons, 1996).
4. "Reclaiming the Future," Allianz Life Insurance Company of North America contracted Larson Research and Strategy Consulting, Inc. and DSS Research to field a nationwide online survey of 3,257 U.S. adults, aged 44–75. The online survey was conducted in the United States between May 6, 2010 and May 12, 2010.

CHAPTER 2

How We Got Here

T he financial services industry has become crowded with advisors focused on helping people prepare for and manage their retirement. The reasons for this are simple. First, it's where the people are; the largest segment of the U.S. population is beginning to enter retirement. Second, it's where the money is; these same individuals hold a large share of wealth in this country. Third, it's where the problem is; there is a retirement crisis developing in America.

Calling the state of retirement readiness in America a crisis may seem like an overstatement, until we look at the facts. Perhaps the crisis closest in magnitude we've experienced in our lifetimes is the public health consequences (chronic illness) due to preventable bad behavior like smoking and obesity. Similarly, we have not come to the verge of a retirement crisis because of a single factor; it's an accumulation and interaction of many factors. In this chapter, we discuss seven factors in detail: demographics (the baby boom), increasing longevity, increasing health care costs, decreasing work-to-leisure ratio, lower savings rates, a weakened Social Security system, and reduced employer-provided retirement. To complicate matters, many of these factors interact in ways we can't always predict, tending to compound the overall effect.

There's one more issue. Most people desperately need help planning for their financial security regardless of whether they can afford professional advisors, so there are often other people involved. There are relationship dynamics between individuals and the advisors that affect the quality and effectiveness of the planning. The less intimacy present between the individual and advisor, the more potential there is for misunderstanding, and the less motivation to correct bad behavior, or reverse bad decisions.

We don't know which of these factors will end up being the one that undoes the retiree, but it is less important that we predict which one it is than to be aware that all of these are potential problems. In fact, the risk of these factors is more likely to be understated here than overstated.

DEMOGRAPHICS: THE BABY BOOM

Just in case you haven't been in communication with the outside world in the past 60 years, here is a brief description of the U.S. demographic trend called the "baby boom." Baby boomers are individuals born in or between the years 1946 and 1964. They make up 25 percent of America, numbering roughly 78 million. The first boomer reached age 65 in 2011, and, as of 2004, they held financial assets, not including home equity, totaling $7.6 trillion. Yet, even though they control trillions of dollars of wealth, that wealth is concentrated and alarmingly so. The top 10 percent of baby boomers own 68 percent of the financial assets in their age group, or "cohort."[1]

Large numbers of individuals reaching retirement at the same time, by itself, may not be enough to cause a retirement crisis. However, the baby boom trend becomes a meaningful factor in the crisis because it amplifies the impact of other converging factors.

The implication of these statistics is that a big problem (the retirement crisis) does not necessarily equal a good business. You need to work with clients who have a high probability of remaining solvent through retirement so that your advisory business is sustainable. Chapter 3 is dedicated to this single issue, finding the right clients.

INCREASING LONGEVITY

Our longevity is increasing; we are living longer than we used to and quite possibly longer than we've planned for. Figure 2.1 shows the expected

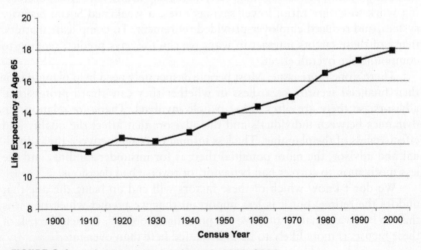

FIGURE 2.1   Life Expectancy at Age 65, 1900–2000

remaining years of life for a 65-year-old during the course of the twentieth century.

Go, Gladys, Go—A case in point for increased longevity: Consider the case of Gladys Burrill of Bend Prospect, Oregon, who caught our attention recently in a magazine targeted to running devotees. Gladys, who is also known as the Gladyator, recently completed the 2010 Honolulu Marathon in just less than 10 hours. Not a blazing time, except when you consider that she is 92 years of age. This was the fifth marathon she completed in seven tries at the Honolulu Marathon; she did not even start participating in marathons until she was 86 (she walks them). Pat Bigold, spokesman for the Honolulu Marathon Association, told us that the Guinness Book of World Records has confirmed Gladys as the oldest female to ever finish a marathon in recorded history. To celebrate Gladys is to embrace the future.

Note: Courtesy of the Honolulu Marathon.

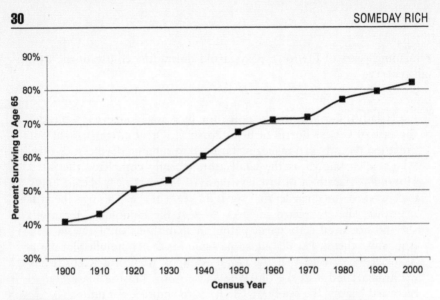

FIGURE 2.2   Percent of Americans Born Reaching Age 65, 1900–2000

These figures are based on U.S. census data collected every 10 years. In 1900, a person reaching age 65 could expect on average to live an additional 11.9 years. In 1970, that figure had increased to 15 years, and in 2000, a 65-year-old could expect, on average, to live an additional 17.9 years. From 1970 to 2000 life expectancy for a 65-year-old increased 2.9 years. That's roughly a 20 percent increase. The reason this is relevant is that the longer we live after our income stops, the more we need to save to fund those years. And, while 20 percent may not seem like a large increase it is significant especially when combined with the other factors we discuss in this chapter that are making retirement more financially challenging.

More of us are reaching old age. Figure 2.2 shows the percentage of the population who have reached age 65. In 1900, just over 40 percent of people reached age 65. In 2000, that percentage had increased to 82 percent (about 78 percent for men and 86 percent for women).

Although the increase in longevity makes retirement more expensive, it's the uncertainty of longevity that makes retirement planning so difficult. Based on RP-2000 tables for healthy annuitants, a 65-year-old male has a remaining life expectancy of 17.6 years. The standard deviation of this figure is 8.2 years. This means that there is a wide distribution of how long individuals might live: 20 percent will not make it to 75 while 20% will live past 90. That's quite a range.

But here's where it gets even more uncertain. Most people reach retirement as a couple. So, using the same actuarial tables, the life expectancy of the second to die of a male/female couple both age 65 is 23.9 years.

The standard deviation is 7.0 years. This means that a male/female couple, standing at the door of retirement (at age 65), has a 50 percent chance that one of them will live to age 90. They also have a two-thirds chance that the second of them will die in a range from 16.9 to 30.9 years. These figures aren't the maximum range; they only represent a roughly 66 percent probability. Another case in point: Willard Scott now gets an average of over 300 birthday notices **every week** for his 100-plus hall of fame!

INCREASING HEALTH-CARE COSTS

Medical advances are keeping us alive longer, and preventing us from dying suddenly in old age as was more common decades ago. Health care costs rise dramatically and disproportionately towards the end of our lives putting our remaining wealth at risk of rapid depletion. Put another way, our extended lifespans are extending our consumption—especially regarding one of the most expensive and inflationary items in the economy, health care.

Baby boomers have demonstrated the ability to over-consume and health care is an area that illustrates this point. Health care could be the single biggest budget buster in retirement and boomers need to be aware and plan for it.

An excerpt from a Rand research report illustrates this point.

Changes in the way Americans die are mirrored in health care cost patterns. The overwhelming preponderance of U.S. health care costs now arise in the final years of life. Indeed, if one were to estimate costs across a life span, the shape of the expenditures reflects the new health and demographic circumstances. [Figure 2.3] presents a rough estimate of health care costs distributed across the average American's lifetime. The final phase of life, when living with eventually fatal chronic illnesses, has the most intense costs and treatments. A similar curve for the U.S. population in 1900 would have been flatter, both because serious illness was more common throughout life and because death often occurred suddenly.

So, although the overall health picture for Americans has improved dramatically, health problems have become clustered in the last years of life. In effect, the average American now lives a long, healthy life, with only intermittent health problems or chronic conditions that are compatible with normal life. However, increasingly fragile health and complicated care needs ordinarily mark the years just before death.

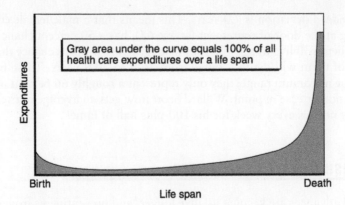

FIGURE 2.3 Distribution of Health-Care Expenditures
Source: James Lynn and David Adamson, *Living Well at the End of Life* (Pittsburgh, PA: Rand Corporation, 2003).

Total expenditures for health-care increase with age but so do total out-of-pocket health-care expenditures. From 1987 to 2004, the average annual per capita out-of-pocket expenditure for personal health-care for individuals 85 years of age or older increased from $2,989 to $4,886. In 2004, the average annual expenditure for a person in the 85+ age cohort was roughly four times that of a person in the 55–64 age cohort.[2]

In Chapter 9 we discuss in greater detail the risk posed to retirees of possible entitlement program cutbacks (Medicare and Social Security). Of the two programs, Medicare is by far the one with the biggest fiscal challenges. It is unlikely that Medicare will continue to pay the percentage of retiree health-care costs that it does today. It is hard to believe that "means testing" is not heading our way.

DECREASING WORK-LEISURE RATIO

Sound bleak? There's good news, too: We are spending less time working and more time having fun. The ratio of time spent working relative to time spent in leisure defines the work-leisure ratio. The data in Table 2.1 comes from Robert Fogel's book *The Escape from Hunger and Premature Death*. (Robert Fogel won the Nobel Prize for Economics in 1993.) It shows the trend of the work-leisure ratio in developed countries over the past century and projects the trend into the future. Fogel explains the data in his book published in 2004:

Thus, contrary to much public opinion, the lifetime discretionary hours spent earning a living have declined by about one-third over the past century despite the large increase in total lifetime discretionary time. In 1880, four-fifths of discretionary time was spent earning a living. [Fogel includes in the earning-a-living category work related to maintaining a household.] Today, the lion's share (59 percent) is spent doing what we like. Moreover, it appears probable that by 2040, close to 75 percent of discretionary time will be spent doing what we like, despite a further substantial increase in discretionary time due to continuing extension of the life span.

Why do so many people want to forgo earnwork (earnwork is defined as work resulting in a wage) that would allow them to buy more food, clothing, housing, and other goods? The answer turns partly on the extraordinary technological change of the past century, which has not only greatly reduced the number of hours of labor the average individual needs to obtain his or her food supply, but also has made housing, clothing, and a vast array of consumer durables so cheap in real terms that total material consumption requires far fewer hours of labor today than was required over a lifetime for food alone in 1880. (See Table 2.1.)

As Fogel surmises, people are working less because the amount of work it takes to buy the necessities of life has decreased. However, at the same time the cost of funding a lifetime of leisure has risen dramatically, both because the amount of time spent in leisure has increased and the expenses

TABLE 2.1 Estimated Trend in Lifetime Distribution of Discretionary Time

Activity	1880	1995	2040
Lifetime Discretionary Hours	225,900	298,500	321,900
Lifetime Work Hours	182,100	122,400	75,900
Percent of Total	(81%)	(41%)	(24%)
Lifetime Leisure Hours	43,800	176,100	246,000
Percent of Total	(19%)	(59%)	(76%)

Fogel's note: Discretionary time excludes time required for sleep, eating, and vital hygiene, which is assumed to average 10 hours per day. The availability of discretionary time is taken to commence with the average age of entry into the labor force and includes chores, travel to and from earnwork, and earnwork. Expected years of life after entering the labor force is 41.9 in 1880, 53.0 in 1995, and 62 in 2040. Expected years in the labor force at time of entry is 40.1 in 1880, 40.3 in 1995, and 33 in 2040.
Source: Robert Fogel.

incurred during leisure (primarily health-care costs and the cost of funding longevity uncertainty) have increased.

If the work-leisure ratio continues to decrease as is estimated, we believe it will have a meaningful impact on individuals' retirement security. The reasons are obvious but worth stating. For most people, all funding for leisure is derived from work; we save a portion of our wage, our employer provided retirement is largely based on our wages, as is our Social Security benefit. As the work-leisure ratio decreases, people must save a higher percentage of their wage to fund their leisure. As we will discuss in the next section, the trend in savings rates has gone down over the past 30 years. Research is clear that outliving one's money is the central boogeyman of the boomer. As yet, however, it is not connected with behavior changes. As advisors to advisors, connecting these dots has become our calling.

The effects of increased longevity on a person's financial security can be shown with a simple illustration. We start with a traditional view of the personal financial lifecycle shown in Figure 2.4. For simplicity, spending is shown as a constant throughout the individual's lifetime. The "income from work" line is smoothed and shows a gradual increase throughout the individual's working career until it approaches retirement, when it drops abruptly. This graphic is an oversimplification of lifetime income and spending patterns, but it illustrates the important point; unless an external source of funding enters the picture, savings (and investment earnings on savings) is all there is to fund debt repayment and retirement expenses.

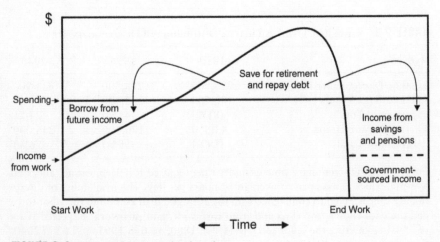

FIGURE 2.4   Personal Financial Lifecycle
Note: For illustration purposes only. Not drawn to scale.

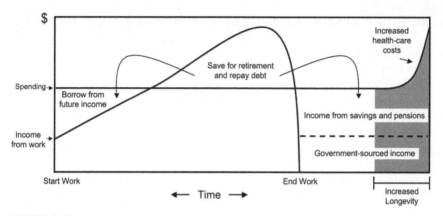

FIGURE 2.5 Personal Financial Lifecycle—Extended View
Note: For illustration purposes only. Not drawn to scale.

Figure 2.5 represents an extended view of the personal financial lifecycle. In the extended view, the size of the area to the right of the end-work point has been increased. This represents both an increase in longevity and a change in the work-leisure ratio. In addition, at the far right side of the illustration, the spending line has been sloped upward to show end-of-life health care costs.

The relevance of the extended view is that it graphically illustrates the added burden placed on an individual's savings. This burden is made greater by the fact that this income is also the subject of competition between generations. For instance, younger generations are experiencing expenses related to starting a family, saving for their own retirement, and assisting the older generation who are experiencing an extended and unplanned for longevity.

Figure 2.5 also shows the increased burden that is being placed on other forms of promised retirement income, namely, Social Security and employer- sponsored pension plans. Any future reductions in these sources of income must be made up for through increased private savings or reduction of spending.

LOWER SAVINGS RATES

The U.S. Bureau of Economic Analysis calculates the national savings rate. From 1952 to 2008 the average savings rate in the United States was just above 7 percent.[3] The savings rate is represented by the after-tax income that is not spent at the end of the year by individuals. Where this money ultimately ends up is another matter altogether and the exact method for calculating the national savings rate is always a popular subject for debate among economists. What's important for our discussion about the developing retirement crisis in America is not merely the absolute value of the national savings rate but how it has changed in the past decades. For example, the average savings rate for the eight-year period from 1971 to 1978 was 9.72 percent. Thirty years later, the average savings rate for the eight-year period from 2001 to 2008 was 2.65 percent. The average for this most recent period is well below the historic average of 7 percent. Given that personal saving is becoming a more important source of financial security, it is concerning to see the savings rate in America trending down, and it is therefore important to confront the origins of clients' aversion to save.[4]

SOCIAL SECURITY

There is a popular analogy of retirement security being like a three-legged stool. The government (Social Security), the employer (workplace retirement programs), and the individual (personal savings) represent each leg of the stool. Next we look at the challenges facing two of the three legs: government and employer-sourced retirement benefits.

Many people we talked with, including some advisors, believe that Social Security will not be around when they retire. They believe it is going broke and they won't receive any benefits in the future. **It is highly unlikely that this will happen.** What may happen is the system will ultimately pay out less than 100 percent of the benefits currently promised. There is a meaningful difference between receiving no benefit versus receiving a reduced benefit. It's impossible to say if Social Security benefits will be reduced in the future, or what form those reductions will take. In general, we believe that a 25% reduction to currently promised benefits (for people under age 50 today) is a reasonably prudent assumption to use for planning purposes.

Keep in mind that future reductions to Social Security payments may also be caused by increased Medicare premiums because Medicare premiums are deducted from Social Security checks. The recipient receives the net amount, their scheduled Social Security benefit minus their Medicare premiums.

Few experts disagree that changes need to be made to keep the system viable. Possible changes include increasing the Social Security payroll tax (although this tax was temporarily reduced by 2 percent in 2011 as part of the government's economic stimulus efforts), reducing benefits, increasing the age when benefits commence, or conditioning benefits on a test of the retiree's means (income level or wealth).

The Social Security Administration has been communicating their concern about the financial future of the system for quite some time. Every year, every American who has paid into the system is sent a benefit statement from the Social Security Administration. Printed on the front page of a Social Security statement from late-2010 are the following two paragraphs:

> *Social Security is a compact between generations. Since 1935, America has kept the promise of security for its workers and their families. Now, however, the Social Security system is facing serious financial problems, and action is needed soon to make sure the system will be sound when today's younger workers are ready for retirement.*
>
> *In 2016, we will begin paying more benefits than we collect in taxes. Without changes, by 2037 the Social Security Trust Fund will be exhausted *and there will be enough money to pay only about 76 cents for each dollar of scheduled benefits. We need to resolve these issues soon to make sure Social Security continues to provide a foundation of protection for future generations.*
>
> **These estimates are based on the intermediate assumptions from the Social Security Trustees' Annual Report to the Congress.*

Calling Social Security a "compact between generations" makes it sound like both parties agreed to the deal. It's not clear that the generations following the baby boom are aware of the size of the obligation they have been handed. A disturbing development on the horizon caused by the retirement crisis is the potential for intergenerational conflict. This conflict would arise from the economic burden that current entitlements place on future generations. Authors Kotlikoff and Burns make this point in their book, *The Coming Generational Storm*, "This is the moral crisis of our age. We are collectively endangering our children's economic futures without giving them the slightest say in the matter.... Worst of all, we are pretending not to notice."

People feel this same way about budget deficits—they want the entitlements now, while simultaneously feeling revulsion for "mortgaging" their children and grandchildren's future.

The relevance of potentially reduced Social Security benefits in the future cannot be overstated. For many Americans, Social Security will be their largest source of income in retirement. Even for marginally affluent people, Social Security represents a meaningful percentage of their retirement income. As stated earlier, any reduction in Social Security income must be made up through other sources of income (private savings) or a reduction in spending in retirement. In Chapter 9 we discuss this topic further and provide an example quantifying the size of possible reductions to Social Security.

REDUCED EMPLOYER-SPONSORED RETIREMENT

Decades ago the most common employer-sponsored retirement program was a defined benefit (DB) plan. Today, however, many employers have either frozen or eliminated their DB plans and now offer a defined contribution (DC) plan as their primary or only employer-sponsored retirement program.

In 1983, 62 percent of workers in the United States were covered by a DB plan only, 12 percent were covered by a DC plan only, and 26 percent were covered by both a DB and DC plan. By 2007 the numbers changed dramatically; 17 percent of workers were covered by a DB plan only, 63 percent were covered by a DC plan only, and 19 percent were covered by both a DB and DC plan.[5] (The most common DC plan is a 401(k) plan. Not-for-profit and government employers sponsor similar plans called 403(b) or 457 plans.)

A larger percentage of workers in the past earned DB pension benefits than today but not all DB plans are the same. There are a couple of significant differences between DB plans. First, not all DB plans have the same benefit formula. Some may pay 100 percent of the worker's preretirement salary for life (and in some cases the life of their spouse) in the form of a monthly benefit while others pay only a fraction of the worker's preretirement salary. Second, beginning in the late 1970s, some DB plans started offering a lump-sum benefit option to their retirees. A lump-sum benefit means the retiree can receive the entire present value of their retirement benefits in a single lump-sum payment rather than monthly checks for life. This effectively shifts the risk of managing the retirement portfolio to the retiree and away from the DB plan managers. The reason for pointing out these distinctions is to raise the awareness that just because an individual was a member in a DB plan in the past does not mean their retirement income problems are solved. It may be that their benefit level is less than their preretirement income, or they received a lump-sum payment and may already spent a significant portion of those funds.

The shift of employers from DB to DC plans is having a meaningful negative impact on retirement security in America because, in general, participants in DC plans accrue smaller retirement benefits than those in DB plans. The reason for this is not because benefit levels in DC plans are necessarily lower than DB plans, although in some cases they are. No, the real reason is because much of the risk associated with funding, investing, and managing a retirement program is shifted to the individual when an employer moves from a DB to a DC retirement program. This fact uncovers yet another source of value you can bring to your client. In a DC plan they need to make decisions about how much to save, how to invest their account, and how to draw down their account in retirement.

With many DB plans, these decisions are made on behalf of the individual. The DB plan sponsor determines the benefit level, regularly funds a trust, invests the trust funds, and pays and guarantees member benefits in retirement including managing longevity risk. In DB plans, the plan sponsor makes up for any shortfalls that may occur as a result of decisions made by the plan managers (by contributing more money to the trust). This is not the case with DC plans. If a DC participant underfunds their account or experiences an unexpectedly poor investment outcome, the plan sponsor does not make up the difference. This is the primary reason individuals today are accruing smaller employer sponsored retirement benefits as a result of the shift from DB to DC programs, because they are being given the responsibility to manage their own retirement and many don't have the skill, temperament, or expertise to do so properly.

However, even individuals who are covered by traditional DB plans are at risk. Federal rules govern the funding of DB plans sponsored by corporations. This ensures corporate DB plans remain solvent. However, corporations sometimes fail to adequately fund their DB plans (usually as a result of corporate insolvency), and when this happens their DB plans are insured by the Pension Benefit Guarantee Corporation (PBGC), a federal agency. The catch, however, is that the PBGC only guarantees benefits up to a certain limit. Participants who have accrued benefits above the PBGC limit will have their benefits reduced if the PBGC takes over their employer's DB plan. In addition, the PBGC does not carry an explicit guarantee from the federal government. It currently carries a deficit of tens of billions of dollars. Just as individuals are beginning to discount the value of their future Social Security benefits, they should be aware that a PBGC backstop is not a sure thing.

Furthermore, state- and local-government retirement-benefit plans are not protected by the PBGC, nor are they subject to many of the Federal rules governing corporate pensions. Many of these plans are underfunded. The Pew Center on the States conducted research on the funded status of state-administered benefit programs and published their report in 2010. What follows is an excerpt from their report.

An analysis by the Pew Center on the States found that at the end of fiscal year 2008, there was a $1 trillion gap between the $2.35 trillion states and participating localities had set aside to pay for employees' retirement benefits and the $3.35 trillion price tag of *those promises. (Pew Center on the States analysis of 231 state-administered pension plans and 159 retiree health care and other-benefits plans.)*

To a significant degree, the $1 trillion gap reflects states' own policy choices and lack of discipline: failing to make annual payments for pension systems at the levels recommended by their own actuaries; expanding benefits and offering cost-of-living increases without fully considering their long-term price tag or determining how to pay for them; and providing retiree health care without adequately funding it.

Pew's analysis ... found that many states shortchanged their pension plans in both good times and bad.[6]

Do we think that government and employer-sponsored retirement programs will disappear altogether leaving the individual totally on their own to provide for themselves? No, that is extremely unlikely. However, it is a reasonable conclusion to draw that the individual is becoming more responsible for the funding, investing, and managing of their retirement.

Again we look at Fogel's observations with an excerpt from his book.[7]

A specter is haunting the OECD nations. It is not the specter of poverty or class warfare, as was the case a century ago, when leisure was the privilege of the very rich and workers toiled from sunrise to sunset to earn enough to purchase meager amounts of food, clothing, and shelter. In 1890, retirement was a rare phenomenon. Virtually all workers died while still in the labor force. Today, half of those in the labor force, supported by generous pensions, retire in their fifties.

To many of today's political leaders this situation, the realization of the dreams of reformers a century ago, is a potential disaster. With baby-boom generation ... approaching retirement, they are confronted with the choice between defaulting on commitments to retirees, delaying the age of retirement, or increasing the taxes borne by young workers. The specter that now haunts OECD [Organisation for Economic Co-operation and Development] nations is not class warfare but intergenerational warfare.

OTHER FACTORS

In addition to the seven factors we've just discussed, there are others that weigh on the state of retirement readiness in America. Humans, as it turns

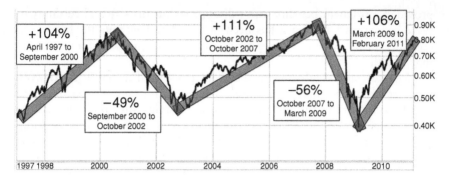

FIGURE 2.6 Russell 3000 Index Returns, April 1997 through February 2011

out, are naturally poor planners. The field of behavioral finance attempts to get at the reasons behind this. It is an area of study that has received much attention recently, as evidenced by Daniel Kahneman's Nobel Prize award for Economics in 2002 for "having integrated insights from psychological research into economic science, especially concerning human judgment and decision-making under uncertainty." Another way of saying decision making under uncertainty is, simply: planning.

In addition, the complexity of the task of planning for retirement continues to increase. This is due in part to the nature of the problem, such as the increasing length and uncertainty of longevity (and the implications to strategies for ensuring against longevity causing financial ruin). However, it is also due to environmental factors, such as the increased complexity of financial products (including how and when they should be used) and uncertainty of the financial markets. Figure 2.6 shows the return pattern of the Russell 3000 index of U.S. equities over a roughly 14-year period. Although Figure 2.6 may show what looks to be a clear pattern, we warn that this graphic represents a relatively brief snapshot of the U.S. equities market and may not be predictive of the future. The purpose of showing Figure 2.6 is to illustrate the environment to which individuals (your clients) have been exposed, which affects their attitudes (and staying power) about the financial markets.

WHERE DO WE GO FROM HERE?

There are three conclusions we draw from all of this.

First, individuals are largely on their own to plan and manage their financial security, and they need your help. Government- and employer-provided retirement benefits won't disappear, but the size and certainty of these benefits is less than it has been in the past. This puts the burden on creating surplus wealth from private sources and the plan for sustaining that wealth.

Second, individuals and financial advisors need a new way to work together becoming mutually focused on the central task of devising plans that best assure the sustainability of their lifestyles after retirement. They don't want to continue doing what they've done in the past and hope things will turn out fine. Much of the rest of this book is dedicated to how advisors and clients can work together in a more effective way.

Individuals and financial advisors need a new way to work together.

Third, fear, complexity, and uncertainty are the norm. This increases the premium for trust, cooperation, and precision in the client-advisor engagement. Advisors who find effective and practical ways to manage or reduce these factors for their clients will have more successful advisory practices, and better (more trusting and cooperative) clients. Again, this book is dedicated to helping advisors with this task.

In the next chapter we talk about finding the right clients for your practice.

NOTES

1. Government Accountability Office, Baby Boom Generation, July 2006.
2. Center for Medicare & Medicaid Services, National Health Expenditure Data: www.cms.gov.
3. Bureau of Economic Analysis web site: www.bea.gov/national/NIPAweb/Nipa-FRB.asp.
4. Matt Smith, *Managing Your Firm's 401(k) Plan* (Hoboken, NJ: John Wiley & Sons, 2010).
5. Center for Retirement Research at Boston College, Frequently Requested Data, Workers with Pension Coverage, by Pension Type, 1983, 1995, and 2007. Source: The authors calculations based on U.S. Board of Governors of the Federal Reserve System, and Survey of Consumer Finances (various years), Washington, DC.
6. "The Trillion Dollar Gap" (Washington, DC: Pew Center on the States, 2010).
7. R. W. Fogel, *The Escape from Hunger and Premature Death* (Cambridge, UK: Cambridge Press, 2004).

CHAPTER 3

The Right Clients

If we've heard the story once we've heard it a thousand times. An advisor starts out in the business and begins searching for clients. The criteria in the early days are simple. As our friend Steve Moore would say, "For some advisors starting out in the business, anyone who can fog a mirror is a prospect." However, as the practice grows, it becomes clear that being everything to everyone isn't even a sustainable business strategy much less a pathway to creating enterprise value.

In this chapter we discuss reenergizing your advisory practice around an ideal type of client engagement. We start by describing the attributes we believe essential for a viable client. The reason this topic is of such great urgency is that, just as society is aging, so is your clientele As they move from earning income and accumulating wealth to spending their wealth, it becomes clearer who among your clients will be able to sustain their standard of living and who will not. This puts you at risk of losing clients and at a minimum the risk in reduction of your fee base if you have (or are trying to move toward) a fee-based (AUM) business model. Knowing how to choose the right clients for your practice, ones for whom you can create real economic value and in turn who will value your services enough to be happy to pay your fee for many years to come, is a skill you need to master.

One of the characteristics we suggest you consider among prospective clients is feasibility; do they have a level of resources that will support a sustainable lifelong funded surplus? However, choosing the right clients is not solely based on asset levels; personality match is also one of the important criteria to consider. We share with you in this chapter a couple of testimonials from advisors on how they consider prospective clients. Client relationships can and should become deeply personal and satisfying for both the advisors and the clients. Life is too short not to have clients you enjoy while you are helping them.

There is a particularly pregnant question around the topic of client segmentation. The question originates from the desire to avoid clients who are in denial of the probability that they will be in ruinous circumstances, either today or in the future, and, even more so, to avoid clients who may seek to assign the responsibility for being in such circumstances to everyone but themselves (and especially you). Also, avoid, if possible, dealing with clients who are ruining themselves despite being able to avoid doing so. Someone who is an overconsumer and/or undersaver and cannot modify their behavior in spite of the recognition that it will have dire consequences. Finally, there is a desire to avoid clients who are in a situation due to injudicious spending who will create anxiety and havoc in their lives even if it doesn't directly lead to ruin. Their spending patterns are one symptom of an attraction to chaos and distraction. Better to leave those genies in their bottles.

FIVE QUALITIES OF VIABLE CLIENTS

You know what clients to avoid, but what are the characteristics of clients we want to attract? There are at least five characteristics we've identified that make up what we will call "the right clients." You may describe your ideal client profile in your own way but we suggest considering these traits in your selection process. You might even consider using this description or one derived from it in your marketing materials under the topic of "Who should join our client ranks?" It may well resonate with prospects who either have, or aspire to have such hallmarks.

Feasible

It is possible to help them. Either they have sufficient wealth to give them a chance of reaching their goal of sustainable financial security, or they have enough working years ahead of them combined with the saving/spending discipline to get there. Later in this chapter we go deeper into this topic by looking at the distribution of households who fall into this category. To every possible extent, you need to consider how to convert this receptiveness to savings into commitment for autodeductions to be directed into their investment accounts.

Receptive

They are looking for help. Not everyone knows that they need help, or will admit as much! Sometimes, events such as the birth of a child, significant change in income, or a disruptive market episode cause people to be receptive to outside help. Receptivity is also affected by people's understanding of how these external events may change their financial security. Your ability to help them see the relevance of such events can significantly change their receptivity. We discuss the topic of relevance more in Chapter 4. People who are frightened seek help instinctively. Maybe asking your client explicitly about their fears is a prerequisite to positioning yourself as the agent of help.

Engaged

They are willing and able to be involved in the process. In order to be engaged the client must sense that you are guided by what's in their best interest at all times. There needs to be a high level of trust between client and advisor. Here again, their understanding of the relevance of your advice and their hunger for it are key to their engagement.

Engagement and trust lead to strong bonds between advisor and client. Peter Rekstad described it to us like this:

> *Relationships where I can be the best advisor are where all of the cards are on the table; all of the issues are out there. I can assimilate ideas to take to the client that are valuable based on my knowledge, experience, and research. But, if the client is simply coming to me looking for information within a box and they've kept me blind to everything else then I have limited ability to give them good advice. Client relationships that don't work are the ones where the client doesn't allow me to see the big picture. This is usually a trust issue.*
>
> *I have a picture in my mind right now of Velcro. Velcro makes a tight bond because it has lots of tiny hooks that are attached to lots of tiny loops. If it had only one hook attached to one loop the bond would not be strong. That is a way I think about my client relationships. I have my hooks into the client loops and we have many points of contact where I can bring them good advice. But if they won't show me their tax return, it's tough for me to figure out how to build a portfolio around their tax situation.*

Adaptive

They are willing and able to make the necessary adjustments along the way, and have the perspective to recognize the world as it is becoming, rather than as they wish it to be. Good and bad news comes in waves. There will be times when they must adapt in order to stay on course. What we are proposing is that it will be easier to keep them on course by using an adaptive asset allocation approach rather than a more conventional strategic asset allocation approach. Asset allocation is a means to an end, not a destination in and of itself.

Match

Seek a personality and philosophical match between you and your clients. It's not healthy for you or your client to work together if you do not agree on the goal of your relationship or if your client is fundamentally unhappy and seeking conflict. Life is too short (for both you and the client) to work with people you cannot agree with. Entering an advisor/client relationship is a voluntary activity, for both parties. You should make it a high priority in your initial discovery process to determine if you are a good match with the prospective client. Jim Warren, an advisor we admire so much that we spoke with him on this topic, put it to us this way when describing how he determines if a prospective client is right for his firm: "My 'blink' or intuitive response is if there is no celebration in the relationship, there is no engagement." What a great way to put it—*celebration in the relationship*. Imagine what would be possible in your business and in your life if that condition was present, or could be brought into being, in every one of your client relationships.

WHY THE URGENCY ABOUT CLIENT SEGMENTATION?

There are several reasons that the idea of client segmentation deserves your attention. As advisors historically were busy collecting accounts for accumulation, fees went up even if account balances started small. Even though advisors' fee revenue went up, this didn't materially change their workload. However, in decumulation, workload increases and economies of scale aren't as easy to create across a large block of modest account sizes. So, even as advisors historically have had "small account" problems, here (in decumulation), the account profitability problems are inverted. Large accounts become small accounts by the nature of the client's circumstances, they are spending down their life savings. This can financially capsize the poorly organized advisory practice.

Also, decumulation is hard enough in and of itself, much less when working with clients who are working against themselves. You need to have clients willing to sacrifice to accumulate enough wealth to fully fund their desired lifestyle. Or, for those clients already in decumulation, that are willing to manage their spending responsibly.

Finally, to the extent you can identify and cultivate clients who you believe have both the assets and the responsible behavior toward those assets such that they are more likely to remain in a funded or overfunded status, those are the clients who will continue to be in a net accumulation status in the future, reversing the advisory revenue conundrum of the business of providing advice to boomers.

You have to think about segmentation even harder than before. If you don't, it won't just be an unaddressed small-account problem; it can threaten the economic viability of your practice. Advisors would do well to refer out clients who cannot or will not cooperate sufficiently to create a reasonable prospect of achieving financial security. Put in a way that doesn't sound so harsh or unfeeling: the risk of continuing to advise a client who refuses to make a rational assessment of their financial condition is potentially very damaging to your practice on various levels, from legal time bombs to psychological sea anchors. All things being equal, if you could choose between one of those clients and a client you could actually help, choose the client you can actually help, even though that client has fewer assets. Why? Because your potential to base the relationship, at least in part, on your ability to create economic value for the client is present. The more the difference that you can make is due to the clients taking your advice, the better your practice will become (and your life!)

Does this mean you should fire all your clients who can't get to a level of wealth necessary to support their lifestyle? No, it certainly doesn't mean that. However, it does mean that conversations with those clients about their ability to dramatically change their contributions to their retirement portfolio and their expectations about their future lifestyle are central to your practice's success in the future. Equally important is their willing-ness to dramatically revise their preconceptions about their independence in old age.

It is not a law of gravity that financial independence should be associated with living one's entire life in one's own private household. In fact, that is a cultural anomaly in America, and it is largely the result of a workforce labor mobility phenomena rather than cultural influences. We've gotten away from the idea that elderly people should live in a multigenerational setting, where they have access to their children and grandchildren who enliven them, and often learn from them, where their children provide them practical assistance (for instance, acting as informal case managers to access their entitlement benefits—anyone who has had a visit to veteran's administration to secure subsidy for an expensive drug therapy knows the value of this service) and their grandchildren provide them some level of inspiration. That is a cultural formula that works very well in many parts of the world. This idea should be introduced and discussed earlier rather than later, while there's still an opportunity to cultivate those multigenerational relationships so they can support that living arrangement rather than it being a last minute imposition on someone who has no expectation of it, when it almost certainly will engender resentment.

FEASIBLE CLIENTS

One of the five characteristics we discussed earlier was feasibility. Figure 3.1 is one way of looking at a distribution of potential clients. What are shown here are U.S. households near or in retirement, distributed by their household assets. The shaded area represents the 9 million households who have between $530,000 and $1,614,000 in assets. What is important here is not so much the absolute value of the household assets (as these amounts will change as time moves forward) but the notion that there is a sweet spot in the distribution of households for which your advisor services could prove most relevant, and a client for whom sustaining a funded status surplus creates true economic value, and, by extension, creates the possibility for you to translate that into enterprise value for your practice.

Households to the left of the shaded area are more likely to have future spending needs that exceed their resources, have less control over their assets,

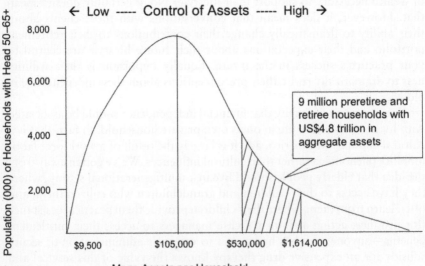

FIGURE 3.1 Distribution of Households by Assets
Source: Adapted from "Strategic Study—Retirement Typology: Charting the Landscape of the Retirement Income Market," Retirement Income Industry Association (2006).

and are less likely to be able to afford an advisory fee. Those to the right of the shaded area are more likely to be able to sustain their lifestyle given their assets and have more control (and options) over their assets. They may make fine (and feasible) advisory clients in accumulation, but their needs are less about helping them maintain their lifestyle than those inside the shaded area. It is for those in the shaded area for whom you can add the most value. This is an illustration of a pool of potentially feasible clients.

In fact, unless the value you bring to their day-to-day confidence of staying on course in an uncertain world is tacit, you should expect them to wonder why their advisory fees represent such a significant portion of their annual income. This proportion is less intuitive when an asset-based fee relates to the entire asset base, versus an annual income target.

In Chapter 6 we talk specifically about how to advise clients based on their funded status (their assets divided by their liabilities). One aspect of that advice is how to protect against longevity risk—the risk of running out of money before you run out of time. Shown in Figure 3.2 is a broad brush-stroke view of sources of longevity protection based on household assets. For households on the far left, it is unlikely they will be able to dedicate any of their accumulated wealth to longevity protection. Most of their assets

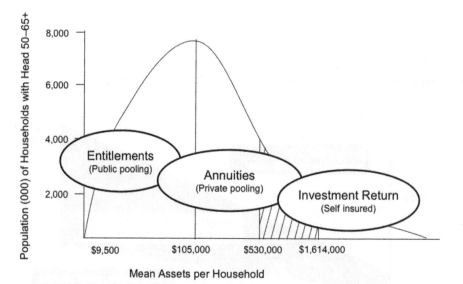

FIGURE 3.2   Sources of Longevity Protection
Source: Adapted from: "Strategic Study—Retirement Typology: Charting the Landscape of the Retirement Income Market," Retirement Income Industry Association (2006).

need to be kept liquid and available for immediate use to satisfy daily living expenses or for emergencies, especially medical expenses. Their longevity protection will rely on Social Security, which is a form of public longevity pooling because the government does this on behalf of those in the Social Security system. Moving to the middle of the diagram, these households may have enough to purchase annuities to cover their living expenses while keeping an amount set aside for emergencies. Annuities in combination with Social Security will provide them longevity protection. Annuities are a form of private longevity pooling because the private sector (an insurance company) provides the mechanism for pooling longevity risk (the annuity). Still further right on the diagram, households who have accumulated greater wealth can afford to forgo annuitization and self-ensure their longevity risk.

IN THE WEDGE

The distribution curve of households we just looked at only represents a single wealth metric: household assets. However, we know that absolute wealth alone does not indicate financial security, although it is a pretty good clue. As we explained in Chapter 1, funded status (wealth relative to desired future spending and purchasing power) is what defines financial security (and of course the ability to remain in surplus status indefinitely). Figure 3.3 is another way to view the feasibility of potential clients. It represents a distribution of individuals based on their funded status. Those in the extreme upper left corner have assets that exceed what is needed to meet their future

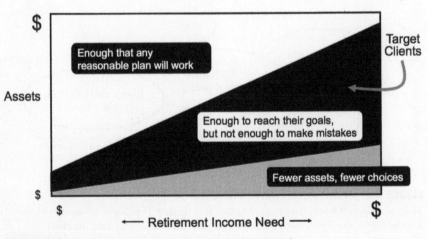

FIGURE 3.3   Assets Relative to Retirement Income Need

expenses. They have the luxury of knowing that any reasonable investment plan will result in success (maintaining their overfunded status) so long as they keep to their spending plan.

Ironically, many of those clients do not actually realize this and worry needlessly about sustainability. Imagine the celebratory dimension of your conversation with them that they may in fact be in a position to spend a little more on what matters to them while they are still alive. Those in the extreme lower right do not have enough assets to meet their future spending needs. They have fewer options and may not be clients whom you are able to help and may benefit from a decision to annuitize right away. The group in the middle, the area we refer to as the wedge, is your target client group.

Our thesis is that the greatest economic value you can deliver to your clients is to help them get into the wedge, to help keep them there, and that the generation of this value has the best chance to increase the enterprise value of your practice. Getting them into and keeping them in the wedge does not necessarily equate to slavishly following a particular investment formula. What is just as important is to bring into their day-to-day mentality this idea that, if they consume now, they get to consume less later: Deferred consumption is the basic premise of investing. You need to begin to break the bonds of hyperbolic discounting (see sidebar) in order to get them to equate consumption later with savings today. If you do this you have a better chance to get them to alter behavior that might get them into the wedge.

> Wimpy's Hamburger—"I will gladly pay you Tuesday for a hamburger today." Hyperbolic discounting describes the tendency to value events in near future more than events in the distant future. This tendency explains why people would rather spend today and pledge to save tomorrow. The "mental" cost of saving tomorrow is less than the mental cost of saving today. For a more detailed description of hyperbolic discounting see the research referenced in the Note at the end of this chapter.[1]

If your greatest economic value as an advisor is to get your clients into and keep them in the wedge (create and maintain a funded surplus), then who are the people who most benefit from that? They are people who have the potential to have sufficient assets because of their existing assets and their saving/spending discipline. It's these people for whom you can deliver the most value.

People who have more money than they could possibly spend in their lifetime have estate-planning problems, not retirement-income problems. For you to present a retirement-income capability as something of economic value to them is a basic mismatch.

How exactly are you supposed to create economic value for people in the wedge? First, identify what they need to do in terms of spending and savings to maximize the ability for their human capital to translate into future financial assets sufficient enough to equal their personalized definition of financial security. Second, manage their assets in a way that preserves their ability to have more than enough assets to purchase an annuity sufficient to satisfy their future spending. Third, have an active surveillance to ensure that they are not slavishly following a plan that was created in the past that no longer reflects their reality.

THREE CONVERSATIONS

Client segmentation has at its center this idea of the funded status; that you should seek clients who are or at least have the potential to be fully funded. But in fact both the funded status and the client's attitude about their funded status are of equal relevance. When the individual is overfunded (for the purposes of this discussion we define overfunded as having 130 percent or more of the wealth needed to meet future spending needs) there's not much of an issue concerning the client's reaction to it because everything is basically on track. The issue arises when there is a large deviation between the client's expected future liabilities and the assets required to fund those liabilities. Issues arise on both the positive side and the negative side. Risk, in this sense, might be summarized as the client's misunderstanding that being 100 percent funded means being 100 percent secure. It does not mean that.

For those in surplus, this can create the potential for a sense of false confidence, an ephemeral wealth effect that can translate into either injudicious or premature gifts, or it can lead to a more general lack of discipline about awareness of their spending. It's like the quote from Ernest Hemingway, "a man goes broke slowly, then all at once." There is a false perception of wealth and then, all of a sudden, there's not enough left to sustain their standard of living. Just like that.

At the opposite end of the spectrum, you have a similar kind of dramatic situation in which, in the very worst case, your clients are despondent and give up because they feel they have no other choice; they have nothing to lose. They feel they only have one more throw of the dice. Lottery ticket time!

Moving inward from these extreme cases, you have the difficult situation of discerning your client's trade-offs in a tighter range around deficit and surplus. Are they willing to accept clear reductions in their standard of living to increase sustainability of their lifestyle? As any experienced advisor is well aware, reductions in standard of living do not just affect the sustainability of a person's financial security, they can cut right to the client's sense of identity, their sense of self worth. If they realize they will no longer be able to bring the sleigh full of toys to their grandkids at Christmas, will they truly be willing to make these reductions?

Creating the framework, the calmness and methods, to have a real conversation with the client who is outside those funded bounds is about how they negotiate the balance between their standard of living and sustainability. This is a competency, a new skill that advisors need to develop, if you have not done so already.

In Chapter 5 we explain how to calculate an individual (or couple's) funded status. Your client's funded status tells you which of the three conversations you need to tailor to your client.

The Happy-Face Conversation

Clients who enjoy plump surpluses (above 130 percent) have plenty of options, because they are either very affluent or very careful spenders, or both (they do tend to go together). It's not that they will never need to concern themselves with having enough, but it does not need to be the key determinant in their investment decisions. If they remain in line with the spending expectations used to calculate their funded status, they should be able to adopt any reasonable investment plan and remain in an overfunded status, barring the dreaded black swans. Their investment decisions should be based on risk tolerance more than their funded status.

The Sad-Face Conversation

Clients who are very much underfunded (below 90 percent) need to consider modifications to their behavior or their expectations more than they need to consider their investment options. For them, saving more, spending less, and working longer should be their primary considerations. If they are unable or unwilling to make these choices, then you should consider whether you want them as long-term clients. Minimally, you should consider a more streamlined service set for these clients. From an investment point of view, (by definition) a conservative portfolio is unlikely to enable these clients to reach a fully funded status. A more aggressive investment approach may be their only hope at getting to a reasonable funded status, and yet asking clients in denial to adopt a risky approach may backfire on you if the markets move against them. Disclosing these risks and ensuring clear acceptance is a compliance necessity. We discuss this approach in more detail in Chapter 6.

The In-Between Conversation

For clients whose funded status is close to 100 percent (for purposes of this conversation we define *close* as 90 percent to 130 percent funded depending on the clients' ages), your conversation can be upbeat but conditional. Their status indicates that they have potential to meet their future spending but they don't have so much of a cushion that just any strategy will work. Their situation needs to be monitored and adapted accordingly. The closer the funded status is to 100 percent, the more conservative they should be invested in order to protect their status. As the funded status climbs above 100 percent, the greater their surplus and more risk they can take, if that is consistent with their preferences. Being overfunded does not mean they should invest more aggressively, only that they have a greater risk budget. Clients in this in-between group need you to monitor their status most carefully as changes to the status (whether because of movements in the market or changes in actual spending) may dictate changes in the risk profile of their portfolio, and a decision to exercise the option to annuitize.

BUSINESS ISSUES WITH BEING OBJECTIVE

We propose you evaluate your clients' circumstances in an objective way, and communicate with them in a direct manner. However, you should know that there are business issues with taking this approach.

First, for clients who are underfunded, you may be asking them to give you a substantial percentage of what they can spend each year in the form of your fee. For instance, if their portfolio can only support a 4 percent withdrawal rate annually with a high probability of success and you are asking them to pay you 1 percent of their assets every year, this amounts to 25 percent of their annual income going to pay your fee. This is a difficult place to be for both you and for them. This may require that you illustrate the difference in their projected future purchasing power with your deferred annuitization strategy compared to actual annuitization. The reality of the situation may dictate that you deliver a different service set to these clients—one that requires less of your time and resources and, therefore, allows you to charge a lower fee.

The second issue you need to anticipate is that not all clients will want to hear an objective assessment of their situation. You may be at risk that your clients will go down the street and get a second opinion from another advisor, one who will be more than happy to show them a deterministic calculation that tells them they are able to spend a lot more than they should. You will lose some business, but will you also be shedding risky clients? Can you make up your mind to do that?

A great advisor in Pennsylvania, told us how this happened to him with a client recently. He said,

> *I had a client who was spending too much money. She always spent more than she should. At one point her best friend came in to see me about it and I told her that I couldn't talk to her without the client being present. So the friend finally talked my client into coming in with her. The friend and I told her that she was spending too much, we had sort of an intervention in my office. It was a very interesting conversation and the next meeting the client told me she was going to reduce her spending and she wanted to know how to do it. She did a pretty good job of curbing her spending but then after this recent market decline she started spending even more. So, when I saw her in my office in December I told her we really needed to think about the option of an annuity. I told her that she needed to really reduce her spending or purchase an annuity, and that another market downturn could really be bad news for her. She said she would think about what I had to say and get back to me. The next thing I know I get papers in the mail that she is moving her account. At that point I couldn't even talk to her about it anymore. Later I heard from a family member that she was upset that I was telling her that she couldn't spend money anymore. I don't know who told her that she was going to be able to spend more money or continue to spend the way she was but I felt like I drove her into the hands of somebody who was telling her a different story.*

These risks were made clear to us by a colleague, Grant Gardner (who co-authored Chapter 11), when he pointed out that in the accumulation stage, advisors only faced bad news when the markets were going down. In decumulation, they potentially face bad news all the time when (some of) their clients don't have enough wealth and they are charging them a fee. The advisors' fees are going down every year in absolute-dollar terms, the clients are unhappy about the amount of the fee relative to the amount of income they can draw, and advisors down the street are telling their clients that they can spend more than they should. It's (potentially) bad news all the time.

Are we suggesting you should not be candid with your clients? No, absolutely not. What we are saying is that you must be careful to choose clients whom you can help (they have sufficient wisdom about using their wealth) **and for whom your fee is commensurate with the economic value you are delivering, which is partly measured by the forecasted benefits of deferred annuitization.** If your clients leave you because other advisors told them happier stories, then maybe they were not viable long-term clients to begin with. Would such a client be likely to enthusiastically recommend you to a friend? You should always work on making your clients conversations as effective and positive as possible, but they need to be "real" conversations as well. Ironically, our market research suggests that these are the very conversations clients now crave and are more likely to engender their trust and collaboration. There are enough great clients out there who want that from advisors that you should not be concerned about losing those few who wanted someone else to tell them they could spend more from their portfolio than they should. Our own experience with advisors offers plentiful examples of practices that moved from many hundreds of modestly profitable client relationships to a couple of hundred valuable relationships, producing greater client satisfaction and referrals as well as more inherently profitable practices in the process. This is a formula for increasing the enterprise value of your practice, which has been demonstrated to work.

MOVING ON

Advisors who will be successful in this new arrangement will have a couple of distinguishing characteristics. First, they will have achieved successful strategic focus as advisors in their community, regarded as advisors who are client-centric, solutions-oriented people, rather than as people who are access points to capital markets or vendors of financial products. As a consequence, they tend to develop reputations with centers of influence in their community, and become identified by their own clients so strongly with that reputation that their clients will become the source of their referrals. Indeed, this is what we've observed with the most successful advisors we work with, like Kirk Greene in Seattle, Washington. They ultimately become so successful at describing what they do, that it allows them *to be found by the market.* This frees them from the fallacious idea that they have to broadcast their services to the market and spend their precious time prospecting for new clients. Instead, what happens is new clients finds them. Successful advisors' practices will have that endemic marketing element, the ability to be known among their communities of clients and potential clients, which allows them to build their book of business with less effort.

The second characteristic they will have is a planning process that can be appropriately tailored to the wealth and complexity of their clients. For clients who have a high level of wealth and need for complexity, they will get

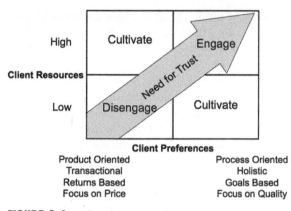

FIGURE 3.4 Client Segmentation

a highly tailored set of services. Those clients with a lower level of wealth and a more homogeneous need will get services that involve less customization, even if they can be reliably characterized as tailored. Finally, for clients who can't afford customization, they will either get referred out of their advisors' books or they will be put on paths of aggressively building up their assets, which will allow them more options moving forward. If it is clear when clients in this third group are put on that path that they don't have either the temperament or the ability to move up that path, then we encourage you to strongly consider having a disengagement conversation with them. Let them be someone else's project.

Say that you actually take all of this advice about client segmentation; what would that look like? It would look something like the diagram in Figure 3.4.

What you are aiming for are clients with the sufficient resources that make it possible for you to deliver value and the preferences that match your advisory approach. Clients who have high resources yet are focused on price and return consider you to be merely a facilitator of transactions, and an access point to products. You may be able to cultivate them into clients who embrace your comprehensive, wealth management approach. If you are unable to move them in that direction you should consider disengaging with them and making room in your practice for new clients who actually want what you are striving to offer.

Other clients may be a good match in terms of preferences but don't have the resources such that your fee is a good value for them. For younger clients in this situation, you may be able to coach them (through saving and spending modifications) to a spot higher up on the graph. If not, you should consider a more streamlined service set for them, one that delivers quality at a lower fee and requires less of your team's time to deliver.

For clients who are not in the upper right corner of Figure 3.4 and who cannot be coached there, disengage. Peter Rekstad described his thoughts on client segmentation to us this way:

I think of my practice like a bookshelf. There is only a limited amount of space on a bookshelf, and in my practice those books are the clients. I can only put so many clients in my practice and take care of them. So my goal should be to find clients worthy of being on the shelf not just anyone to fill the shelf. So I've become a lot more discriminating in the discovery process.

Jim Warren, who we heard from earlier in this chapter, described to us in detail the types of clients he and his team enjoys working with. We asked him to describe to us the client relationships that he felt were the most mutually satisfying and contrast them with client relationships he felt were not satisfying. Here is what he had to say:*

My response to the most satisfying clients is confirmed through periodic surveys we have sent in the past to them. We have always been curious as to why they chose our particular firm versus the many other choices available to them. Their responses have been consistent: "They want to transfer implicit trust and confidence and allow us to apply our expertise. They require competence, integrity, objectivity, combined with a sense of personal care."

When considering the client relationships that were not enjoyable, they relate to when we were developing the practice and doing business with anyone in order to meet our cash flow requirements during our first ten years in business. There are certain profiles to whom we are not committed. Those lessons have been learned over the years. We terminated 400 clients in 1993 when changing our paradigm to become more selective and disciplined.

For example, we are not committed to moguls whose profile is to control the professional relationship as a priority. Investing is another way of extending personal power. They enjoy leveraging their power over people without regard.

We are also not very good with VIPs. Their profile is investing with the ability to purchase status possessions where prestige leads

---

*The source for the profiles that Jim refers to in his description: Russ Alan Prince and Brett Van Bortel, *The Millionaire's Advisor*™ (2003). Analysis: CEG World-wide, LLC.

the way. They are more interested in their image than their values and have a tendency to be self-centered and self-indulgent.

We are not committed to gamblers who run the risk of losing it all without regard to those they value. They enjoy investing for the excitement of it. They like a high-risk tolerance and can be volatile.

We don't work well with innovators who focus on leading-edge products and services, analyze the complexity of the products, technically savvy and highly motivated to change directions without notice. They are sophisticated investors who like complex products.

Our primary profile today is family stewards whose dominant focus is to care for their families, be conservative in their personal and professional lives and transfer the trust and confidence to us so they can do the things that are most important to care for them.

Accumulators are also meaningful relationships that focus on making their portfolios larger and who are performance-oriented. They tend to live below their means and spend frugally in order to meet specific goals. They value competent advice and work to understand what we are talking about in greater detail.

We enjoy the profile of the independent. They seek the personal freedom money makes possible and feel investing is a necessary means to an end. They are not interested in the process of investing. They value our relationship and transfer trust and confidence easily.

Ironically, we like phobic profiles that are confused and frustrated about wealth. They dislike managing investments and technical discussions. They choose advisors based on the personal trust they feel. They avoid meeting unless it is absolutely necessary.

We are committed to making sure we are compatible, which begins with the discovery meeting before proceeding regardless of a prospect's wealth today.

Again, we would like to thank Jim for his thoughtful response and for his generosity in sharing his thoughts with us. This is an advisor that really knows what he is doing.

AGE

The entire foregoing discussion leaves out an important observation, namely, that these clients who we are talking about as a monolithic group actually exist along a broad age spectrum. The younger they are, and, therefore, the further they are away from their retirement anniversary date, the greater the opportunity they have with regard to wealth creation and the contribution of that wealth to their retirement. Likewise, younger clients have the greatest potential for things to interrupt those plans. Therefore, there is still a significant level of uncertainty even with a very high potential earner in the young part of the development curve who has a high interest in spending.

Being young and having high earning potential do not by themselves create a successful outcome. This is like the joke about how to help doctors double their wealth: stop getting divorced. It merely creates better conditions for a successful outcome. We encourage you to think about accumulating for retirement income very much in the same way as saving in a defined contribution plan. The more emphasis there is on automatic contribution the less opportunity there is for momentary abnormalities in the life of the client to interrupt their programmatic wealth accumulation. Keep in mind that what we refer to as momentary abnormalities in the life of the client may be in fact events such as the birth of a child, or an opportunity to start an exciting business. In the moment, these events may not seem threatening to their wealth accumulation, but in the long stretch of time they might. The point we are making here is that the tolerance bands around an acceptable variation of a client's funded status is in reverse proportion to their age.

* * *

Choosing the right clients is the key to creating a sustainable advisory practice, not to mention a satisfying profession and a happy team committed to a community of clients, not just a "book." It ensures that you will have long-term relationships that are mutually valuable because they are based on the economic value you are providing, that your clients are able to sustain their financial security and that you and your team are able to make a decent living and have satisfying careers and potential to generate real (and therefore potentially sustainable and transferable) enterprise value. Delivering the right advice to the right clients is something that we've collectively spent decades learning to do. We've had a lot of help along the way and also skinned our knees plenty of times. In Chapters 5 and 6 we explain in detail the personal asset liability model and how to apply it to your clients. However, before that, in the next chapter, we talk about the events, experiences, and people that shaped our thinking about the model. We also share mistakes we've made and songs we loved that in the end belonged to the sirens.

NOTE

1. D. Laibson, "Golden Eggs and Hyperbolic Discounting," *Quarterly Journal of Economics* 62 (May 1997).

CHAPTER 4

Connecting the Dots

Providing effective advice to individuals is clearly a multidisciplinary task. We have been fortunate in our careers to have worked with and have access to many talented people who have collaborated (sometimes unwittingly) in our effort to help advisors. As Albert Einstein said, "A hundred times every day I remind myself that my inner and outer life depend on the labors of other men, living and dead, and that I must exert myself in order to give in the same measure as I have received and am still receiving." We share this sentiment.

In large part, our job is to bring together great thinking from a variety of perspectives in a way that better enables advisors to help their clients realize sustainable financial security. The different approaches we've assembled here represent researchers looking at the problem from different angles and in some cases building on one another's work. We don't claim that this is the only research that has informed our approach to creating sustainable financial security; they happen to be the pieces of research we are familiar with and were involved with as they were developed. If a tree fell in the forest and we happened to be out of town—we know that it still made a sound.

As we discussed in the first chapter, the financial crisis of 2008 made the advisor's job more difficult, but it also made it more pivotal, more valuable. It became clear to us that we needed to help advisors in new ways. The tools and methods we've developed over the past few years (many of which are still being developed today) were inspired by the needs of our advisor clients that came about as a result of the financial crisis of 2008 and the client service urgencies that the crisis catalyzed. Several needs emerged: advisors needed help talking about the crisis with their clients, they needed help explaining to their clients how the crisis was affecting their financial expectations, and they needed help understanding the impact the crisis would have on the profitability of their advisory businesses.

DASHBOARDS

To help advisors talk about the crisis with their clients, Russell Investments developed an economic recovery dashboard (see www. helpingadvisors.com). The number and types of economic and market data being discussed as the cause of the crisis or the clues to the future became unmanageable; no one could keep track of all the data that was being discussed. Our economic recovery dashboard originally tracked seven key metrics that advisors could use in their client meetings to keep the conversation from slipping into a quagmire of worry over what might happen next.

Advisors also needed help explaining to their clients the impact of the crisis on their financial plans. Mathew Greenwald and Associates helped us understand the end investor's perspective. With Greenwald's help we learned that, until advisors could specifically articulate to their clients how the crisis had impacted their own situation, their personal financial security, the clients seemed to tune out. This clarified for us the importance of communicating the impact of the crisis to the end investor, but we still did not fully understand how we might do this persuasively. Meir Statman from Santa Clara University provided us with a framework for how an advisor could talk about the crisis with their clients based on the individual's unique personality temperament. To further round out our communication approach, we turned to the firm of maslansky luntz + partners who helped us develop the right language to be used in these conversations. Maslansky taught us that it is not what you say but what others hear that matters. These bodies of work—Greenwald, Statman, and Maslansky—have broader applications than merely how to talk to end investors about financial crises; they form the core of the communication advice we offer to you on how to talk about sustainable financial security with your clients.

Finally, we found that advisors needed help understanding how the crisis (and the new environment extending beyond the crisis) impacts their advisory business. For help in this area we turned to Steve Moore. In particular, the Client Engagement Roadmap that Steve developed years ago with several advisor clients, notably Kirk Greene and Russ Hill, is now more valuable than ever before. The value of the roadmap is it ensures that the advisors address their clients' most important needs first, that advice is being delivered with consistently high quality across the advisors' books of clients, and that advisors' clients are constantly reminded of the value they are receiving for the fee they are paying. If the Client Engagement Roadmap was useful before the crisis, it's imperative now in the aftermath.

A continuation of our efforts to help advisors has been the development of the personal asset liability model, which is the focus of the next chapter. The framework is a process for an advisor to help their clients determine their funded status based on the present value of their assets and liabilities and create an investment plan centered on this status. The framework has technical pillars, each of which we explain briefly in this chapter. The fully detailed versions of each are provided in the chapters that follow.

ADVISORS SEEKING HELP

One of the ways we routinely interact with our advisor clients is through conference calls. The rapid-response call is a special type of client call or webcast that is intended to provide advisors information regarding a market event that is more urgent or serious (or both) than typical. We had established rapid-response calls years before the 2008 financial crisis. Tim Noonan developed guidelines to determine when a rapid-response call was appropriate (i.e., not an overreaction). Tim believes that the only time we should do these calls is when three conditions are met. The first condition is when the crisis is material, that it is not just an event the media portrayed as a crisis but rather one that could have some actual implications to the capital markets in the long term. Second, when what we have to say about the event is not duplicative to what can be found on a more commonly accessed source of public information. If we are just adding to the CNBC commentary on the event, it isn't worth our clients' time to have the call. The third condition is when what we have to say must have an advice hook; there has to be some advice we are offering that the advisor can, in turn, offer to their clients that is relevant. When those conditions are met, we conduct rapid-response calls.

Prior to 2008 we had conducted these calls on topics such as the dot-com bust, the meltdown of Long-Term Capital Management, etc. . . . It was typical to have a few hundred advisors attend these calls. The technology we were using allowed us to see not only how many attendees we had but also how long they remained on the calls. It wasn't unusual for us to lose half the audience by the end of the allotted time. Maybe this didn't mean the audience was uninterested in what we had to say, although that could have been true at times, but rather it was more likely an indicator of how busy they were. Not every advisor can spend a solid hour in the middle of the day on a conference call without an important interruption, like a call from a client. However, when we started doing the rapid-response calls related to the financial crisis in 2008 we began to notice a significant change. First, the attendance skyrocketed; there were times when we had thousands rather than hundreds of advisors on the call. This was 5 to 10 times our normal attendance. Just as surprising, nearly all the attendees remained on the calls for the duration.

It was this experience that made us believe that the advisors were more than just seeking knowledge about an event; they felt like they had to be there, that in some way they drew comfort from being part of a group experiencing the same crisis they were experiencing.

The Bandura Moment

It was then, in October 2008, during the unfolding of the financial crisis that it was becoming clear how serious the crisis was from a systemic-failure perspective. Leading up to that time, there were multiple failures: Bear Stearns failure, Lehman Brothers failure leading to the collapse of the money markets, all happening in quick succession. The crisis was snowballing, and it began to show the expanse of the problem. It began to show the degree to which the system was in free fall. At that very time (October, 2008) we were conducting a practice management session for our advisor clients in Phoenix, Arizona with Steve Moore and Kevin Bishopp. At this meeting, it was obvious that unless these advisors hadn't committed months in advance to being at this meeting, there was no way they would have shown up. They would never have left their offices and their clients given what was going on in the markets.

However, they were at the meeting and, as luck would have it, Steve Moore had arranged to have Albert Bandura, professor from Stanford University and world-renowned expert on self-efficacy, speak to that advisor group. The scene at this meeting was tense. The advisors in attendance were, to understate the obvious, distracted. They were distracted with what was going on in the marketplace and with their clients. They were spending quite a lot of time on their phones and laptops, texting and e-mailing back to their offices and checking the latest financial headlines. Into this scene steps 83-year-old Professor Bandura, making his way to his place in front of the audience. He started talking about the nature of anxiety and how there are certain behaviors that are counterproductive and tend to fuel anxiety. One of the examples he cites is the constant checking of news on a frequent basis. Individuals become engaged in a pattern of behavior in which their attention is drawn deeper and deeper into the crisis of the moment causing a collapse of their perspective. And this was the individual's undoing, because as he or she becomes absorbed in the minutia of the crisis, perspective on time collapses and the individual becomes part of the drama. He went on to explain that, right then, what individuals needed was for their advisors to remain outside the drama; to be observers of the drama and to retain a level of calmness in order to avoid making a catastrophe out of the situation alongside their clients.

It was impressive not because of what he was saying but the way he was saying it. He was completely unflappable. He was basically saying, "I know you can't hear me when I'm telling you what you need to do right now, but I'm obligated to tell you anyway." For us, that morning was a critical turning point when we took the concept of helping advisors into execution. Upon returning to the office, we decided we had to focus everything that we were doing on helping advisors get their perspective back so they could keep their clients, while the financial crisis resolved itself. That moment in Arizona was the pivotal point when our efforts to help advisors were put on the path that led us to much of what we discuss in this book.

We quickly identified three things we could do to help advisors through the crisis. The first was to help them talk to their clients about the crisis itself. The second was helping them help their clients understand the impact the crisis was having on them personally and immediately. The third was to help advisors understand the impact of the crisis on their own businesses, staff, and families, and what they needed to do to keep the doors open, serve their clients, and keep their cool.

How to Talk about the Crisis

As a result of our first priority, to help advisors talk to their clients about the crisis, Russell developed the Economic Recovery Dashboard and made it available to any advisor, client or not, in the United States (later dashboards were developed for Canada, the U.K., and Australia). To do this, we went to our analysts and suggested that we find a fixed number of things that we could continually reference as economic indicators that advisors could follow. The conclusion we came to was that the more specialized topics that advisors opined to their clients, the greater the risk that the advisor would appear as a "phony" to their clients. Our reasoning was that their clients would ultimately conclude that it's impossible for any advisor to be an expert on so many arcane topics. One day you needed to be an expert on TED spreads, the next day about CMOs, the next day the relationship between crude oil prices and inflation expectations. It went on and on. No one could possibly keep track of all of this data. However, we believed that it would be credible for them to keep track of seven things. And we picked seven things because there are seven digits in a phone number; it was no more complicated than that.

Those seven items became the seven factors in our economic-recovery dashboard. The dashboard included factors such as levels of corporate debt, market volatility, mortgage delinquencies, interest rates, and so forth. Our hope was that these seven things would be constants, and as they were continually refreshed they provided advisors with a consistent outline for conversations with their clients. It was a format that did not allow clients to take over the conversation by challenging the advisors' knowledge about the latest news item they had just heard. The economic-recovery dashboard caught on like wildfire. There were times when there were more hits to it on the Internet than the rest of Russell.com.

That was the first part—how to talk about the crisis in a way that didn't allow the advisor or the client to collapse their perspective into the minutia of the crisis. This was inspired by what Professor Bandura said that morning in Arizona and the capital-market insights of many great analysts at Russell (but Erik Ristuben, Doug Gordon, and, above all, our head economist Michael Dueker stand out). Two ingenious web designers, Joe Lizee and Austin Dienst, carried a great pass over the goal line. Thus, HelpingAdvisors.com was born.

Explaining the Impact of the Crisis on the Individual

We also knew we had to help advisors help their clients understand the impact of the crisis on them. At this very same time we were engaged in a comprehensive consumer market research project, the purpose of which was to gain insight on advisors' and individuals' perspectives on planning for retirement. This project had begun in early 2007, but many of the focus-group sessions overlapped the 2008 financial crisis. In the fall of 2008, we were sitting behind the glass of the focus-group rooms watching both advisor and investor audiences try to talk about retirement-income-related issues, but they were understandably overwhelmed by the unfolding meltdown in the markets. The crisis was dominating their psychology. Clearly, advisors were unable to articulate to their clients what all this stuff (the maelstrom that was the financial crisis) meant to them personally. Because of that, investors would tune out. They would look for their own sources of information. The only time advisors seemed successful at recentering the discussion was when they could say to their clients, "This is what all this means to you."

An example of what it was like for advisors in the midst of the crisis is seen in a story related to us by Andrea Shenocca, an advisor in New Jersey. She said,

> I had a real interesting situation with a client in March 2009. It was March 2nd, it was a Monday and snowing here. I was working at home because of the snow, and I was getting lots of calls from clients because of what was happening in the markets. This one client calls me and said that he knew we had just met in January and we weathered everything that happened last fall (2008) but he said, "I just can't do it anymore, you've got to get me out." I

suggested to him that rather than pulling out of equities completely that we adjust his asset allocation to mostly bonds, he agreed. I don't recall exactly what the mix was but it was something like a 30/70 mix (of stocks to bonds). The market bottomed within a week of this. On Thursday, March 12 he called me because the market was going back up quickly, and said, "Put me back in." I said, "You're kidding, right?" He said, "No, put me back in." I asked him what was going on, what's different, what has changed since we last talked. He said, "I don't know what is worse, watching the market go down (when I'm in it) or watching it go up and not being in it." I reminded him that we would be going back into the market 6 percent higher than when we came out just a few days earlier. He said he understood. I thought that was one of the most poignant things a client has said to me, "I don't know what's worse, watching it go down or watching it go up and not being in it." I share that anecdote with everyone.

Mathew Greenwald and Associates (Greenwald) conducted the 2007–2008 consumer market research. A summary of Greenwald's research results can be found in Appendix A. The Greenwald work yielded several important observations. The most compelling was that the fear of impoverishment in old age was overwhelming and all-consuming. Unless advisors were able to talk to their clients in a way that addressed that fear, everything else that they said seemed to be discounted. The next was that investors intuitively understood that the asset allocation strategies they needed to employ to produce reliable and steady income were different than the ones they had relied on to accumulate wealth, but they didn't understand what precisely to do about that. The final observation was the importance of flexibility and liquidity. They knew that the downside to annuities was the loss of control of their wealth and the upside of traditional investments was the ability to change their minds at any time. The preservation of flexibility was key because they had a new level of skepticism about forecasts that suggested they were smarter if they kept their options open (didn't lose control of their assets), and adopted a strategy in which they could change their mind. Those ideas were more or less consistent and continuous throughout the several studies Greenwald conducted for us.

The Greenwald experience inspired us to build a client analyzer tool. The client analyzer tool was our first mass commercialization of a personal asset liability model. It was designed to allow an advisor to profile the retirement readiness, or funded status, of all their clients in a simple and fast way so that they could triage their clients. We used a color code to indicate that green clients were those who were fully funded, yellow clients were slightly underfunded, orange clients were in trouble, and red clients were in big trouble. So let's say you were an advisor with 500 clients and 100 of those clients were green and 100 of those clients were red. Those are the 200 most urgent conversations you need to have, to reassure your green clients that they are still okay and to warn your red clients that they're not. The client analyzer tool did the trick, but because it was such a technical approach it didn't include the softer bedside-manner element. By sorting their clients by funded status, the advisor knew which clients they needed to talk with about which topic, but they didn't know *how* their clients might react to what they had to say. The tool was missing the psychological framework for how to talk with different personality types about the central question.

We recognized that the data output of the client analyzer tool might be insufficient to motivate investors to modify their behavior (in the case of an investor who was put far behind in their financial goals by the crisis), and this is why we called Meir Statman. Meir Statman is the Glenn Klimek Professor of Finance at the Leavey School of Business, Santa Clara University. His research focuses on behavioral finance. Our request to Prof. Statman was to help us understand how advisors should communicate with their clients about the financial crisis based on the personality type of the client. The result of this work is described in greater detail in Chapter 8.

Statman's work provided us with the psychological framework for communicating with individuals based on their personality temperament. However, the piece we were still missing was the language element. What were the words that would resonate with individuals? Or, maybe even more importantly, what words should we avoid? For this we turned to the communications firm of maslansky luntz + partners (Maslansky).

By this time we had already been developing the idea that individuals needed to solve their retirement income problem with a better process rather than more or more complicated products. "Process before product" is one of the tenets of our personal asset liability model discussed in later chapters, and it is the byproduct of Russell's decades of experience advising institutional clients on their pension plans. There are many lessons borrowed from the institutional world that help us solve the individual's retirement income problem, but the nagging question remained. If this process approach is so good, why aren't more people using it? We thought the brilliance of the idea was all that the marketplace needed to embrace the approach, but it didn't. Maybe we needed more proof points or more clever PowerPoint slides. But this was the wrong way of looking at the situation. Both advisors and individuals were tuning out because it wasn't immediately obvious what the process approach meant to them. We were talking about the problem and the solution in the wrong way. This is what we were hoping Maslansky could help us fix.

In 2010 Maslansky conducted research into the language to use when talking about retirement income with financial advisors and end investors. Their work convinced us that it isn't just what you have to say that is important but also how you say it. The Maslansky experience had the same profound impact on us as did the Bandura experience, because out of it came these three important points.

First, they introduced us to the primacy of presenting a proposed solution for a client in terms of personal "tailoring." Embedded into the idea of tailoring was the premise that, if you can't explain to your client how something affects *them,* then they won't listen. Tailoring is the intersection of personalization and expertise. It incorporates both the idea of clients being seen and understood and that they're being seen and understood by experts. More importantly, by experts who know what to do with their information. The experts (advisors) are able to turn the individuals' information into a plan tailored specifically for each of them. Maslansky is making the point that if you don't make it clear that what you're saying is tailored to your audience, your audience tunes out. This seems obvious, but as advisors, we still don't do it much.

They refined and developed our previous, more primitive thought that if the advisors couldn't say to their clients what the crisis meant to them that they would stop listening, or worse: listen cynically, not cooperatively.

The second thought, maybe as big as the first one, was lifestyle planning. They helped us see that when we were talking to people about retirement (as if it was a good thing), the audience was hearing something different. We thought that, by talking about our decades of experience managing large institutional pension plans, we were credentialing ourselves. What was in fact happening was the audience heard *retirement* and had an instant negative reaction. They thought they were about to be lectured to and told they had to retire the same way their parents did. When they heard *institutional*

FIGURE 4.1 Maslansky's Three Ideas

pension the first thing that came to mind was "failure." Their reaction was to ask, "Aren't institutional pensions all under water? Why would I want to model my retirement income plan after that?" The words *financial planning* also elicited negative reactions. When end investors hear *financial planning* they assume they are about to be sold something.

The terms *retirement planning* and *financial planning* are negative receptors that turn off clients' listening, whereas *lifestyle planning* excites the listener. They don't want to hear about how bad they've screwed up their retirement plans or financial plans. However, they think that planning their lifestyle is still a positive thing. A realization that is hard for people like us in the money business is that people don't want to talk about their money, they want to talk about their lives. Money is just a means to live the *lifestyle* they want. Just the same way that tailoring is the intersection of personalization and expertise, lifestyle planning is the intersection of financial planning and retirement planning.

The third big idea to come out of the Maslansky work was flexibility. Retirement planning involves the use of long-term projections into the future, yet people have lost confidence in long-term forecasts, and, at the moment, many people haven't much faith in the sustainability of the planet, much less their nest eggs! So there's a question of how you construct a plan (that requires forecasting) knowing that people don't believe you when you tell them the likelihood of something happening 20 years from now.

One approach is to tell your clients you're going to wake up every morning and decide whether they should be in the market. However, we know too much about this sort of market timing fantasy—it doesn't make any sense. Another approach is to ignore their concerns about forecasting and construct their plans based on a set of beliefs about the long-term behavior of the markets and not revisit their plans for another 20 years. We also know this purely strategic approach may make less sense to clients than a purely tactical approach.

So, what does make sense? The intersection of a tactical and strategic point of view is adaptability. You establish a long-term goal with your client and using your long-term beliefs about capital markets (and more importantly about your client's behavior), you construct a plan of how much risk to take with their portfolio. Rather than set the strategy and walk away, you continue to monitor what's going on in the markets and with your client's behavior and goals to observe if they remain on track (funded status). Based on these observations, you may choose to adapt along the way. This adaptive approach seems to resonate with end investors as long as it is intimately tethered to their tailored goal of financial security.

Maslansky was also instrumental in helping us avoid the negative, what they call language landmines. And, in helping us increase the receptiveness of the listener by using language that is more universally viewed as optimistic. A more detailed version of the Maslansky research results is provided in Appendix B.

The Impact of the Crisis on the Advisor's Business

As we stated at the beginning of this chapter, the advisor's job became permanently more difficult as a result of the financial crisis of 2008. End investors have become more skeptical of the capital markets, their anxiety levels have risen, and their needs have become more acute and more immediate as time marches on.

A key difference in how advisors and their clients perceived the global financial crisis relates to their confidence in the global financial recovery. At first, the low point of the global financial crisis meant more or less the same thing to advisors and their clients: a sudden, cataclysmic disruption in the orderly functioning of the capital markets, followed by a deep and lasting economic contraction. As the markets and most developed economies sought to establish policies that would create some traction on their path to recovery, advisors' confidence in the markets was gradually reestablished (concerns about future inflation notwithstanding). However, investors' confidence has lagged.

In the fall of 2010, as part of their Financial Professional Outlook, Russell Investments began surveying advisors about their and their clients' optimism about the capital markets. The Financial Professional Outlook is a survey-based study about the conversations between advisors and investors. Each quarter, Russell collects the opinions of hundreds of advisors working at national, regional, and independent advisors firms.[1] The results shown in Table 4.1 illustrate the wide gap in optimism between advisors and their clients about the capital markets.

TABLE 4.1 In general, are you/your clients optimistic or pessimistic about capital markets broadly over the next three years?

	May 2011	Feb 2011	Nov 2010
Sentiment Gap (advisor–investor optimism)	48%	50%	51%
Advisor: Optimistic	76%	86%	59%
Advisor: Uncertain	14%	6%	28%
Advisor: Pessimistic	10%	8%	13%
Investor: Optimistic	29%	36%	7%
Investor: Uncertain	52%	50%	48%
Investor: Pessimistic	19%	15%	45%

For the third straight quarter, advisors remain far more optimistic (by nearly 50 percentage points) about the future of capital markets than their clients. Although 76 percent of advisors polled were optimistic, only 29 percent believed their clients shared that positive outlook. The gap in optimism has remained large since the inception of the survey, implying the difficult task advisors must be having in convincing clients to reenter the market.

Let's think about why this is, as it has important implications for how advisors coach clients who sold off financial assets during the crisis (at depressed prices, with potentially little chance to recover full value) to now "reengage." By reengage we mean to agree to invest again in financial assets. The clue to this riddle is not, in our view, found in a dramatic difference in economic literacy between advisors and their clients, although that certainly may be a factor. The answer is to be found in recognizing the recovery's seminal idiosyncratic feature: the jobless recovery.

For investors, especially those who lost jobs or had friends and family members who did, the global financial crisis is not yet a thing of the past; it is a dominant feature of their present. For them, not just the economy needs to improve, but employment, too. Not recognizing this insight is risky for advisors trying now to reengage their clients. It runs the risk of not recognizing the origin of their reticence to reenter capital markets, whose misbehavior may have been the catalyst of the real pain and demoralization that accompanies job loss or forced early retirement.

As a result of the impact of the global financial crisis, advisors must find more effective ways to manage their client relationships. Steve Moore, author of *Ineffective Habits of Financial Advisors: And the Discipline to Break Them* (John Wiley & Sons, 2010) has worked with advisors for over a decade helping them build more valuable practices. Steve is a former NFL coach, our long-time mentor, and management consultant. One tool Steve co-developed with advisors is the Client Engagement Roadmap. The roadmap is explained in greater detail in Chapter 7.

The purpose of the Client Engagement Roadmap is to eliminate from the advisor/client dialogue careless, haphazard, or reflexive conversations and to replace them with procedural and methodical planning conversations. The reason why that's important is that many people, even educated, wealthy, and sophisticated people, do not have a clear sense of what their financial advisors are doing for them or, more instrumentally, how to explain its benefits to others (namely, their affluent friends and colleagues). The Client Engagement Roadmap reduces that uncertainty by creating a clear understanding and a literal roadmap for those activities to take place between you and your client. This has various beneficial outcomes. For the investor, the roadmap increases their certainty of reaching their desired destination. It also allows the investor to understand how to collaborate in the advisory process and thus engenders greater enthusiasm to that process. The investor, then, is able to articulate to other people why the process is so fulfilling with the effect of bringing those other people to the advisor's doorstep (this is the essence of endemic marketing). For advisors, it allows the ability to create a much higher level of quality control in the client engagement by following a defined process for their client conversations. Sometimes this is referred to as institutionalizing the client-service process. Another benefit for advisors is to be able to convey to their staff what materials are required for those client meetings such that the clients' outcomes might be better assured and assured continuously.

Underserved Individuals

We hope we have insights about how advisors can improve their communications with their clients. However, even with the use of tools such as the Client Engagement Roadmap, the ability to automate these insights is finite. We come back to the thought that the personal interaction between the advisor and the client is the foundation of a positive and effective relationship, and it explains the advisor's fee. There are enough large providers of financial services that, if these insights and methods could be automated to the satisfaction of affluent clients, they already would have been. The larger point to be made here is that the advisory process cannot move forward to the future that we are describing without the end investors' tailored outcomes being actually seen. Not just perceived as being seen but actually being seen, and continually monitored.

However, many individuals aren't being seen by their advisors. In March 2007, McKinsey & Company conducted an online survey of 3,673 people throughout the United States, asking them about their plans, concerns, and patterns of interaction with financial firms.[2] The following is an excerpt from the results of the survey.

> *Those consumers who have an advisor are not necessarily getting what they need. About a quarter of affluent consumers say they are seeking advice on a range of financial topics, including choosing investment products, guaranteeing sufficient income in retirement, and protecting themselves from rising health-care costs. However, only a small percentage say they are receiving the help they need from financial providers.*
>
> *Advisors are also not drawing up financial plans for their customers frequently enough. This phenomenon is particularly true for women. Two-thirds of women with advisors say their advisors have not helped them develop a financial plan for their retirement—a shockingly high number.*
>
> *Consumers' unmet need for help explains a surprising finding about the anxiety levels of affluent pre-retirees who currently have*

financial advisors. It turns out that they are actually more anxious than people who do not have advisors. This may be partly because some people who don't use advisors are unaware of the financial risks they face. But it also sends a clear message that the typical advisor is not doing enough to make his customers feel confident about their financial futures.

So here is the watershed difference. Up until now it's been possible to have various strategies that cause individuals to think that they are being seen (mass customization is an example of this). However, the future of wealth management is to *actually* see the client, and to do something with what you are observing. *Seeing them* first means that you understand what their funded status is, and second that you know how to advise them based on their funded status. This is inseparable from the idea of customer intimacy. It can't be done with fake sincerity. There's no such thing. The challenge, of course, is that, if you have 1,000 clients, it's not possible to advise them all in a sincere way. You certainly will have to become more efficient in your client-facing activities and more selective with whom you accept as clients.

TECHNICAL FOUNDATION PILLARS

The next chapter of this book is dedicated to the personal asset liability model; a process for determining an individual's funded status relative to their future needs and building an investment plan accordingly. The framework did not spring forth out of the blue. It is a continuation of many previous technical insights, some directly associated, others less so. Often though, the challenge with technical insights is that they are not accessible to the end investor, because, to be appreciated, they require a broad contextual understanding of investment, economic, finance, and pension technology that end investors do not have. What the personal asset liability model tries to do is provide a process whereby these technical insights can be abbreviated and summarized by advisors. What follows is a brief overview of some of the technical insights that have informed the personal asset liability model. A fully detailed version of each can found in the chapters that follow.

Building a Simple and Powerful Solution to Retirement Saving (Grant Gardner and Yuan-An Fan)

Gardner and Fan's theoretical framework (reproduced as Chapter 11) breaks ground in two ways. First, it incorporates human capital into the asset- allocation decisions for individuals accumulating wealth for retirement (originally applied to the design of target-date portfolios). Second, it uses for its definition of success a wealth target sufficient for the individual at retirement to purchase an annuity equal to their targeted replacement income. They create rules for an intelligent way for individuals to balance the value of their human capital with a basket of financial assets throughout the course of their career. This definition of "rich" that people want to get to someday, is a translation of their insights.

In this framework, success equates to a perpetual call option on annuitization. The reason the framework is based on an option to annuitize rather than actual annuitization is to account for a pervasive behavioral aversion that exists toward annuitization; the fear of the loss of control of wealth and the flexibility to deal with an uncertain (and mistrusted) future. The individual works their entire life to accumulate their nest egg and then is faced with the prospect of giving their nest egg to someone else, even a trusted insurer. The individual has a desire to avoid the regret that arises from the possibility that the insurance company will somehow benefit from their early demise (even though the individual may ultimately benefit from the longevity protection provided by the annuity). This creates a further incentive to defer annuitization if possible. There is also a sense that the individual understands, more clearly than previously thought, the counterparty risk of buying an annuity by recognizing that there is no guarantee that the insurance company will outlast them.

The Annuity Puzzle: In Chapter 2 we documented the decline of the traditional (DB) pension in America. For decades, employers bemoaned that, despite their efforts to educate their employees of the value of their pensions, few fully understood or valued them. Now, people near or in retirement long for the guaranteed income of a traditional pension. However, here's the head-scratcher: even though people say they want the guaranteed income provided by pensions and they can buy annuities directly from insurance companies that replicate traditional pensions, they choose not to buy annuities. This is called the "annuity puzzle." Annuities are often tremendously valuable solutions—why do people (even advisors) love to hate them?

Richard H. Thaler is a professor of economics and behavioral science at the Booth School of Business at the University of Chicago. In a *New York Times* article from May 2011, Thaler discussed the annuity puzzle and the reasons why annuities do not appeal. "Some people think that buying an annuity is in some way a bad deal for their heirs. But that need not be true."

With a life-only annuity, when the annuitant dies, the payments stop and there is nothing left to pass on to their heirs. But, a bequest does not have to come only from residual capital at the time of a person's death. The annuitant could take a portion of their monthly payment and set it aside as a bequest or spend that amount on their family while they are still living (sometimes called a "living bequest"). It's true that if the person buys a life-only annuity and dies early, her heirs will have a smaller bequest than they would have otherwise, but using this set-aside method to create a bequest could also result in a higher bequest (than self-insuring longevity) if she lives longer than average.

From the heir's perspective, it's not so much that an annuity is more or less risky than self-insuring longevity, it's just that the risks are different. With an annuity, their bequest is at risk of being smaller but they have the peace of mind of knowing their parent will have a reliable stream of income for as long as they live. When self-insuring longevity, their bequest remains intact if their parent dies early, but if the parent lives a long time there is a chance they will run out of money before they die. As Thaler explains, "If you have aging parents, you might ask yourself how much you'd be willing to pay to insure that you will never have to figure out how to explain to your spouse, or whomever you may be living with, that your mother is moving in."

Thaler goes on to talk about other reasons for the aversion to annuities including the perception that buying an annuity is a gamble that only pays off if one lives a long time.

Investment Aspects of Longevity Risk (Don Ezra)

According to Don Ezra,

> After retirement, wealth is no longer the yardstick (for success). Rather, income becomes the yardstick. The trade-off is now between higher expected income (good news for obvious reasons) and higher uncertainty of income (bad news, because it can result in low income). But in retirement, unlike in pre-retirement, it is no longer acceptable to have an approximate time horizon for planning. The time horizon extends until one's death–and that is unpredictable.

In Chapter 12, wearing his actuary's hat, Ezra evaluates the danger to individuals when they're left out of the strong and loving arms of the pension plan and lose their ability to pool their longevity risk. He identifies the disadvantages to the individual on his own versus being a member of a pension plan or owning an annuity. The key insight is that once the individual has lost her ability to pool longevity risk, deferring annuitization as long as possible is crucial because the cost of annuitization is high, not only because of the expense, but also due to the loss of control and flexibility over one's assets. The individual's inability to pool their longevity risk is the seminal issue that led us to the development of the personal asset liability model discussed in Chapter 5. It is the primary way our expertise leaps from working with institutions to addressing the individual's dilemma.

Mismeasurement of Risk in Financial Planning (Richard Fullmer)

In Chapter 13, Richard Fullmer discusses the pervasive mismeasurement of risk in financial planning. He explains,

> *Financial planning is complex. Modeling tools have proliferated as a way to help wade through the complexity and facilitate sound decision-making processes. The selection of the risk measure in these tools is all-important. Poor decisions can result if the risk measure is faulty or incomplete.*

Fullmer argues the risk that should be focused on when planning for retirement income should be the risk of income shortfall rather than volatility of portfolio return. The total risk measurement he proposes is the product of the probability of shortfall times the magnitude of shortfall. In real life this means that missing by an inch may matter less than missing by a mile.

Modern Portfolio Decumulation (Richard Fullmer)

Fullmer's modern portfolio decumulation piece is a logical extension of his mismeasurement of risk work (Chapter 13). It "describes a new framework for efficient portfolio construction in the 'decumulation' phase of the investment lifecycle, in which an investor who has accumulated assets over time wishes to use those assets to fund ongoing living expenses. It combines elements of both investment theory and actuarial science, introducing an effective way to manage longevity risk in the portfolio." The key thought here is that the conventional standard for accumulation of wealth is not optimal for decumulation. Besides just identifying that, he comes up with an alternative approach for investing in the decumulation phase, developing his thinking along lines of dynamic asset allocation models (we use the term *adaptive* rather than *dynamic* in this book, except where the content is written by contributors).

* * *

What we've attempted to do in this chapter is to connect insights from the diverse perspectives of psychology, language, practice management, portfolio construction, actuarial science, and financial planning so they appear in a context that is relevant to both you as the advisor and to your clients. In the next chapter we connect the dots further in our discussion of the personal asset liability model.

NOTES

1. The latest print and video summaries of the Financial Professional Outlook is on Russell's Helping-Advisors website at www.russell.com/Helping-Advisors/YourBusiness/FinancialProfessionalOutlook.asp.
2. "Winning the Retirement Race," The McKinsey & Company Consumer Retirement Survey 2007.

CHAPTER 5

The Personal Asset Liability Model—Funded Status

I n this and the next chapter we describe the steps of the personal asset liability model. As we mentioned in the previous chapter, this model is the result of an accumulation of insights. In particular we would like to recognize our colleague at Russell, Sam Pittman, PhD, who is responsible for much of the content in the two chapters on the personal asset liability model. We thank Sam for his generosity in allowing us to incorporate his work into our description of the model and for his effort in pushing the larger project ahead.

By now you know that the personal asset liability model is a process for determining an investors' funded status relative to their future spending needs and for developing investment plans accordingly, and surveillance of those plans.

Our great teacher, Randy Lert, former Chief Portfolio Strategist at Russell Investments, distilled the essence of the personal asset liability model by saying:

> *The model, using the funded status approach, is fundamentally different than the modern portfolio theory idea about risk preferences. Here the risk preference function is transferred not to some general sense of return volatility but to the volatility of the funded status. Now your client's actual ability to tolerate variation in spending becomes the new risk.*

A key point we are making in this book is that individuals should make informed decisions about whether to annuitize. Deferring annuitization buys them time in hopes that their situation improves. So long as that deferral is an informed decision (by the fact that you know your funded status is greater than 100 percent), it is a sound decision. The big risk of course is not being informed—being underfunded and not knowing about it or your clients having less discretion in their spending than they imagined. The personal asset liability model provides you the steps to accurately inform your client of their present funded status and how to make investment decisions based on that.

We've broken the model into two parts: Part one discusses how to calculate an individual's funded status, and part two discusses how to create, implement, and maintain an investment plan based on the individual's funded status. Later, in Chapter 7 we discuss the business of giving good advice and suggest how to incorporate these steps into a Client Engagement Roadmap.

RETIREMENT REALITY CHECK

We could have named this chapter "the retirement reality check." By doing the math at the level of detail we suggest here, the individual's *real* situation becomes clear. The three key questions we discussed in Chapter 1—How much do I need to spend to live the lifestyle I desire? Will my money last as long as I will? Am I invested accordingly?—are all addressed as a result of going through the steps described in the model. Even so, this process may not be right for every individual. It requires trust between the advisor and the individual investor, for a couple of reasons. First, the process relies on accurate inputs from individuals, particularly with regard to future spending and (if applicable) future savings to be contributed to the individual's portfolio. In addition, if individuals withhold information from their advisors, (e.g., assets, liabilities, objectives, motivations, etc.) or deceive themselves and others about savings commitments, the results of the process can be undone.

Because individuals' funded status is the fundamental metric that helps determine the amount of risk individuals can or should take with their investment portfolio, naturally, it is the most important metric to be monitored going forward. However, the funded status can only be accurately calculated if all the individuals' assets and liabilities are included in the calculation. To reinforce a previous point, if information is withheld from the process, the resulting funded status may be inaccurate and will misinform any subsequent decisions on which the funded status is based. Astute advisors will recognize in this both the opportunity for asset consolidation and the benefit of securing future funding promises with autodeposit, when possible.

TAX CONSIDERATIONS

Tax implications, when ignored, can cause an otherwise sound financial plan to be suboptimal or insufficient for meeting the individual's future spending needs. It is beyond the scope of our description of this model to factor all possible tax circumstances that might arise—plus, we are not tax accountants. Therefore, anyone using this model must factor the necessary adjustments according to the individual's specific tax circumstances. For example, for the case in which an individual preliminarily has just enough wealth to buy an annuity to meet their future spending needs, they might not have enough if, upon liquidating their assets to purchase the annuity, the net proceeds are significantly reduced because of taxes. We recognize the importance of tax considerations when applying this model, however, it is not possible to build into the steps every conceivable tax situation that might arise. That means that if you are not also your client's tax advisor, you should know who is and get acquainted.

DETERMINING THE FUNDED STATUS

Funded status is simply a ratio of assets to liabilities (when both are expressed in present-value terms). There are numerous ways this calculation may be made. What follows is one example of how to perform this calculation. Afterwards we discuss special considerations when valuing an individual's assets and liabilities.

Measuring the Amount of Wealth Needed for Retirement

Note: the following section in this chapter, through to the section titled "Other Considerations When Determining Assets," was written by Sam Pittman, PhD. Sam uses the term *funded ratio* rather than *funded status*. The terms mean the same thing. A funded status is expressed as a percentage whereas a funded ratio is expressed as a ratio with 1 equating to 100 percent funded. Sam thanks Grant Gardner for many insightful discussions that helped shape this content.

A funded ratio provides a quick, accurate feasibility assessment of an individual's spending plan. Funded ratios are used by pension funds to compare their liabilities—the future payments going to the participants—to their assets—the amount of wealth the fund holds to generate those payments. Adequately funded spending plans have funded ratios greater than one, meaning they have more assets than liabilities. The following approach we discuss will enable you to quickly show your client whether his proposed spending plan can be adequately funded by his investments.

Many advisors turn to retirement planning tools to analyze a spending plan. So why would they choose a funded ratio? Because, **it's a quick** calculation that addresses longevity concerns, doesn't depend on forecasts of market returns, and it doesn't require an investment plan to determine the adequacy of one's wealth to fund retirement.

A weakness of relying on market-return projections to determine spending feasibility is that the assessment is then dependent on forecasts, versus known values. If the market-return forecasts are incorrect, such as an overly optimistic equity return assumption, the investor's plan is at greater risk of failure than indicated by the planning tool. Hence, prior to tailoring your client's investment plan using a retirement-planning tool, a good practice is to check spending feasibility by comparing the asset values to spending liabilities using a funded ratio.

Let's consider an example of Phill and Wendy Rogerson. Phill, age 61 and will retire from EFD Corporation in six months. Wendy is 62 and retired a year ago. Neither has a pension, but between them they've saved $760,000. Phill hopes to add another $15,000 to his retirement account during his final six months of work. They're depending on their nest egg and combined $38,000-per-year Social Security benefit to support their retirement lifestyle. Wendy, the budgeter for the household, says that they'll need at least $60,000 to support their essential living needs, but this would mean making some cutbacks. Like most couples, they're looking to enjoy a comfortable retirement. Wendy figures that $72,000 per year would provide a lifestyle that includes travel and other activities they're looking forward to, but she's unsure if this is attainable.

Throughout our description of the personal asset liability model we make the distinction between spending needs that fall into the categories of essentials, lifestyle, and estate. Essential spending is that which the individual (or couple) believes is necessary to meet their basic needs. Lifestyle spending is the amount above and beyond essentials to provide for a desired quality of life. Travel, dining out, club memberships, and so on might be examples of lifestyle spending. Estate spending is the wealth the individual wishes to give away (typically to family members or charities). Estate spending may take place during the life of the individual or simply be a targeted amount to be dispersed upon the death of the individual (or the second to die of a couple), so long as it is discretionary.

Categorizing expenses in these categories is subjective. What one individual considers an essential, another may consider a luxury. We posit that much can be learned about a client's actual tolerance level for variability of spending through an advisor's probing of what are really, truly, non-negotiable essentials. The importance of the distinction will become clearer as we continue to describe the personal asset liability model. Most importantly, many of your clients will not have sufficient wealth to meet all their spending needs. Therefore, it is critical to know the spending needs by category, and critical for the client to understand that the smaller the base of essential expenses, the greater their flexibility is. Having said that, the top priority and therefore the baseline definition for the annuitization hurdle is essential spending.

We owe a debt of gratitude to Don Ezra for his contributions to our thinking on this subject (not to mention his tutelage to each of us throughout our careers) and for his detailed explanations of how to consider expenses in this way. Don is Co-chair, Global Consulting at Russell Investments, recipient of the Lillywhite Award from the Employee Benefit Research Institute for "extraordinary life contributions to Americans' economic security," and the first-ever Fellow of the American Savings Education Council. Don has written extensively on investing, including his much acclaimed 1998 book: *Pension Fund Excellence* (New York: John Wiley & Sons) and his 2009 book: *The Retirement Plan Solution* (Hoboken, NJ: John Wiley & Sons). In the latter book, Don first introduced us to the idea that individuals should consider investing their retirement assets based on their level of wealth relative to their future liabilities (funded status).

Phill and Wendy are interviewing wealth managers and visit your office. They're more prepared than most clients, but they need investment advice and want to know if their spending plan can be supported. If the Rogersons follow their essential spending plan, they'll need to withdrawal $60,000 – $38,000 = $22,000 per year from their retirement portfolio. If they use the higher lifestyle spending plan, they'll need to withdraw $72,000 – $38,000 = $34,000 per year. Both of these withdrawal rates seem reasonable at 2.8 percent and 4.4 percent considering the 4 percent rule.[1] However, Phill and Wendy are young retirees; they likely have long lives ahead of them. This needs to be considered. Using the funded ratio, which factors in longevity, you can quickly assess their spending plans. Figure 5.1 shows the value of their spending liabilities and their portfolio value. The liabilities in Figure 5.1 account for a 2.5 percent annual cost of living increase and mortality expectations. The method for calculating these values are discussed later in this chapter.

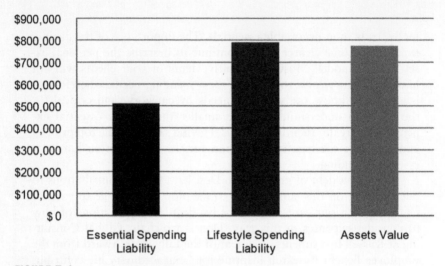

FIGURE 5.1   Assets and Liability Values

Figure 5.1 shows the liability amount for two different spending plans and the assets' value available to support them.

Fortunately, the proposed essential spending liability is smaller than their portfolio value; the lifestyle spending plan liability is slightly larger than their total assets value. The funded ratios for their proposed spending plans are stated here:

Essential Funded Ratio : ($15,000 + $760,000)/$510,591 = 152%

Lifestyle Funded Ratio : ($15,000 + $760,000)/$789,100 = 98%

The surplus values, assets less liabilities, for each spending plan are shown here (Note: A negative surplus amount is a deficit, which will also result in a *funded status* of less than 100 percent or a *funded ratio* of less than one).

Essential Plan Surplus : $15,000 + $760,000 − $510,600 = $264,400

Lifestyle Plan Surplus : $15,000 + $760,000 − $789,100 = −$14,100

Using the criterion of a funded ratio of 1 as feasible, the lower (essentials) spending plan is feasible, but the higher (lifestyle) spending plan is slightly infeasible. Although there are risks and investment strategy implications to choosing one spending plan over another, these can be addressed in a comprehensive retirement planning process. **What the funded ratio provides is an objective measure of the spending plan feasibility relative to the client's assets, while accounting for inflation and longevity.**

We now examine how to calculate the values on which the funded ratio depends.

Assessing Retirement Liabilities　Retirement liabilities are future payments required to support living expenses and other expenditures. The primary liability of a retired person is the income stream to replace the paycheck received from his employer. In this illustration we focus our discussion on consistent retirement spending. For example, the necessary essential income of $60,000 per year adjusted for inflation required by Phill and Wendy to replace their preretirement salary. To determine if clients have enough wealth to cover their retirement expenses, we need to determine the value of their liabilities. In conventional analyses, future obligations (liabilities) are discounted and summed to obtain a present value. In simple terms, that's how we proceed in the following pages, but we also address mortality and inflation, because we don't know how long the investor will need to provide income nor the purchasing power of money in the future.

> Explaining to your client that your approach accommodates these uncertainties simultaneously reveals that you are preoccupied with two of their central anxieties—living too long and the cheapening of their purchasing power.

One method of valuing future liabilities is to use market prices. Insurance companies provide a market for individuals to exchange a lump sum of cash for a stream of future payments that last for life. Prices for annuity contracts are readily available.

However, there are some issues to consider with using market prices of annuity contracts to value liabilities and as a result, we caution you to regard such prices as indicative only. Contracts may not exist that perfectly match your client's liabilities. As an example, it may be difficult to find an insurance company that will guarantee future payments linked to inflation. Often insurance companies provide step-ups, where the future payments increase at a fixed rate, but this does not perfectly hedge the risk of inflation growing faster than the provided step-up. Additionally, buying an insurance contract subjects your client to counterparty risk. If the insurance company goes out of business, then it may default on the annuity contract, though, in fact, this has been rare. An alternative to using market prices is to employ the pricing methodology used by insurance companies.

Insurance companies employ actuaries to price insurance contracts. Actuaries have essentially transparent methods for pricing liabilities that can be replicated and amended to address investor-specific liabilities. Counterparty risk can also be addressed in the valuation by making an assumption that the portfolio backing the annuity payments is invested in riskless treasury bonds that perfectly hedge the liability of the investor.

Given a mortality table and a yield curve, the actuarial net present value of a stream of future payments can be calculated according to equation 5.1:

$$L = \sum_{t=R}^{t=\infty} \frac{(1+i_t)^{t-1} D_t p_t}{(1+r_t)^{t-1}}$$

where D_t is the distribution in period t expressed in today's dollars.

r_t is the yield of a zero coupon treasury maturing in t years.

p_t is the probability that the liability in period t will have to be paid. For a single person, it is the probability that they are alive in period t; for a couple it is the probability that at least one of them is alive in period t.[2]

i_t is the expected annualized inflation rate from the beginning of the current period to the beginning of period t.

R is the first year in which a future payment is made to support retirement spending. For someone already retired, R will be 1, otherwise it will represent the number of periods until the first retirement distribution.

In equation 5.1, we assume that retirement distributions occur at the beginning of the period.

As is often noted, it's a mistake to plan only to your client's life expectancy, because your client may live past it. Planning to the average outcome isn't what we're suggesting here. An insurance company can ameliorate longevity risk by selling contracts to a pool of investors that will have an aggregate life expectancy close to the average. Although an individual cannot diversify mortality risk like an insurance company, **an individual can preserve the option to purchase insurance.**

This is, in fact, an acutely valuable insight Sam is describing, namely, the idea is that we can create and design around a concrete definition of financial security in retirement by perpetuating the client's option to purchase an annuity sufficient to cover "essential" expenses, but deferring the decision to do so as long as possible. It may be possible to defer annuitization forever because the annuity will decrease in price as the client ages. (You might model the economic value such a strategy affords in case your client wants to know what you have done for him lately to earn your fee.)

In Chapter 14, Richard Fullmer shows that, if an individual maintains enough wealth to purchase an annuity, then he maintains the option to cover their liabilities using an annuity contract. This means that retirees who decide not to insure through the purchase of an annuity should ideally maintain a funded ratio greater than 1. As long as insurance companies are willing to sell annuities, and your client maintains more assets than the cost of an annuity contract, a funded ratio of greater than 1, your client has at least one option to cover their spending needs for life. (However, concerns around counterparty risk will need to be considered if an annuity is actually purchased.)

Tallying Up Current Assets   The value of current assets is the sum of all assets the investor owns that can be used to offset liability payments. For most investors, this will include their financial assets and human capital. Other assets such as inheritance or other contingent claims can also be included, but here we limit consideration to financial assets and human capital. (As used in this description, human capital means future savings to be added to the couple's retirement portfolio, typically as a result of saving a portion of their paychecks, hence the name "human" capital.)

The value of financial assets is simply the sum of the value of the current assets someone owns. This is the value of all of your client's available financial accounts, the equity value that would be obtained from the sale of any businesses, the equity value of any properties, and any other assets that contribute to net worth and could be made available to fund future spending. This is expressed mathematically in equation 5.2:

$$V = \sum_{i=1}^{N} V_i$$

where V_i is the equity value of financial asset i
N is the number of financial assets

Financial assets represent the value of wealth accumulated plus anticipated growth. Because our goal is to assess whether an individual has enough to retire, we also need to include the value of additional savings (human capital that has not yet been converted into financial capital).

To calculate this value, we find the present value of future retirement savings. This is the sum of future retirement contributions discounted at an appropriate interest rate. We make the assumption that future savings contributions are similar in risk to coupon payments of an AA bond, leading us to use the AA yield curve to obtain discount rates. However, this assumption may be inappropriate for some occupations, such as a stock trader, whose future contributions may be more equity-like.[3] **The chosen yield curve used to discount future payments should be risk adjusted to match the risk of human-capital payments.**

The formula for calculating the present value of future human capital contributions is given in equation 5.3:

$$H = \sum_{t=1}^{t=R-1} \frac{a_t S_t}{(1 + \overline{r}_t)^{t-1}}$$

where S_t is the projected salary in period t

a_t is savings rate in period t

$\overline{r}_t$ is the interest rate on the yield curve for a payment with duration t

Note that human capital payments are deposited at the beginning of the period, and there is no mortality risk factored into the calculation of human capital in this example.

Following are a few notes regarding human capital:

- When an investor has retired (and, thus, is no longer generating income from work) the value of human capital is zero.
- Be on the lookout for unrealistic savings plans. If a client forecasts an unusually high savings plan that he is unlikely to meet, then the value of his human capital will be overstated. This would defeat the purpose of using the funded ratio to assess feasibility, because the value of the assets would be artificially inflated. This problem is similar to basing a retirement plan on overly optimistic future market returns.
- A method for ensuring the value of your client's human capital is to get them to commit to automatic funding of their portfolio. A variation of this method is for them to contribute to employer sponsored 401(k), at least to the level that gives them the maximum employer match contribution.

Defining Funded Ratio and Surplus   Because the funded ratio is simply the ratio of assets to liabilities, and assets and liabilities have been defined, the funded ratio can now be stated as shown in equation 5.4:

$$F R = \frac{V + H}{L}$$

If the value of the investor's assets (the numerator) is greater than that of the liabilities (the denominator), then the investor's retirement plan is fully funded (**at that moment in time**). However, if the funded ratio is less than one (i.e., the denominator is larger than the numerator), then the plan is underfunded.

The difference between an investor's assets and liabilities is the surplus, given in equation 5.5:

$$S = V + H - L$$

An investor with a surplus greater than zero has a funded ratio that is greater than one, indicating a fully funded retirement plan. An investor with a negative surplus has a funded ratio that is less than one and, ergo an underfunded plan.

Managing Your Client's Funded Ratio   Although the funded ratio provides an indication of the viability of your client's retirement plan, it requires management. If your client's funded ratio is less than one, his plan is not feasible and needs adjustment. If the investor has not yet retired, they have several options to obtain a feasible plan—one with a funded ratio that is greater than one:

- Save more to increase the value of their human capital.
- Scale back proposed retirement spending to reduce future liabilities.
- Delay retirement to increase human capital and reduce liabilities.

Retired clients with an underfunded plan will also have to make adjustments to achieve a feasible retirement plan. The options are:

- Adjust liabilities by spending less in retirement.
- Return to work to reduce retirement liabilities, and potentially increase human capital if some of the wages can be saved.

An individual (or couple) who are unwilling or unable to make adjustments to obtain a feasible spending plan are, by default, accepting the risk of outliving their assets.

Advisors may want to tailor their clients' investment strategy according to the clients' funded ratio. Take the example of a retired investor with a surplus. Two factors that could cause a drop in the funded ratio are:

1. A drop in the market that decreases asset values—the numerator of equation 5.4.
2. A drop in interest rates that increases the liability of the plan—the denominator of equation 5.4.

Investors wanting to avoid falling into deficit can tailor their investment plans to manage surplus risk. For example, they could buy immediate annuities to cover expected liabilities. Investment risk and longevity risk would be eliminated, but there would still be exposure to inflation and default risk. If they have a sufficient surplus, there is value to deferring an annuity purchase,[4] and instead manage the client's wealth to control surplus risk. Pension funds and insurance companies do this by matching investments to liabilities. In doing this, investment managers construct a portfolio to move in tandem with the value of the liability to reduce the risk of having a surplus drop below a certain threshold.[5]

One approach to managing the risk of having your client's surplus drop below zero is to use an adaptive investment strategy that dynamically manages surplus risk—the risk of shortfall relative to the spending liabilities. In Chapter 14, Richard Fullmer describes managing surplus risk dynamically resulting in a decrease of shortfall risk relative to a static strategy. Although there are various benefits to reducing surplus risk, one that may resonate with most advisors is reducing the odds of an uncomfortable conversation around spending cutbacks due to a negative surplus after the client is in retirement.

> We discuss in further detail managing an individual's investment plan relative to their funded status in part two of the personal asset liability model–investment plan (Chapter 6).

We perceive tremendous benefits for advisors who adopt a reliable, unbiased, and, above all, consistent approach to determine if retiring clients have enough wealth to retire or to validate a preretiree's spending plan. In fact, we imagine a whole slew of new advisory practices sprouting up that will offer this capability as their competitive edge. The funded ratio, which has been used by pension managers, provides such an unbiased answer to the question of plan feasibility. In addition it's simple to compute; and it has minimal dependency on future projections. The computation of the funded ratio requires you to determine just three values: financial assets, future savings (human capital), and retirement liability. Upon obtaining these three numbers, it is a simple calculation to determine whether your client's plan is well funded or needs altering.

> What's novel is the adaptation of the funded status concept to the individual and focusing the ongoing client-service conversation on it as a proxy for addressing the client's central concern: "Am I on track?"

The actuarial table used in this example is the U.S. Basic Individual Annuitant 2000 Table, Society of Actuaries. In addition, Tables 5.1 and 5.2 show the yield curves used in this example.

TABLE 5.1 Treasury Yield Curve

Duration	1	2	3	4	5	10	12	15	20	30	50
Yield	.31%	.64%	1.09%	1.56%	2%	3.61%	4.04%	4.33%	4.61%	4.75%	4.81%

TABLE 5.2 AA Investment Grade Yield Curve

Duration	1	2	3	4	5	10	12	15	20	30	50
Yield	.75%	1.23%	1.80%	2.35%	2.86%	4.61%	5%	5.35%	5.62%	5.71%	5.69%

OTHER CONSIDERATIONS WHEN DETERMINING ASSETS

For the funded status calculation to be reliable, both total assets and liabilities must be properly valued. You should exclude from the asset side of the ledger any investments or property the individual does not intend to make available for future spending. The most common asset to be excluded is owner-occupied real estate (the family home). If it is unlikely the individual or couple is willing to spend the value of their home (through a reverse mortgage or an outright sale), their home equity should not be included in the value of their assets. However, people who are underfunded or on the cusp of underfunded status may not have a choice but to spend their home equity. In our conversations with advisors and individuals in preparation for this book, we found that many people consider their home equity as part of the estate they intend to leave to family members or charity. Some also feel their home equity is their cushion; they don't intend to tap into that asset during their lifetime but know they can access the equity if needed.

Another area of caution is the risk of overstating future savings. Whether due to overconfidence or lack of discipline, evidence is rife that it is much easier to pledge to save than to actually do it. Conservative assumptions should be made regarding future savings unless you have a long history with a particular client and are confident of their future savings estimates. Or better still, encourage your clients to commit to an automatic funding (saving) program. Involuntary retirement can also cause the estimate of future savings (and liabilities) to be inaccurate. Some people may retire involuntarily which will affect their ability to meet their savings plan, either because they no longer have income or, when they try to reenter the workforce, they have less earning potential and, therefore, less saving potential.

This fact is made clear in the following excerpt from the book *Managing Your Firm's 401(k) Plan* (Smith 2010):

> *People are spending more years in retirement because they are retiring earlier than planned and living longer than in the past. While the normal retirement age most people think of is 65, research shows that many are retiring earlier. According to the Employee Benefit Research Institute's (EBRI) 2010 Retirement Confidence Survey (RCS), 28% of individuals surveyed who were still working indicated that they planned on retiring before age 65. However, of the individuals surveyed who were already retired, 61% said they actually retired before the age 65. An excerpt from the survey report sheds light on why people are retiring earlier than planned.*
>
> *The RCS has consistently found that a large percentage of retirees leave the workforce earlier than planned (41% in 2010). Many retirees who retired earlier than planned cite negative reasons for leaving the workforce before they expected, including health problems or disability (54%); changes at their company, such as downsizing or closure (26%); and having to care for a spouse or another family member (19%). Others say changes in the skills required for their job (16%) or other work-related reasons (11%) played a role. Some retirees mention a mix of positive and negative reasons for retiring early, **but just 5% offer only positive reasons**.[6]*

The point we want to make clear is that future estimates of savings must be carefully qualified. It is an easy temptation for individuals who are still in the accumulation phase to try to solve their underfunded status by increasing their savings assumption or by lengthening the number of years they intend to work (and save). Even when you are dealing with well-intentioned and disciplined individuals, their estimates may be too optimistic due to external and involuntary factors. These factors merit highlighting in your client contracts and disclosures.

OTHER CONSIDERATIONS WHEN DETERMINING LIABILITIES

We offer a similar caution when estimating future spending; take pains to be as realistic as possible and err on the side of being conservative. Self-deception, lack of discipline, lack of foresight, and inability to accurately predict inflation are all potential causes of inaccurate spending plans. Later in this chapter, we describe four methods for helping your clients develop a spending plan. We are sure there are other suitable ways to do this as well. We spoke with an advisor in Florida, Ilene Davis, who has been developing her spending-plan calendar for decades. We asked her to tell us about how she helps her clients create a spending plan. She said:

> I found when I met with clients, even if they brought in a list of what they spend money on, they leave out things like gifts, personal care, or donations. To help both the client and me create a more accurate spending plan, I designed a calendar, called the Personal Financial Planning Calendar, to help us remember categories that might have been forgotten. It's a checklist for them to use to look at their monthly, quarterly, and annual expenses. One problem people have is they can tell you what they pay for their mortgage or their utilities, but it's the other 30 to 50% they spend that they have no clue what they're spending it on. I have them go through at least six to twelve months of their credit cards and checking accounts to try to account for where their money has gone. I also have them track their cash so they have a good feeling of what they've been spending. But more importantly, I asked them to describe the lifestyle they expect to have in retirement. They are suddenly going to go from 40 to 60 hours a week working, that they're getting paid for, to 40 to 60 hours a week that they will need to fill, golfing, gardening, working part-time, volunteering, or whatever. So, I want them to think about what they're going to do with those 40 to 60 hours a week that they used to spend working. It could be a very expensive 40 to 60 hours.

We asked if this results in improved accuracy in the estimates. She responded:

It depends on the individual. Because I work with my clients to really determine what they want to do in retirement the estimates are pretty good. The men are the biggest challenge because they are accustomed to their life being centered around their work. So it's more difficult for them to think of what they are going to do with their time. I've had male clients who said that they are going to paint the house, etc., and then I asked them what they're going to do with the other 120 to 140 months of their life. I try to help them understand that what they said they're going to do in retirement usually takes about a year and they need to think about the rest of their time. I haven't seen my clients spending plans change much because I really try to get them to think about what they want to do. Some go back to work because they're bored. Others will travel more than anticipated. But I don't see major changes.

Even when your clients are able to articulate their spending plan accurately, they may struggle with staying on plan. As an advisor in the U.K., Marlene Shalton, explained to us:

You need to probe deeply and try to understand why clients spend compulsively or on impulse. Usually there are deep seated fears and/or insecurities that drive these behaviours in the same way that being afraid to spend can be. For instance, I had a client who admitted that she liked to spend money on clothes, but felt she lacked discipline with her spending and looked to me to instil this. I suggested she clear her credit card debts and then, instead of paying £X to pay off the bills each month, she pay this amount into a clothing and footwear savings account. Only when she had sufficient money in the account was she allowed to buy. This system seemed to work for her. She still consults me on any major spending she might want to do and we both recognise and acknowledge, that this is the only way she can manage her finances.

FOUR APPROACHES TO CREATING A SPENDING PLAN

Here we discuss four ways to help your clients create spending plans. One method is to begin with their current income (their paycheck) and work toward replacing this amount. Another is to help them build a spending plan independent of their current income levels, say to target some level of certainty that they will not outlive their assets. Still another approach is when your clients are already confident in their spending needs and have prepared accurate plans. Here, your role is to help them verify the accuracy of their plan. Finally, your clients may want to solve for their spending level and their investment plans as part of an iterative process; evaluating trade-offs between spending level and certainty of sustainability. It's an interesting discussion to have with clients in and of itself—what approach seems to them the best fit. This is an obvious example of *tailoring*.

Replace Their Paycheck

For some people, it is easier to begin with their current paycheck and work from there to determine the amount of income they need in retirement. The resulting spending plan should equal the value of their preretirement after-tax take-home pay. However, they don't need to fund this entire amount. Income from sources such as Social Security and employer pensions should be subtracted from the spending plan as we saw in the detailed example earlier in this chapter. Figure 5.2 is a simple example of a replace-my-paycheck calculation.

In our example, Bill and Jane Smith have a combined gross monthly income of $13,000. However, after subtracting taxes and retirement savings that will cease once in retirement, and adding back the value of other benefits they are receiving from their current employers such as health insurance, the after-tax value of their net monthly take-home pay is $8,860. (Note: The

	Bill	Jane	Combined	
Income Before Retirement				
Monthly gross pay	$10,000	$3,000	$13,000	
Monthly taxes	−2,800	−840	−3,640	
Monthly retirement savings	−1,000	−300	−1,300	
After-tax value of benefits such as health insurance			800	
Net after-tax value of monthly take-home pay			8,860	**(A)**
Other Sources of Income in Retirement				
Estimated Social Security payment	2,200	1,100	3,300	
Bill's monthly defined benefit payment	1,850	0	1,850	
Jane's monthly state pension	0	750	750	
Retirement income from other sources	4,050	1,850	5,900	**(B)**
After-tax monthly cashflow needed to replace their paycheck			$2,960	**(A–B)**

FIGURE 5.2   Bill and Jane Smith's Replace-My-Paycheck Calculation

amount that should be added back into their monthly take-home pay for health insurance is not likely to be the value of their current employers' health insurance contributions rather the cost of health insurance they will incur once in retirement in order to supplement their Medicare benefits.)

Bill and Jane can expect a combined $3,300 per month in benefits from Social Security as well as a $1,850 per month pension Bill earned earlier in his career and a $750 pension benefit Jane earned as a public school teacher. After subtracting these amounts from their preretirement net after-tax monthly take-home pay, Bill and Jane need another $2,960 of after-tax monthly cash flow to replace their paycheck.

Please note that in a real-life scenario there may be other (many other) tax considerations that must be factored into this calculation. The example we described here is solely for explanation purposes and is therefore unlikely to be representative of any individual's actual tax circumstances.

Help Them Build a Spending Plan

Some individuals may wish to build their spending plan without reference to their current paycheck amount. For people whose income fluctuates significantly, this method may be preferable than the replace-my-paycheck method. The best place to start is to look at how much your client is currently spending today. If they have not tracked their spending before it would be a useful exercise for them to do so for at least twelve months in order to get an accurate picture of how they spend their money. In addition, as we heard from Ilene Davis earlier in this chapter, the more accurately your client can describe how they will spend their time in retirement the more accurately they will be able to determine their spending plan. Figure 5.3 is a simple example of Bob and Sue Jones' spending plan estimate. There is nothing like fingering a box full of receipts to help concretize spending, and create a practical linkage between planning for the future, and how one spends in the present.

The top portion of the spreadsheet shows Bob and Sue's annual budget to be $70,000 resulting in a monthly spending goal of $5,833. As in our previous example, we determine how much of this spending they need to fund from their retirement assets by subtracting other sources of income in retirement. In this example they are estimating they will receive $2,200 per month from Social Security. They do not have any other form of retirement income such as employer provided pensions. Therefore, they need to be able to support $3,633 of spending per month from their retirement assets. This is, of course, after-tax. The same caveats we made in the previous example about tax considerations apply here—this example is only for explanation purposes and might not represent the complexity of your client's actual tax situation.

Annual Budget

Housing	$12,000
Transportation	10,000
Food	8,000
Healthcare	6,000
Property Tax	5,000
Utilities	4,300
Entertainment	3,500
Insurance	3,000
Household Miscellaneous	2,500
Clothes	2,400
Gifts	2,000
Furnishings	2,000
Reading and Education	1,600
Personal care	1,000
All other	6,700

Total Annual Budget	$70,000	**(A)**
Monthly Spending Goal	$5,833	**(A)/12**
Other Sources of Income in Retirement		
Est. Monthly Social Security	$2,200	**(B)**
After-tax monthly cashflow needed	$3,633	**(A–B)**

FIGURE 5.3 Bob and Sue Jones's
Help-Me-Build-a-Spending-Plan Calculation

The example shown here of Bob and Sue's spending plan is merely an example. We are not suggesting an individual (or couple) spend their money on these expense categories or in these amounts. Two important points to remember when helping your client build a spending goal are (1) it should be based on the way they live their lives and not someone else's suggested categories and amounts, and (2) it should be realistic. Again, looking at where they currently spend their money is a good starting point for creating a spending plan.

If you are interested in how Americans spend their money, you can go to the U.S. Government's Consumer Expenditure Survey web site at www.bls.gov/cex/. There you can find data on consumer expenditures broken down by consumer type (age, race, income level, etc.) as well as by expense type (food, housing, clothes, etc.).

They Already Know What They Need to Spend

For you as the advisor, this is the easiest of the methods to create a spending plan for your client; they already know how much they need. It is still worth your time to discuss with them how they determined their spending plan. Help them check their work. Their funded status and subsequent investment decisions will be based in part on this spending plan.

Solve the Spending Plan and Investment Plan Simultaneously

A final approach is to create investment plan scenarios using the client's assets and show the sustainability of various spending plans based on each investment plan scenario. In many ways, this is a vastly more understandable approach to discriminating among various asset allocation strategies than the prevailing convention of approximating risk tolerance. Using this method, clients can iterate back and forth between the desire for spending and the desire for certainty (sustainability of spending). If this method is used, a preliminary spending plan should be created using one of the previous methods described so clients have a point of reference later when they are comparing possible spending plans.

* * *

This chapter introduced you to the concept of the personal asset liability model and described in detail the first part of the model: determining the funded status. The next chapter describes in detail the second part of the model: how to create, implement, and maintain an investment plan based on the individual's funded status. As we discussed in the final section of this chapter, there are times when the creation of the spending plan and the investment plan interact with each other. This may happen when an individual wants or needs to optimize between two competing desires: the desire to spend and the desire for certainty. The next chapter deals with this topic in greater detail.

NOTES

1. The 4 percent rule is to withdraw 4 percent of the portfolio value each year.
2. To keep the formula simple, we assume that the benefit to a survivor is 100 percent. The formula would be altered to account for other survivor benefits, such as 75 percent.
3. R. G. Ibbotson, M. A. Milevsky, P. Chen, and K. X. Zhu, "Lifetime Financial Advice: Human Capital, Asset Allocation and Insurance," The Research Foundation of the CFA Institute (2007).

4. M. A. Milevsky, and V. R. Young, "Optimal Asset Allocation and the Real Option to Delay Annuitization." Working Paper (2002).
5. Bob Collie, and John Osborn, "LDI's Role in Pension Plan Strategy: Risk and Return Considerations," Russell Research (May 2011).
6. Matt Smith, *Managing Your Firm's 401(k) Plan* (Hoboken, NJ: John Wiley & Sons, 2010).

CHAPTER 6

The Personal Asset Liability Model—Investment Plan

In the previous chapter we described how to calculate a funded status based on your client's assets and liabilities. This chapter discusses how to create an investment plan. First we will talk about ways an individual can improve on their funded status, then about the implications of their status on their investment plan. Individuals fall into three broad categories based on their funded status: materially overfunded, materially underfunded, and everyone in between. As we will explain, it's those in the middle category whose financial security you can most greatly affect.

We teach you in this chapter a straightforward way to determine a client's asset allocation based on a hypothetical couple's funded status and risk preference. In this example, we discuss sustainability of withdrawal rates and the appropriate risk metrics to consider when making investment-plan decisions. The final topic we cover is how to use goals-based reporting in the ongoing maintenance of your client's funded status. We give an example of what a goals-based report looks like and the value of using this approach with your clients.

WAYS TO IMPROVE THE FUNDED STATUS

Some people have so much wealth that any reasonable investment strategy will keep them in surplus. Others are so underfunded that betting the ranch on a high-risk portfolio is their one and only chance at coming close to closing the gap in their funded status. For these two groups, their investment decisions will be based more on personal preference than on managing their funded status. For those moderately overfunded or below, depending on their age and stage of life, they may have options for improving their funded status (other than using investment methods). Before moving to the step of creating an investment plan, your clients should consider options for improving their funded status: working longer, saving more, and spending less.

Advisors tell us routinely that many of their clients find it difficult or impossible to make these adjustments. However, a reduction of spending in retirement will be forced on them eventually if they allow their funded status to remain low. Peter Rekstad lamented, "The real tragedy I see is that people, rather than making realistic assessments at the start, make decisions about spending in the first five years of retirement that totally change the rest of their life. Then, the adjustments they need to make later are so extreme they always feel impoverished."

It may be that your client simply needs to save more during their working years or reduce their spending expectations for retirement. We say "simply" with the understanding that this simple suggestion is not easy to implement. Spending less before retirement results in increased savings. Spending less in retirement results in a reduced present value of future liabilities. Both improve the individual's funded status. Another way your client can improve their funded status is to work longer, either full time or part time.

The traditional view is that a person works full time until their day of retirement and then stops working, forever. Today this scenario is less common. It is more often the case that a person's human capital declines gradually. Human capital, we remind you, is a term used to describe a person's ability to create income from work rather than from passive activities such as investing. In financial literature, human capital is often specifically defined as the amount of income not immediately consumed but saved for the future.

Human capital is an asset, for sure, but it is an unusual one. When researchers refer to the economic value of human capital, they are describing the transformation or exchange of one's labor into some equivalent amount of fungible assets. In this sense, people who retire, never to work again, fall off a sort of human capital retirement cliff: The day they retire becomes the riskiest day of their lives. It assumes that, after retirement, their human capital cannot ever be reengaged, and, indeed, this is often so. Most people don't want to work again after they retire! However, there is a world of difference between a preference not to have to return to work and an inability to do so. In the case of the latter—where the possibility to reenter the work force even partially is assumed to be out of the question, the risk of a precipitous decline in retirement nest-egg value is all the more catastrophic; one of the three remedial options (remaining in the work force longer) is foreclosed.

In fact, for people who retired in 2007–2010, this is exactly what they experienced—the decline in value and the spike in unemployment combined to amplify the sense of panic among recent retirees whose options for prolonged work—whole or part time, were modest. This is euphemistically referred to in academic literature as "end-point sensitivity," but we think David Bowie said it (actually sang it) best in his song Young Americans:

"I got a suite and you got defeat." Do you remember learning in elementary school science class about the two forms of energy found in nature, kinetic and potential? The economist's measurement of human capital is like the kinetic form; it is observable and measurable. Yet, outside of the economic domain there may be a much more important question in the potential, not the kinetic domain. What is the psychic value (perception of security) to your client to preserve the potential of their human capital to be reengaged (wholly or part time) should they need to do so?

Connecting this to the earlier visual image of the retirement cliff, as well as to a body of research detailing the desire for baby boomers to think (and talk about) retiring differently than their parents, you may wish to promote planning scenarios with clients that, where feasible, model wading into retirement as a more gradual process, versus diving (or being pushed) off the human capital retirement cliff. If your client cannot separate his or her value from his or her paycheck, it is unlikely that even the most robust and sustainable income-replacement strategies will address a longing some boomers experience for doing something significant for at least a portion of what is expected to be a much, much longer and vital postwork life span than their parent's had.

As you saw in Sam Pittman's funded ratio equation in Chapter 5, human capital is part of the numerator (for individuals still working). If people have low funded status, they can improve it by working longer. This is, by far, the option that can have the greatest positive impact on a person's funded status, so much so that it is worth counseling your clients who are close to 100 percent funded (and, therefore, must be vigilant about managing their funded status) that keeping their income-producing skills viable into retirement is a valuable call option on their human capital that they may wish to exercise later.

Although not a popular option for many people, working longer has many benefits: It allows them to postpone withdrawals from their retirement account (or, at the very least, decrease the amount they need to withdraw until they stop working for good), it may result in additional savings added to their retirement account, they may be able to continue to receive employer-provided benefits such as health insurance, and it may allow them to postpone taking Social Security resulting in a higher benefit later.

USING AGE AND FUNDED STATUS AS A GUIDE TO ASSET ALLOCATION

As we discussed in Chapter 3, your client's funded status tells you which conversation to have with them about their investment plan. Later in this chapter we take you through a detailed example of creating an investment plan for a hypothetical couple. In this next section we look at how age and funded status influence asset allocation decisions.

Investing in a Personal Asset Liability Model World

Note: This section, up to the section titled Other Adaptive Methods, was written by Randy Lert.

In a world in which we are investing to achieve a funded status greater than 100 percent, the statement of the investment objective is different than the fairly straightforward world of Markowitz portfolio construction and what I will call traditional asset allocation. There are two primary reasons for this. First, and to some degree the most difficult issue to address, is that we have entered a multi-period world. Multi-period problems are those where we need to make decisions or take actions during the course of the journey, if you will. In the world of simple and traditional asset allocation there are only two time frames, now and then, and as such we only make one original decision concerning portfolio construction. This is not the case in the personal asset liability model world. Why? Because we are concerned with an investment objective of achieving a funded status of 100 percent or more and that is influenced by a number of things, including current interest rates, current investment returns, changing savings rates, and even the passage of time itself. For example, our funded status changes as a function of time. If in retirement everything stays the same, the value of the liabilities decline.[*] (I refer to this in a jocular vein as the Pink Floyd effect, "one day closer to death.") Another way to say this would be that, in a personal asset liability model world, the target constantly moves. The result of this is that if we are to successfully achieve a funded status of 100 percent or more, we may well need to make interim decisions, both with respect to things like savings levels and, as we shall see as the chapter unfolds, our investment strategy.

In addition, since the numerator of the funded status includes both our financial assets and our human capital, the variance of the funded status is a function of the variance in both the value of the financial assets and the value of our human capital. Here is the time issue again; everything else being held equal, the value of our human capital declines over time.

---

[*]Of course, liabilities in retirement decrease as time goes on because they are being paid. Presumably they are being paid for with the client's assets therefore the client's asset value goes down as well. In general, the funded status for an individual who is underfunded on their retirement date will trend down over time, and the funded status for an individual who is overfunded on their retirement date will trend up over time.

As a result of this, we make an important observation concerning the development of an investment plan in a personal asset liability model world: *Investment strategy is not the only driver of success and to some degree it is the crudest and riskiest tool available to influence the funded status.*

It is a big mistake to think there is a magic investment wand that can be waved to make up for excessive spending plans and/or retiring earlier than can be reasonably achieved. This has been discussed elsewhere in this book, but it is very important to keep it in mind as we discuss the investment issues in this chapter.

Investment Risk in a Personal Asset Liability Model Framework Remember that the risk we are most focused on is the risk of the funded status. We can define that risk in the same way that we normally define investment risk, that is, as the variance of the status as an analogue to the variance of return. However, the variance of investment return is only one of the items that drive the variance of the funded status. The variance of the funded status is also a function of the variance of our human capital and the variance of our liabilities. It is worth noting that more than one thing influences the value of the liabilities besides interest rates (such as a change in projected real spending). Interest rates are not independent of the return of the portfolio, so we already know that we have complex interactions driving the variance of the funded status in relationship to the variance of the portfolio. As a practical matter, we can say that some of the risks of the funded status are independent of the risks of the portfolio, and some are not (namely, interest rates). However, by examining the funded status more carefully, we can arrive at some observations that allow us to think about managing investment risk in a manner that is aware of some of the other risks of the funded status.

Because we are in a multi-period framework, one of the things we can think about is time. Specifically, we can arrive at some conclusions concerning the relative contribution of investment risk to the funded status at various points in time. (Some of this material is looked at in a more formal matter in Chapter 11, where Grant Gardner and Yuan An Fan discuss a methodology for the calculation of a target date "glide path.") The discussion here is more focused on the intuition underlying that chapter as well as parts of the discussion in Richard Fullmer's two chapters (13 and 14). Our goal here is less formal and more heuristic, so as to provide you with intuitive guidance for helping your clients reach the appropriate asset allocation. Later in this chapter, Sam Pittman takes you through an example of determining the asset allocation for a hypothetical couple.

As noted, human capital declines over time. What is the practical impact of that when all else is equal? One thing we can observe is that, over time, human capital provides a smaller and smaller contribution to funded status volatility. That suggests that investment risk contributes more to the volatility of the funded status later in life than it does earlier in life. This in turn suggests that we can be more aggressive (more exposed to higher risk assets like equities) early in life and less so as we reach retirement. To some degree, this is considered conventional wisdom, although, it is often erroneously stated as being true because "risk declines over time." This is factually incorrect as Richard Fullmer explains in Chapter 13.

What is not generally considered conventional wisdom, however, is to think about the funded status once we have hit retirement (I am using retirement as a proxy for the time when the value of an individual's human capital is effectively equal to zero, which, although not strictly true, is close to true the longer we are retired). Once in retirement, the variance of the funded status is a function of both the investment portfolio but also the value and variance of the liabilities. Here, we see something interesting and normally ignored, namely, the fact that for an underfunded individual the value of the liabilities now start to decline as a function of time, and the funded status increases. In other words, everything else equal, the funded status goes up in retirement due to this temporal effect. This has an interesting outcome. This means that the contribution of investment risk to funded-status risk starts to decline at some point in retirement, even though this occurs fairly slowly. If we were to graph the influence investment risk has on funded status over a person's lifetime, the line on the graph would increase as it approaches retirement and fall after that date as it moves into old age. What can we say about investment strategy based on this intuition? It turns out we can say quite a bit.

First, we can see that, to the degree investment strategy has an impact on the funded-status risk, it has its most significant impact roughly 7 to 12 years before and after the event of retirement. Before that and after that, other factors are equally or more important. I state this in terms of a range because many client-specific factors are relevant here. For example, a financial plan based on an aggressive savings rate in the final few years before retirement faces a significant risk, namely the ability to achieve that aggressive savings level. Failure to achieve the targeted level of savings could be driven by health issues (a significant number of early retirees become so because of unanticipated health problems), an unexpected business downturn, job changes, or any number of other factors. Therefore, it is critical that you exercise judgment in this realm based on your intimate knowledge of your client.

Second, by extension, it suggests that those clients who are either significantly underfunded or overfunded will likely find that investment strategy has only a limited impact on their status. Basically, the overfunded can pretty much do what they want, and the underfunded are unlikely to find help in the markets and will basically need to get lucky or utilize other levers to change their funded status.

Finally, those clients who are fully funded, plus or minus a bit, are most exposed to investment risk and, therefore, need to be the most carefully monitored.

With that intuition in our back pocket (that investment risk influences funded status more the closer a person is to retirement—coming or going) we examine asset allocation decisions for individuals in the three funded-status conditions (underfunded, overfunded, and close to 100 percent funded).

Later in this chapter Sam Pittman provides a detailed analysis of sustainable withdrawal rates in retirement. Therefore, I am going to focus the majority of my analysis on the **preretirement period**. As should be clear by our discussion, while the intellectual framework is the same for the pre and post retirement periods, the actual calculations differ when there are no longer positive cash flows entering the portfolio but in fact, we have withdrawals.

Essentials, Lifestyle, or Both?   The baseline funded status that should be contemplated first is the one covering essentials; that's the first-order starting point. If the client is near retirement and is 100 percent funded or barely (to cover essentials), then **they should seriously consider some level of annuitization, without delay.** Such a client is extremely exposed to a short-term negative market movement, as I hope is obvious. The other alternative is for you to have a conversation with your client that is not an investment conversation so much as a spending, savings or deferral of retirement conversation.

After that, the funded status should be calculated based on essentials and lifestyle. Including lifestyle spending in the funded status gives the individual the extra option of being able to reduce spending to improve their funded status if needed. **If the funded status is only based on essentials, the option to reduce spending to improve their funded status does not exist.**

Underfunded Individuals   If we look at the extreme cases, seriously underfunded clients are in a fundamental bind because there's really not that much an advisor can do for them. The correct thing to do is first try to get them to modify their spending expectations for retirement. After that, they may need to roll the dice by having an aggressive asset allocation. The odds in this situation aren't great but they're better than any other strategy if the objective is to get them somewhere close to a fully funded status.

Having said that, advisors must be very careful doing this because, if such clients don't have a very clear understanding of why you are taking so much risk, you may be setting yourself up for potential litigation. You must be very clear with your clients that they are not in good shape (low-funded status) and, to the extent that they have a chance of being successful (getting back to a fully funded status), they must be aggressive with their investments. By aggressive of course I mean a higher allocation to equities and as such the clients have a higher chance of having some bad outcomes but also a higher chance of having some good outcomes. If clients understand this and are prepared for those possible outcomes, then you may want to proceed with aggressive plans, but that understanding needs to be well documented for your and your clients' benefit.

Advisors must keep in mind that, although the rational investment strategy in this situation may be to increase equity exposure, this may be regarded dimly by compliance officers who are attuned to what has conventionally been perceived as an inverse relationship between a client's age and their equity allocation.

Overfunded Individuals   On the other extreme are the seriously overfunded clients who are perfectly good clients but also uninteresting from an investment challenge perspective. They really can do just about whatever they want and still have a funded surplus. They can let their risk tolerance guide their decision because their funded status is not a factor. The challenge with these clients is to determine what they are most comfortable with, securing their surplus or reaching a higher level of wealth through a more aggressive allocation to meet some other long-term objectives.

Individuals Close to 100 Percent Funded

What does it mean to be close to 100 percent funded status?—The bad news is that there is no simple rule of thumb for determining when someone is so near 100 percent funded that they require more careful monitoring. The good news is that this is exactly why it is such a potentially fertile client conversation, especially considering that engaging in it is inseparable from your client experiencing you as a partner in helping them to reason through their big concerns.

Markets can drop precipitously, causing a person's funded status to drop in a very short period of time. A rough guide to consider is that individuals whose funded status is between 90 percent and 130 percent (in our opinion) should be monitored more cautiously. (Note that we reflect the asymmetry of risks in stating this range. We are implicitly stating that the result of bad outcomes is much worse than the result of good outcomes is nice.) This does not mean that clients whose funded status is outside this range do not need to be monitored on a regular basis. It means that for clients outside this range, their investment decisions are more likely to be based on risk preference than funded status.

The interesting investment problems exist with clients who have a funded status slightly above or below 100 percent, and are within the 7 to 12 years of retirement timeframe we discussed earlier. That is because for these clients investment risk is the primary risk they face with respect to their funded status. Consider an individual who is already saving at a high rate, say 25 percent of income, works in a profession where as a practical matter there is effectively a mandatory retirement age (which exists more than one might think as a matter of business or corporate culture), and has already outlined a desired retirement lifestyle that is comfortable but hardly lavish or inappropriate. It should be clear that investment risk is the dominant risk in this example without doing a lot of math or simulations. The normal response to this scenario based on the analysis we have presented so far would be to place this client into a fairly conservative asset allocation. Note that this is exactly what well-designed target date glide paths do and for the same reasons outlined above. (You might recall the public uproar in 2008–2009 over those glide paths that did not do this.) The problem however is clear. Conservative portfolios probably will avoid catastrophic outcomes (in the mathematical sense of the word probable) but, they also make it very hard to generate a larger surplus and in turn an enhanced lifestyle because basically, without going through an analysis of every asset class, upside potential comes from equities or other high volatility assets, most of which embed some significant level of equity risk. Therefore, these are portfolios with a low probability of significant upside increases. Is there something we can do for these investors, who could well make up the bulk of an advisor's practice?

The answer is a tentative yes, we probably can, but in order to do so we need to think about the investment issue differently than we often do. We also need to realize that we can utilize strategies that **may** result in a better outcome than a static asset allocation, but it is not a "sure thing" that they will. However, if they are correctly implemented they also should not produce an outcome that is worse than the conservative static mix strategy. Let's return to the target date glide path for just a moment to illustrate our potential opportunity to provide a real value to these clients. Glide paths (e.g. when used in target date funds in defined contribution plans) operate under a significant constraint, namely, that the asset allocation be proscribed in advance. This is because most of the payroll and other administrative systems used in retirement plans cannot provide highly specific information about each participant. Therefore, one size has to fit all. In addition, it is much easier to communicate a pre-established asset allocation to a large group of people. Neither of these constraints applies to working with an individual client. You have the ability to be responsive to your clients' changing situations and the impact of shorter-term market movements. Clients whose circumstances match the ones we have just outlined can potentially benefit from an adaptive asset-allocation method, in which the advisor dynamically adjusts their portfolio risk with respect to their funded status.

The idea here is not to use tactical market timing but rather to pursue a dynamic hedging strategy, raising the risk in the portfolio when the individual's funded status increases and lowering the risk when their funded status decreases. In other words, we are arguing that this is a scenario where a form of "portfolio insurance" can be effective. Why? Because it is a mechanism that allows for the possibility of higher equity (risk) exposure when it can be tolerated and reduces it when it cannot. The result is that, on average, such a strategy will average higher equity exposure than a static strategy of equivalent risk over the specified time frame and therefore can outperform a static mix that is pegged at the most conservative level. In fact, it can be demonstrated, in a mathematical sense, that dynamic strategies, properly implemented, can always do at least as well as static strategies and may do better. Note that there can be market conditions that will be so negative that higher equity exposures are never used, but when done correctly, the result should be no worse than the very conservative static mix. Also note that this would never be a conclusion of an analysis that was conducted in a traditional Markowitz world, because there, variance of return is the only risk considered. In the Markowitz world, there are only single period problems and risk aversion is assumed to be fixed. However, in our personal asset liability model world, there are multiple time periods, there are multiple sources of variance in our funded status, and while our overall risk aversion may be fixed (it does not have to be but that is a level of technical complexity outside the scope of this book), we can alter the mix of risks to achieve the same level of overall funded status risk in each time frame.

Now to be fair, this is not an easy investment problem to solve. There are many ways to set up dynamic hedging strategies and one could articulate the problem in different mathematical forms. Creating and providing such an array of algorithms is well beyond the scope of this book. However, some directional heuristics can be provided that you might find useful as a practicing advisor.

First, however, to make the results of our heuristics more accessible, I am going to do a quick conceptual overview of dynamic hedging strategies.

To make it easier to follow I am going to assume a simplified environment of a risky asset and a risk-free asset. As we note in a sidebar, there is no "risk free" asset available for the retirement income problem. So everything we do here is in the context of improving the "second best" outcome. With that out of the way let's recall the ideal of such a dynamic hedging strategy. It is to place a "floor" on the overall result, albeit at an upside cost compared to a fully invested strategy in the risky asset. However, our objective is not to do as well or better than a strategy that is fully invested in the risky asset, it is to do better than a static mix that would with high probability deliver a floor in a worst-case scenario.

Because we are protecting against a worst-case scenario the static mix solution must be very conservative indeed. The logic is to do better than that but to have a roughly similar truncation of downside risk. One way of defining this is to say that what we really want is a put option on the risky asset that protects us from dropping below our established floor. This might let us maintain a higher level of exposure to the risky asset if we define an appropriate floor and a reasonable time frame for the put option. (I am not trying to provide a complete overview of option pricing theory here but if our desired floor is too high and our time frame too long then the cost of the option is prohibitive and the problem we want to solve may not be solvable, so choice of floor and time frame is important in such investment problems.) The key insight that drives dynamic hedging strategies is that since options are derivative securities their return pattern can always be replicated via a trading strategy in the actual underlying assets (ignoring trading costs and other practical constraints).

As mentioned earlier there are many ways to set up a dynamic hedging strategy for this or any other type of investment problem but as you might intuit from thinking about the paragraph above, they all have some common elements.

- The hedging period must be defined; it cannot go on forever, as options have a finite life.
- The initial allocation is a mix of the risky and the risk-free asset.
- As investment results are realized the investment mix is modified. The outcome is, directionally, that if investment results have been good then the exposure to the risky asset is increased, if they are bad then exposure to the risky asset is decreased. The level of increase and decrease is a function of the specific objective of the hedge and other factors unique to each algorithm. However, everything else being equal, the further the client is from their retirement date the greater the magnitude of asset allocation change should be in response to investment results, and the

closer they are to their retirement date the smaller the magnitude of
asset allocation change should be.

Risk-Free Retirement Asset—The perfect risk-free retirement asset
would be one that is guaranteed to keep pace with inflation, has no
default risk, and pays a monthly amount for the length of the asset-
holder's life. In the United States, such an asset does not exist because
the only entity that could issue this kind of asset is the U.S. government, and they don't. The U.S. government could help retirees by
issuing guaranteed lifetime annuities that have payments indexed to
inflation. Or, as a second-best, a fully amortizing 30-year bond would
be a very helpful asset to work with in a post-retirement context.

So, let's figure out what this means for you as an advisor interested in
an informal heuristic providing some of the benefits of a dynamic hedging
strategy. First, a good baseline for your asset allocation might be the static
target date glide path allocation for the same time out relative to your
client's targeted retirement date. (This is open to a lot of latitude since target
date glide paths are normally calculated with a number of assumptions,
the most critical being the savings rate. If you can find out what those
assumptions are you may be able to make sensible adjustments, such as, if
your client's savings rate is much higher than that assumed by the glide, your
equity exposure could be higher. Learning the assumptions in the glide path
calculation will prove very useful to you in this exercise.) Second, the closer
the funded status is to 100 percent the lower the equity exposure should
be. Third, if the funded status improves you should consider increasing the
equity exposure. Fourth, if the funded status declines you should consider
decreasing the equity exposure.

Combining these we get the following proposed heuristic for advisors,
which is not a technical dynamic hedging solution but might be a good
starting point for clients "nearing the retirement zone" and close to a funded
status of 100 percent. (We discuss in more detail what we mean by " close
to a funded status of 100 percent" in a sidebar, which is essentially in the
range of 90 percent to 130 percent.)

- Establish a baseline asset allocation using a well-constructed target date
  glide path adjusted for known client factors such as savings rate.
- If the funded status increases significantly, increase the equity exposure
  from the baseline level.
- If the funded status decreases significantly, decrease the equity exposure.

▪ Adjust yearly for both the baseline equity exposure proscribed in the target date glide path and in response to unanticipated large market movements.

This should result in an investment strategy that combines a baseline of declining equity exposure as your clients approach retirement with variations from that baseline based on changes in your client's funded status. The key is, the better the funded status the more equity exposure can be accepted while the lower the funded status the less equity exposure can be accepted. While this is not necessarily as "optimal" a strategy as a fully fleshed out dynamic hedging algorithm, you should realize much of the same benefit.

Remember, this approach is only recommended for clients with a funded status close to 100 percent. The key is to first determine their funded status and consider providing them with an adaptive asset allocation if they fit this definition. For other clients, more traditional approaches are probably more appropriate.

Other Adaptive Methods

What Randy has described is one idea for how to incorporate an adaptive model of asset allocation. There are certainly other methods that may be appropriate and could include:

▪ Utilize a principal protected fund with a time-frame that is a reasonable match for your client
▪ Buy a series of rolling broad equity market puts
▪ Utilize one of the newly available "retirement income" products for part of the portfolio while investing the remainder of it in a more traditional manner
▪ Buy an annuity that covers a significant proportion of the essentials budget and in so doing allow for a more aggressive implementation of the rest of the portfolio, or
▪ Implement your own form of "intelligent rebalancing" where on an annual basis you modify the risk of your clients' portfolios based on their current funded status.

The list above is provided to show you that there are many ways to dynamically hedge your client's funded status risk. We are not recommending one strategy over another. Only you can make the determination of what strategy is best for your client. There are many reasonable approaches to take and there may well not be a one-size-fits-all solution. The important takeaway is that a simple static rebalancing strategy may not be optimal for clients in the later-stage preretirement zone who have a funded status of roughly 100 percent. Remember, we are not advocating such an approach for clients that are extremely underfunded or overfunded.

For clients still working but nearing retirement, it's important to remember that the day they retire is likely to be the riskiest day of their lives (see sidebar) **and they may not be in control of when that day happens.** This is significant because, if you are managing the portfolios of clients who are well-funded and still working, but then they suffer involuntary job interruptions, this may rapidly change their funded status and may be cause for adjustments to their asset allocation. Depending on their prospects for future work-related income, you may even need to consider annuitization or partial annuitization.

> The Riskiest Day of Your Life—From a retirement perspective, the day people retire could well be the riskiest day of their lives. It is on this day that they have theoretically exhausted their human capital (the ability to create income from work), they have the longest period of time for which to fund their living expenses, and they have the greatest longevity risk. This fact largely explains the reasoning behind reducing investment risk as one nears retirement (despite many other popular explanations). It's also why target date funds, for instance, have a progressively conservative asset allocation as they move toward retirement. Despite the fact that some target date funds continue to become more conservative after reaching retirement, we know of no reasonable investment explanation for doing this. In fact, as discussed in the body of the chapter, you can make an argument that as a client ages, and if they are so inclined, the risk of their portfolio can be increased with little fear of damaging their funded status. A more detailed discussion on constructing a glide path for target date funds is provided in Chapter 11.

APPLYING THE MODEL

The main point of our discussion about individuals in the adaptive zone is that these are the people for whom you can deliver the greatest value. By this we mean that your interventions are the most meaningful in averting outcomes in which the clients' standards of living and flexibility are the most constrained. If, by closely monitoring their funded status and adaptively managing their portfolio accordingly, you are able to help them sustain their financial security, avoid the cost of annuitization, and retain the control over their wealth, then you have truly earned your fee and your clients' loyalty and trust.

What we've been discussing up to this point is how the funded status influences the level of risk a person should take in their portfolio and focusing primarily on the preretirement portfolio management issues. Another decision point, one that is influenced by the amount of investment risk taken, is how much a person can withdraw from their retirement portfolio and still have a high level of certainty that they will not run out of money in their lifetime. You need to be able to answer your client's question, "What is a sustainable withdrawal rate from my portfolio?"

For an example of how to answer this question, we again turn to Sam Pittman. As you will see in his example, there are degrees of sustainability, and individuals with just enough wealth to meet their spending needs must make trade-offs between their level of spending and certainty of success.

What's a Prudent Withdrawal Rate for Retired Investors?

Note: This section, up to the section titled When to Annuitize, was written by Sam Pittman, PhD. Sam thanks Grant Gardner for many insightful discussions that helped shape this content. Tables 6.6 through 6.8 at the end of this section contain the return and yield curve assumptions used in this section.

No one wants to outlive their assets. However, as people plan for the lifestyle they want when they retire, knowing how much they can withdraw from their portfolio each year is clearly top of mind. "What is a prudent withdrawal rate?" can only be answered probabilistically, because the future of markets is unknown, as is each individual investor's lifespan.

A common rule of thumb is not to exceed 4 percent of the portfolio's principal value (principal value being defined as the portfolio value at the time of normal retirement, i.e., somewhere close to age 65). However, given today's markets with low interest rates, high volatility, and uncertain inflation, does this rule of thumb produce a prudent decision?

When planning for retirement, prudent decisions can only occur if both the advisor and the client understand the risks inherent in the plan. Naturally, most people don't want to think about risk, let alone talk about risk. No one wants to think that there's a chance their plans could fall far short of their hopes. However, addressing risk by having honest conversations about it is an essential part of planning. As distressing as facing risk can be, we know that, to produce the best outcomes, it's necessary to face risks squarely and plan accordingly.

Many advisors today are helping their clients who are near or in retirement understand the implications and correlations between their spending goals and investment decisions. To illustrate, take Ed and Sally Jones, a recently retired 65-year old couple with three grown children. Ed and Sally have saved $560,000 for retirement, and they need to know how much money they can withdraw from their portfolio annually to help fund their lifestyle without exhausting their savings over their lifetimes. A commonly used recommendation would be: an asset allocation of 60 percent equity 40 percent fixed income (also known as 60/40) and a 4 percent annual withdrawal rate to fund spending goals.

On the surface, this seems like a rather benign recommendation, but did you know the odds of a 4 percent spending plan with a 60/40 allocation succeeding are 76 percent given current market conditions? Fortunately, there are other asset allocation recommendations that may be more appropriate to help Ed and Sally achieve their goals in retirement.

Our intent within this paper is to help advisors and investors understand how to factor in current market conditions on spending rates and asset-allocation decisions. We'll show you how spending rates and different investment portfolios translate to metrics that measure retirement success.

As an example, we'll show the likelihood that a 40 percent equity /60 percent fixed-income portfolio with a 5 percent withdrawal rate will fail to provide sufficient income for the retiree, by how much it is likely to fall short, and also the potential wealth it will accumulate. These metrics can help you help your client make more informed investment decisions.

Generating Retirement Income in Poor Market Conditions There's no question that markets have ventured into an area that makes retirement planning challenging. The difference in the yield curve for two time periods separated by a mere four years, shown in Figure 6.1, illustrates the risk of end-point sensitivity: Market conditions at the date someone retires greatly influence their chances for success.

Low interest rates have a meaningful impact on retirement spending sustainability. In a lower interest rate environment:

- Investors earn less interest on their investments.
- Under the assumption of a constant equity risk premium, expected equity returns are lower.
- The cost to fund retirement increases due to a lower discount rate used to discount future cash-flow needs. In other words, annuities become cheaper as interest rates rise and vice versa.

Given the low-interest-rate environment, as well as uncertainty regarding the direction of inflation and other unknowns, it's important to

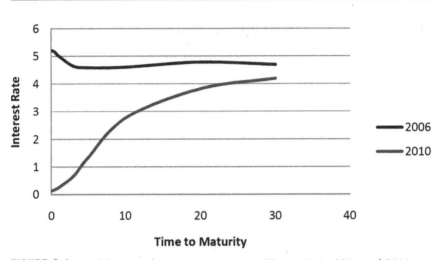

FIGURE 6.1 Yield Curves for Constant Maturity Treasuries in 2006 and 2010
Source: www.federalreserve.gov/releases/h15/data.htm.

understand the implications of spending goals and investing decisions. One of the realities of low rates is that more investors need to draw cash flows from their portfolios that will exceed the yield generated from bond portfolios and other dividend- and interest-producing positions. At the same time, portfolios need to grow to lessen the risk of outliving assets. The bottom line in today's environment: planning is essential, which is why advisors who are expert in helping clients build and execute sound plans are so valuable.

What Does It Mean to Have a Sustainable Retirement Income Plan? To characterize the sustainability of a retirement plan, we examine a couple that withdraws money from their portfolio to support income needs between ages 65 and 85. At age 85 we compute the difference between their portfolio value, and the theoretical cost to purchase a joint life annuity that will cover their cash flow needs adjusted for 2.1 percent inflation for the remainder of their life. The use of the annuity is a modeling device rather than an investment plan. This approach to managing longevity risk is discussed in Chapter 14.

We realize few 85-year-olds will purchase a life annuity. However, we don't know how long people will live and we need to factor this uncertainty into our calculations. If the investors have enough to purchase an immediate life annuity at age 85, then they have the means of insuring they will not run out of money. If their portfolios have values that are greater than the cost of the annuity, the plan is recorded as successful, meaning it has met the retirement income needs. If the portfolios' value have less wealth than

TABLE 6.1 Examined Asset
Allocation Portfolios

Equity	Bonds
0%	100%
20%	80%
40%	60%
60%	40%
80%	20%
100%	0%

the cost of the annuity at age 85, the plan is recorded as unsuccessful. This is a more conservative approach to measuring success because there is a chance that the investors may not live to age 85 to purchase the annuity. Our approach plans for the scenario in which the couple lives to age 85 and needs to fund the expenses for both of them beyond that.

To capture the impact of market uncertainty on the sustainability of a withdrawal plan, we use Monte Carlo simulation to produce hypothetical equity returns, bond returns, interest rates, and inflation rates. For each of the simulated market scenarios, we examine the evolution of wealth over time for selected withdrawal rates and asset-allocation models.

In this report the amount withdrawn to support spending is the withdrawal rate times the initial portfolio value. Each year the withdrawal amount is grossed up for a 2.1 percent cost of living increase. This means that the amount withdrawn does not change with time other than an annual cost of living adjustment of 2.1 percent. Additionally, the cost of the annuity at age 85 assumes that the distributions will grow with the inflation rate of 2.1 percent.

The same starting asset-allocation policy is implemented each year between the ages of 65 and 85. The portfolio is rebalanced back to the policy allocation annually.

Examined Asset-Allocation Portfolios We show sustainability results for six different equity to bond allocations, listed in Table 6.1. (Please refer to Tables 6.6 through 6.8 at the end of this section for expected return, standard deviation, correlation, and yield-curve assumptions.)

Hypothetical Performance for Different Withdrawal Rates Here, we present the modeled retirement sustainability and accumulation metrics for selected withdrawal rates and equity/bond mixtures (asset allocation policies).

We use several metrics below to characterize retirement-plan success:

- Probability of Success: The percent of time the portfolio had enough value in it to purchase an annuity when the investors reached age 85.
- Surplus: The difference between the final portfolio value and the cost of the annuity less any missed distributions. Below this value is expressed as a percent of the initial wealth.
- Expected Wealth: The mean amount of wealth when the investors reached age 85. Below this value is expressed as a percent of the initial wealth.
- Shortfall: The maximum of zero and the surplus. Below this value is expressed as a percent of the initial wealth.
- Expected Shortfall: The mean of shortfall. Below this value is expressed as a percent of the initial wealth.
- Magnitude of Shortfall: The mean of the positive shortfall outcomes. Below this value is expressed as a percent of the initial wealth.

Figure 6.2 shows the probability that different asset allocation portfolios meet the sustainability requirement based on selected withdrawal rates. One obvious pattern is that more conservative portfolios have a higher chance of

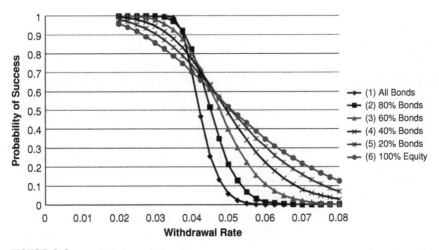

FIGURE 6.2 Probability of Plan Success
IMPORTANT: The projections or other information generated by this analysis regarding the likelihood of various investment outcomes are hypothetical in nature, do not reflect actual investment results, and are not guarantees of future results. Other investment not considered may have characteristics similar or superior to those being analyzed.

meeting the payments at lower withdrawal rates and that more aggressive portfolios have higher chance of success at higher withdrawal rates. An example of this is the all-bond portfolio curve being above all other curves for low withdrawal rates and lower than the other curves for withdrawal rates beyond 4.25 percent. This is a rather intuitive outcome. The dispersion of outcomes for a conservative portfolio is lower than for an aggressive portfolio. At low withdrawal rates, the income hurdle is low enough that most or all of the simulated outcomes are above the summed income hurdle. Alternatively, at high withdrawal rates, the only chance of meeting the income hurdle is to invest aggressively, increasing the dispersion so that some of the outcomes exceed the income hurdle.

Although the probability of success is an important metric to examine, as Richard Fullmer points out in Chapter 13, assessing a retirement plan based on the probability of failure alone is dangerous. All shortfalls are not equal, nor are all successes. Falling short of the ending annuity hurdle by a few dollars at age 85 and accepting a slightly lower standard of living going forward is a far different outcome than running out of money at age 75. To gain perspective on the magnitude of shortfall across the different portfolios, in Figure 6.3 we plot the mean shortfall, when it occurs, as a percent of initial wealth.

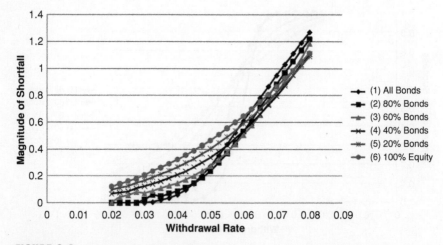

FIGURE 6.3 Magnitude of Shortfall
IMPORTANT: The projections or other information generated by this analysis regarding the likelihood of various investment outcomes are hypothetical in nature, do not reflect actual investment results, and are not guarantees of future results. Other investment not considered may have characteristics similar or superior to those being analyzed.

We have a strong intuition that the prevailing consumer concerns about sustainability of lifestyle is inadequately captured in this one risk measure (the probability of success). It does not proxy the actual concern: not simply depleting the nest-egg assets, but doing so by such a significant amount that radical lifestyle changes would be forced on the individual, conceivably lasting many years, if not the rest of their life.

The magnitude of shortfall shows a different facet of sustainability. At lower withdrawal rates, when there is a shortfall, its expectation is greater for more aggressive portfolios. At high withdrawal rates, more conservative portfolios have higher expected shortfall, when it occurs. Considering the magnitude of shortfall together with the probability of shortfall can help investors make informed spending and investment decisions.

For example, if retirement income is the only goal, we can see that at low withdrawal rates, conservative portfolios are superior because they have a higher success rate and less expected shortfall. At high withdrawal rates, aggressive portfolios are better, because they have higher success probabilities and lower expected shortfall. In the middle range of withdrawal rates it is less clear which portfolios are superior. That leads us to Figure 6.4, where we factor in both the probability of shortfall and the amount of shortfall.

The probability of an event doesn't reflect its magnitude, and the magnitude doesn't reveal the chance of the event occurring. However, when we multiply the two, we get a sense of the combined effect of chance and magnitude. Figure 6.4 shows that conservative portfolios have less expected shortfall for low withdrawal rates and that aggressive portfolios have less expected shortfall at higher withdrawal rates. Additionally, expected shortfall also helps us rank the portfolios in the middle of the withdrawal-rate range where a clear preference cannot be found in Figures 6.2 and 6.3.

Together, Figures 6.2–6.4 help us assess the attractiveness of the portfolios at different withdrawal rates when retirement income is the only goal. Although retirement income is the primary goal for most retirees, many may want to consider bequest and other goals that rely on accumulated wealth beyond income needs.

Figure 6.5 presents the expected surplus for the different withdrawal rates and investment strategies. Although the previous charts give a sense of the risk involved in trying to meet retirement income needs for different withdrawal amounts, Figure 6.5 shows the surplus wealth that can fulfill other goals. The curves cross zero on the vertical access where the portfolio is expected to produce no surplus. A surplus below zero means the investor

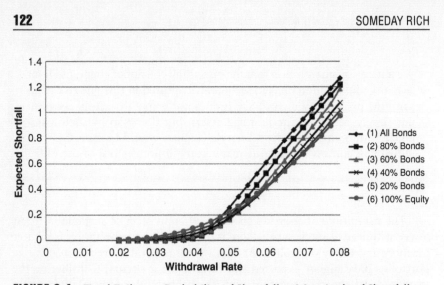

FIGURE 6.4 Total Failure = Probability of Shortfall × Magnitude of Shortfall
IMPORTANT: The projections or other information generated by this analysis regarding the likelihood of various investment outcomes are hypothetical in nature, do not reflect actual investment results, and are not guarantees of future results. Other investment not considered may have characteristics similar or superior to those being analyzed.

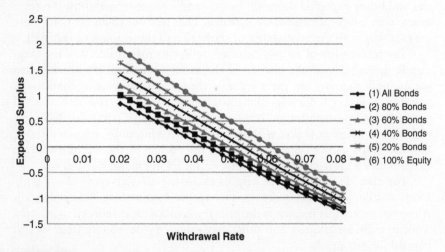

FIGURE 6.5 Expected Surplus
IMPORTANT: The projections or other information generated by this analysis regarding the likelihood of various investment outcomes are hypothetical in nature, do not reflect actual investment results, and are not guarantees of future results. Other investment not considered may have characteristics similar or superior to those being analyzed.

will not have enough wealth to purchase an annuity and, therefore, fails to meet the test for financial security. Financial security in retirement equals the perpetual ability to annuitize, without actually doing so. This graph preserves our natural intuition about investing—that higher portions of equity lead to higher expected wealth. Naturally, the higher the withdrawal rate the less expected ending wealth.

Each of the previously mentioned metrics pertain to a single aspect of retirement success that should be examined. Though, looking at a single metric isn't enough to produce an informed decision, trying to weigh all the metrics across the different withdrawal rates and asset allocation portfolios could be daunting. Below we demonstrate an approach that can help you efficiently wade through the data behind these charts.

Helping Clients Make Informed Investment Decisions Based on Relevant Data   Let's revisit Ed and Sally Jones again to make a few points. Recall that they are a newly retired 65-year-old couple with $560,000 saved for retirement. Obviously the amount they spend is going to impact their quality of life in retirement. Consuming $35,000 per year (6.25 percent of $560,000) from their portfolio to supplement retirement income from other sources such as Social Security would provide a very high quality of life for the Joneses, but they're capable of making it on $20,000 (3.6 percent of $560,000) of consumption annually. They also have three kids, whom they would like to leave an inheritance if possible. How should the Joneses invest their wealth and how much should they withdraw to supplement their other income?

We presented four metrics, six investment strategies, and various possible withdrawal rates. However, we still need a way to translate the investment and withdrawal decision to risk and bequest implications, in a way that quickly gets Ed and Sally in the best portfolio with the right withdrawal rate. We take a straightforward approach to accomplish this based on a simple search algorithm commonly used in computer science. We start with the midpoint of the two implied withdrawal rates behind the Joneses spending options (listed above), showing the potential outcomes for three of the different investment choices. We limit the number of portfolios to three to avoid displaying too much data at one time.

Table 6.2 shows metrics discussed earlier for the 5 percent withdrawal rate (the midpoint of 6.25 percent and 3.6 percent), which corresponds to $28,000 of income per year.

None of these plans look very appealing. The highest success rate of 52 percent from the all equity portfolio is simply too low. It's obvious that the Joneses will need to withdraw less money.

To obtain the next withdrawal rate using the search algorithm, we take the midpoint of the lowest withdrawal rate, 3.6 percent and the one that we

TABLE 6.2   Five Percent Withdrawal Rate

Portfolio	100% Equity 0% Bonds	60/40	20/80
Success Rate	52%	49%	21%
Magnitude of Shortfall	46%	34%	24%
Expected Surplus	49%	13%	–14%

just determined was too high, 5 percent. Had we determined earlier that the Joneses could spend more than 5 percent, we would take the midpoint of 5 percent and the maximum withdrawal rate, 6.25 percent. Proceeding with the simple algorithm, we consider the new withdrawal rate: 4.25 percent ($24,080 annually), which is the midpoint of 3.6 percent and 5 percent, and show the same metrics.

TABLE 6.3   4.25 Percent Withdrawal Rate

Portfolio	100% Equity 0% Bonds	60/40	20/80
Success Rate	66%	70%	69%
Magnitude of Shortfall	36%	23%	11%
Expected Surplus	84%	44%	14%

Decreasing spending substantially improves the plan. All the plans show a positive expected surplus and the success rates are significantly better than 50 percent. However, Ed and Sally want to play it safe. Although the numbers at a 4.25 percent withdrawal rate are palatable, Ed and Sally prefer taking less risk; even a 30 percent chance of failure is too much for them.

We find the next candidate withdrawal rate of 3.75 percent (21,000 annually), as the midpoint of 3.6 percent and 4.25 percent.

The Joneses believe these numbers are in the ball park for their needs. In the 20/80 portfolio they have a high chance of success (92 percent), with very little expected shortfall, should that occur. Further, the expectation is that they will have a surplus of 34 percent, $190,000—in today's dollars—when they are 85. Although the Joneses are comfortable with this portfolio and spending decision, they would like to create potential for more expected surplus. Because we have found the appropriate spending decision, we now show them other candidate portfolios that we left out thus far. All five portfolios are shown in Table 6.5 for the 3.75 percent withdrawal decision.

Ed and Sally like the additional expected ending wealth of the 40/60 portfolio: $274,000 versus $190,000 obtained with the 20 equity/ 80 fixed

TABLE 6.4 3.75 Percent Withdrawal Rate

Portfolio	100% Equity 0% Bonds	60/40	20/80
Success Rate	75%	83%	92%
Magnitude of Shortfall	29%	18%	7%
Expected Surplus	107%	66%	34%

income. Moreover, little additional risk is taken. They decide to invest in the 40/60 portfolio and withdraw 3.75 percent annually.

One of the nice aspects of this plan is that Ed and Sally are able to target two of their objectives: meeting retirement income with high probability and creating an expected inheritance for their children. If market conditions are favorable during the first years of retirement, they can revisit the decision of increasing their spending. Had they chosen to spend more early on, they would have increased the chance of running out of money and given up the expected surplus. This example shows how the goal of being able to spend more in retirement competes with sustainability and the goal of bequeathing.

By using the simple search algorithm rather than asking the Joneses to fill out a questionnaire to elicit their preferences, we let them choose their preference between achieving certain goals and risk. This eliminates the potential for misinterpretation, giving the Joneses a better understanding of the implications connected to their choices.

The search algorithm ensures that we don't get lost in the data, and provides the best portfolio with relatively little work—four versions in this case. The algorithm works like this:

1. Obtain the possible spending range from essentials to enhanced lifestyle.
2. Choose the midpoint of this spending range, and show them the plan metrics for a collection of portfolios (don't show too many).
3. Let the response dictate whether to increase or decrease the spending rate. Always set the new spending rate at the midpoint of the last

TABLE 6.5 3.75 percent withdrawal rate/all portfolios

Portfolio	100% Equity 0% Bonds	80/20	60/40	40/60	20/80	0/100
Success Rate	75%	79%	83%	88%	92%	91%
Magnitude of Shortfall	29%	24%	18%	13%	7%	4%
Expected Surplus	107%	85%	66%	49%	34%	21%

spending rate and the highest if the answer is increase spending (the lowest if the answer is decrease spending).

4. Stop adjusting the spending rate when your client tells you they are comfortable with the risk level of the spending decision.
5. Fine-tune the portfolio selection for the selected spending rate and show the metrics associated with other portfolios near the one they chose.

If there are special client circumstances that need to be considered, such as a large inheritance, the sale of a business, or others, the algorithm may need to be altered or abandoned. What we presented above is tailored to the simple case of drawing down a portfolio to meet consistent income needs.

Humans don't like uncertainty, but the world and markets are filled with it. As much as we want to believe our retirement plans will succeed, there is a possibility that they won't. We can either choose to face this uncertainty and manage it, or ignore it and hope for the best. Advisors have the opportunity to enhance the value they add by understanding a client's circumstances and accounting for market conditions. Advisors can help clients understand what their retirement possibilities are and then align the portfolio with their preferences

At the beginning we posed the question: What's a prudent withdrawal rate for retired investors? The answer is *it depends*.

It depends on their preference between risk and meeting goals. Perhaps another question to ask is whether investors can make prudent spending and investment decisions without understanding the implications. To help them understand the implications we need to change and sharpen both our definition of risk (not having enough to buy an annuity) as well as the precision of the goal—running out of money by an amount large enough to really matter to the client.

Return and Yield Curve Assumptions

TABLE 6.6 Expected Returns and Standard Deviations

	Equity	Bonds	Cash
Expected Return	6.84%	3.84%	2.58%
Standard Deviation	16.98%	4.34%	2.00%

TABLE 6.7 Correlation Matrix

Portfolio	Equity	Bonds	Cash
Equity	1	0.2609	0.0904
Bonds	0.2609	1	0.4901
Cash	0.0904	0.4901	1

TABLE 6.8 Average of Yield Curve Used to Price Annuity Target 20 Years in the Future

Duration	1	2	3	4	5	10	12	15	20	30	50
Yield	4.39%	4.57%	4.69%	4.78%	4.86%	5.13%	5.20%	5.28%	5.39%	5.54%	5.68%

WHEN TO ANNUITIZE?

The Joneses in our prior example had to choose between spending and certainty. They came to a compromise between the two based on their personal preferences. In some cases, however, the client's risk aversion may be so great that they should consider buying an annuity to cover all or part of their spending needs. Another way to look at this or even explain it is that the funded status of the client is so low, that they have no risk budget left to spend. This makes the prospect of deferring annuitization to a later date, when either the markets might bail them out or at least the annuitization cost is expected to be lower, simply not a strategy they can afford.

There is no clear answer to exactly when someone should annuitize their wealth. We can provide a guideline, but the final decision will be based on personal preferences, most notably whether the clients are comfortable losing control of their nest egg assets to create the income security they might direly require. The guideline we use is the *annuity hurdle*. A funded status is calculated by dividing the present value of an individual's assets by the present value of their liabilities. The denominator of this equation (the liability value) represents the theoretical cost of purchasing an annuity to fund future spending. The liability value can be seen as a hurdle the individual always wants to stay above, a threshold for staying fully funded. The liability value does not remain constant, it decreases over time as there are fewer days in the individual's life left to be funded. If we were to plot the value of the liability over time it would be a gradually downward sloping line. We've done this in Figure 6.6. We call this decreasing liability value an "annuity hurdle."

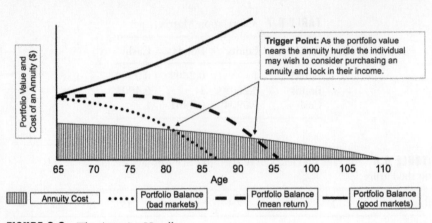

FIGURE 6.6 The Annuity Hurdle

So long as the individual's wealth remains above the hurdle, they can afford to essentially self-insure their future spending and longevity risk. We've drawn three hypothetical wealth trajectories on the chart in Figure 6.6. They represent what an individual's wealth value might be in the case of bad markets, normal markets, and good markets. If clients' portfolio values near the annuity hurdle, they may wish to consider buying an annuity or at least partially annuitizing.

We asked several advisors how they incorporate annuities into their client recommendations. One advisor's response was representative of what we heard in general:

> *I can't say that (an annuity) is the first thing we choose, but we do use them, mostly in cases where the client doesn't have much choice. We will do a single premium immediate annuity for clients where they need a certain amount of income and they just don't have the assets to get there by taking three or four percent of their portfolio each year, and they can't afford to take much risk.*
>
> *We use annuities sparingly and just in the right places. In some cases where the client is really worried we will use an annuity on top of their Social Security and pension from work to get them to a point where they can meet all of their basic expenses. That way we can cover all of their household expenses in a guaranteed way and take the rest of their wealth and invest it for growth. More often than not, we use them in places where we just don't have any other choice.*

Develop a Proactive Strategy With Your Client About If and When to Convert to an Annuity

In addition to commissions and expense, individuals should be aware of the fact that buying an annuity is an irrevocable decision (with the exception of some variable annuities). Unlike an asset allocation that can be adjusted if the individual's circumstance or preference changes, the decision to buy an annuity cannot be undone. The individual might be able to sell the annuity to a third party for a lump sum amount, but the proceeds will likely be at a deep discount to the fair value of the annuity's future payments. Also, annuities carry counterparty risk, the risk that the insurer and the entities backing them cannot make the annuity payments. This risk may be extremely small, but we are talking about a person's life savings here, and in most cases the person annuitizing has little or no other wealth to fall back on. The occurrence of default only has to happen once for it to be catastrophic for the person affected. Therefore, we recommend use of annuities from highly rated insurance companies, whose balance sheet strength provides a relative measure of protection from default as well as the ability to price competitively. The decision to annuitize for your client may often be the correct decision. As a fee-based advisor, it will often be your final one—so measure twice because you only get to cut once.

Deferred Annuitization—Some experts suggest that individuals consider deferred annuities (sometimes called advanced life deferred annuities, ALDAs) bought before or close to retirement with payments beginning at an advanced age, such as 85. This type of annuity is considered pure longevity insurance because it only pays to individuals who live to an advanced age. As such, premiums for ALDAs are deeply discounted compared to immediate annuities.

An individual 65 years of age who purchases an ALDA with payments beginning at age 85 eliminates the bulk of their longevity risk while at the same time creating a finite window of time for which they have to manage their remaining wealth, 20 years. This may serve to remove considerable uncertainty and complexity from their retirement plan (which is a good thing), but again, there are costs involved in executing this strategy.

The point of mentioning this deferred annuity technique is to show that there are many ways to use annuities in combination with other assets to solve the retirement income puzzle. Still, the individual's funded status influences the decision to use a strategy like the one described here. Clearly, a person who is so underfunded that the ALDA premium would exhaust their entire wealth should not consider this strategy. And, a person whose funded status is well above 100 percent may choose to use this strategy out of personal preference, even though they may be able to afford to self-insure their longevity risk.

SUMMARY OF FACTORS INFLUENCING PORTFOLIO RISK

We argue that individuals' funded status should be the single most important metric influencing their portfolio selections. Their funded status is determined in large part by their ability or willingness to make adjustments in their saving and spending, and whether they can control the length of employment. Ultimately they must make trade-off decisions between spending and sustainability; between standard of living and sustainability. Because the decisions are so personal, advisors are smart to consider both their clients' stated ability to modify their behaviors (when needed) as well as the advisor's intuition of the client's ability to actually do so.

Finally, age plays a role in the decision as well. Younger people still have the option of saving more or deferring retirement and thus may be able to afford to take more risk. Older people have fewer years left to fund and their longevity risk is lower. They also may be able to take on more risk if they are in an overfunded position. It's the person closest to their retirement date and closest to 100 percent funded who must be the most careful in selecting their portfolio risk.

GOALS-BASED REPORTING

Calculating your clients' funded status and matching their investment plan accordingly is only the beginning of helping them create sustainable financial security. The ongoing surveillance of their financial security is equally important, and equates to tailoring. Advisors we've worked with tell us that one of their biggest challenges is keeping their clients on the right track once their goals and investment plan have been set. An effective way to do this is by using reporting methods that show your clients' goals and their progress toward those goals as opposed to typical benchmark-relative quarterly reviews, which research confirms to be of scant value to the typical client. Regular feedback relative to goals not only keeps your clients apprised of their status, it also cultivates a greater sense of the advisor's ownership of their goals. Advisors who use these methods have told us that their clients' behavior changes when they see their goals (and progress) reported to them every month or quarter. They begin to *want* to stay on track rather than feel like they are being *told* to stay on track.

Dan Baker, an advisor in Texas, told us,

> *One of the things that seems to help is benchmarking the client's progress toward their retirement goals as opposed to some market benchmark. Clients like it when we provide them with regular progress reports showing their goals and where they are relative to their goals, to determine if they are on track. When clients have worked this way for a while, they like to stay on track with a spending plan that's going to allow them to live out their lives in dignity. One thing that helps is making (goals-based reporting) a regular part of client meetings. It's also important to have a realistic number (goal) in the first place. If we test their goals and verify them, they seem to be more committed to using those numbers, by having a process that makes it realistic and getting to the right number in the first place. Clients who use that process try to stay in the zone (of being on track).*
>
> *Where it's more difficult is where they see it as a less serious process and they feel like all the inputs are very much subject to change, either because of their own assumptions about market rates of return, or more likely, their tendency not to plan or budget, and they have no control over their spending. Those client situations get hard. They want to spend for today... I wish I could say everyone listens and takes our advice but there are some that just won't.*

The annuity hurdle is one way to track your client's status. This is a form of goals-based reporting. The goal is to stay above the annuity hurdle. Reporting to your client where they are relative to the hurdle keeps them informed about whether they need to make decisions to annuitize or partially annuitize. Remaining above the hurdle can reinforce their sense of financial security.

Another goals-based reporting method is to chart your clients' target wealth over their remaining lifetimes then post their actual wealth against this chart on a regular basis. Figure 6.7 is an example of this type of chart. In our example, we show the individual's actual portfolio values as columns. Our example shows annual amounts for the individual's actual portfolio value, but monthly or quarterly amounts could be reported as well. The solid line represents the individual's target wealth based on data they provided about their future savings and spending and using a deterministic assumption

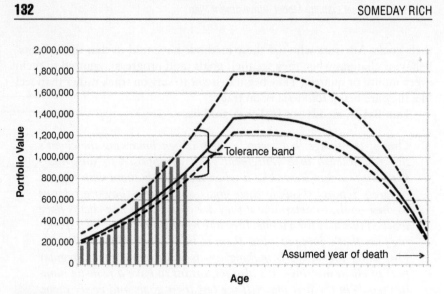

FIGURE 6.7   Example of Goals-Based Reporting

for investment returns. The broken lines define an upper and lower control limit within which we would like to see the clients' portfolio values remain over time. The control limits represent a range between 90 percent and 130 percent of target wealth. You may choose whatever control limits you think make the most sense for your client's situation.

You'll notice in our example that, in the first few years, the clients' portfolio values fell below the target wealth but recovered nicely and even reached the upper control limit just a few years later. The control limits exist to make certain that clients stay within a specified range. In the event that their account values move outside these limits, adjustments may need to be considered. If they fall below the lower control limit, they may need to save additional funds or revise the goal. If values rise above the control limit, it may mean they could increase withdrawals from the account or take more risk in their asset allocation—an opportunity for a happy-face conversation.

* * *

Chapters 5 and 6 make up the steps of the personal asset liability model. In the next chapter, we talk about the business of giving good advice. We start the chapter with our thoughts on what a successful advisory practice looks like based on our observations of successful practices. Later in the chapter, we introduce the idea of the client engagement roadmap. With the roadmap as your base, we show how to incorporate the steps of the personal asset liability model into your client management.

CHAPTER 7

Making a Good Business of Giving Good Advice

Giving good advice obviously requires far more than knowing the correct technical answers to your client's questions. To be a good advisor, you must purposefully and profitably be in the business of giving good advice. This sounds obvious but probably less than 20 percent of advisors do it. This is a skill we observe can be learned, and learned best by advisors with a lifelong curiosity for acquiring it (see Chapter 10). In this chapter, we've organized our comments on the business of giving good advice into three categories.

First, the credibility of advice is inextricably tied to the advisor or advisory firm that is providing it, so we begin with the characteristics that lead to the reputational success of an advisor's business. A strong team with a unified vision for what type of advice they want to give is essential, as is having an accurate assessment of the regional economy and being an active member of the community. Successful advisory firms know what they are good at and stick to it. They are also judicious resource allocators, doing what they do best and outsourcing the rest.

Second are those characteristics that cause the advice to be valued by clients. Of foremost importance is suitability. Suitability is the result of deeply understanding your client's facts. Good advice is also holistic; it considers the "interactive" effects of the various discussions and aspects related to clients' desired outcome. Wealth management is unlike other advice because advisors need to look at clients' entire lives. In addition, good advice must also be able to adjust to contingencies and it must be practical to implement. Finally, advisors must bring a level of attentiveness to their clients to ensure they are focused on the most important goals and stay on track to meet them.

The items in these first two categories are separate and distinct, but they support each other in a way that is unique to each advisor and that advisor's book of clients. Into the third category, we place characteristics that are overarching in nature, and that cover both the advisory practice and the advice. They are the external factors advisors must deal with including global and regional economic conditions and required technical expertise.

After discussing the characteristics of a successful advisory practice, good advice and the external factors that influence them, we turn our attention to the practical steps of delivering good advice. In the second half of this chapter we introduce the client engagement roadmap. Your clients need a clear understanding of where they are going and how you are going to help them get there. That is what they are paying you for. They need a roadmap. The client engagement roadmap helps you focus your client meetings on the highest priority tasks and allows you to take control of the agenda for your client dialogs. It provides your client a clear picture of the value you deliver and enables them to tell their family, friends, and associates what you are doing that is so valuable they should seek out your services as well. It's practical in institutionalizing the basis for client meetings; your staff will come to understand what they need to prepare for each client interaction to be high quality. It allows you to deliver consistent high-quality advice to a large number of clients while keeping you, your team, and your clients all on the same page. And, it makes it possible for you to turn a sufficiently reasonable profit to continue to motivate you and your staff, and to be able to invest in your growing practice.

CHARACTERISTICS OF A SUCCESSFUL ADVISORY PRACTICE

We'll start our observations on what drives success for an advisory practice. These are the characteristics we've concluded after observing the traits most successful advisors have in common. We define successful as the ones who have built the most enterprise value and long-term retention of clients.

Overwhelmingly the most important characteristic of firm success is individuals and teams who are unanimous in their vision for their advisory practice. The people running the firm are unified in their vision of what type of advice they want to give and who to give it to. What breaks apart many advisory firms is the same thing that destroys many other would-be successful organizations, namely, a number of high-ego, high-energy people working in the same enterprise who cannot converge on the same vision of the future. They each have their own idea of where the firm should go and what kind of clients they should seek. And they can't reconcile those visions, so they begin to argue, they begin to develop their own agendas with their parts of the business, and ultimately those agendas are brought into conflict in a way that brings the firm down. We learned this from our study of money managers over many decades.

A strong and unified leadership team is the number-one characteristic of a successful advisory firm. A strong unified team is only possible if there is both a shared idea of what they're doing in service of the client and a shared idea of what actions, literally what products and services, equate to that. This sounds like a very simple thing, but we believe that characteristic would apply to a very small percentage of advisor teams today, somewhere in the range of plus or minus five percent.

Next in primacy is a distinct and accurate assessment of the *regional or local economy* that the advisory practice operates in. The great advisors are keen observers of and participants in their regional economies. They are likely to be able to tell you the names of the probate judges in the adjoining counties, they know who is selling businesses and who the business brokers are, they know the main centers of influence in their region. They are in the stream of information about what's going on in their regional economies, and they are regarded as experts in their particular field. The reason they are in the stream is because they are regarded, not as salespeople, but as genuine experts by the people in their community, particularly those in a position to influence referrals to them. These referrals may relate to the sale of a business or the movement of executives within companies in their region.

Over a period of time, because of the network of those relationships that have been developed, these practices are seen to be **reliable destinations** to bring one of those target clients **who is terribly important to the referring party** (for instance, someone who is a successful small-business person or someone who is possibly a mobile executive). Usually, in the case of a small-business person, that life event is the sale of a business, the building or expansion of a new business, the partitioning of equity in a business to a potential successor, or a significant personal issue such as the dissolution of a marriage. In the case of a corporate person, it is more often than not the change of a job or the occasion of a serious and concerted estate planning effort because they're looking at retirement with a definite time frame. Therefore, this characteristic is a regional command, the access to and connective insights about the flow of information affecting the regional economy.

The hallmarks of this characteristic are obvious. When you walk into an advisor's office and there is a picture of him or her at the Rotary club, or there's a picture of the Little League team that the firm sponsors, these are all positive earmarks. When the advisor tells you that she or he is on the Board of Trustees for the local zoo or community college, this indicates that she has been able to punch her way through the earlier stages of practice development and has become a valued part of the community. These advisors have graduated from the idea of selling things to the idea of servicing clients for long periods of time in order to achieve their objectives and their clients' objectives. Is this you? Do you want it to be, if it is not already?

The last characteristic to consider in this category is whether the practice has a sense of *efficiency*. Great advisors understand the requirement to be judicious resource allocators within their own businesses. How this takes shape is generally through outsourcing; great advisors know what they do well and they want to put all their chips on the bet where they have the unique ability to do something special for their clients. They want to refer out everything else. The most obvious illustration of this is advisors who move to a platform where they get all the custodial and reporting services provided to them by the platform. These advisors know they can't add unique value to these services that are clearly a matter of scale and data processing, so they spend their time on creating and delivering personalized added value to their clients. This goes one step further in that it helps them to establish their brand in the market when it's clear that they do one thing uniquely well.

Marlene Shalton, told us:

> *What I learned is to find out what you are good at, stick to it and not be distracted by thinking the grass is greener elsewhere. I have made these mistakes from time to time and realised that I had just wasted time, energy, and money only to return to what I was already doing quite successfully. There are a host of opportunities within financial services and it is finding out which of those you are more attuned to or skilled for.*

HOW TIM NOONAN MET MARLENE SHALTON

If you just go by the awards and recognition that Marlene Shalton has received in her professional life, you could conclude that she's one of the best Independent Financial Advisors (IFA) in the UK. (What we call RIAs in the US, are called IFAs in the UK) Beginning in Spring 2009, I had been seconded to Russell Investment's London office—it is our second largest operation, globally. Russell executives in Europe had concluded that the time was right for us to build an IFA-oriented business in the UK similar to the model I had helped to establish in the US. The catalyst for wanting to do so was a major regulatory change in the UK, known as the RDR (Retail Distribution Review). The essence of the RDR was to accelerate adoption of fee-based advisory business models, reduce product churning and commission-driven abuses, and in general promote more fairness and transparency in the advisor-client relationship. Because of my affinity with advisors, I was assigned to London to help them develop the product and service strategy, build the sales and marketing teams, work with the financial and trade press, etc.

Now, if you could put out of your memory for a minute how abysmal that timing was to launch a new advisory oriented business, I'd say that working with advisors in the UK was one of the most important learning experiences in my professional life. The epitome of that experience is summed up in my acquaintance, and subsequent friendship, with Marlene Shalton and her husband Richard. Having recently sold her firm, Marlene was not about to ride off in the sunset—although I recall there was the temptation of her tasteful little getaway in Provence. Marlene is an advisor that loves advising, and loves to teach other advisors. I met her for the first time in connection with the advanced study group of the UK Financial Planning Association when I presented to that group. We did not instantly hit it off, indeed, like most great advisors, Marlene is a cautious evaluator. But over the course of a year or so as we were launching our Helping Advisors initiative in the UK, I would call to ask her advice, get her views on an industry event, or on her expectations of how regulatory reforms would be implemented. We saw each other occasionally at dinners and industry award banquets, most notably the year that I was lucky enough to accept Russell's award as a leading educator of the year at the 2009 Institute of Financial Planning's award ceremony in Wales, not far from where she and Richard reside.

What I admire most about Marlene is that she is not only a great advisor, but quite passionate about teaching others to be, as well. She has lectured extensively on cash flow modeling and the importance of installing higher levels of technical discipline in the planning process. I asked her to distill the experiences of her amazing career into lessons for my clients. That's why some of her thoughts are included in this book.

An example of how these two characteristics of regional command and efficiency come together in a powerful way can be seen in an advisory firm we are familiar with. UMA Financial Services operates in Salt Lake City, Utah and works with medical professionals in that area. They focus exclusively on local medical professionals. So, if a medical professional in that metropolitan area has a life event, and asks around the community where to go to get advice, their name will almost certainly come up. Their name will be mentioned because they are so specialized in that region (and that profession) as the firm to go to with a financial issue.

This introduces an important point: We believe there is a fallacy among advisors that in order to become successful they must become good at marketing, and that they need to broadcast their message to the market. We think the opposite is true. If they become very specialized in a particular skill and are focused on articulating that skill to their clients, **this endemic marketing approach allows the market to locate them**. It's the ability of the market to find them that sets them apart and perpetuates profitable growth.

We're talking about strategic focus. If we break down the term *strategic focus* it has two halves. The focus part is obvious; it is the service that makes the firm unique from other firms. This is the way that somebody who is referring new clients to your firm would talk about your firm. The strategic part is the decision that is made by the people running the firm about how they're capable of being genuinely unique. Normally that decision is not simply a product of their deciding to be good at something; it's actually a product of their experience. Successful advisors experience doing something well for their clients and as a result they begin to believe that they are good at that thing. This strengthens their self-efficacy toward that skill and produces an even greater skill and competence in that thing.

The final characteristic we observe is a passion for *measurement* of the factor that defines the firm's success. Whatever way the firm defines success—number of clients, size of clients, revenue per client, profit per client—that definition of success must be broadly shared within the firm. *Shared within the firm,* means specifically that all the people who work in that firm understand the same definition of success. It's not a mystery to them, it's not something only known by management. By knowing the definition of success, they all can contribute to it. By knowing what constitutes success, all the team members in the firm will want to play their part and find a way to apply their skills to help the firm and their clients achieve that success. This is what happens in high-performance teams: contribution to goals becomes exciting, voluntary, nonthreatening, rather than done to avoid punishment.

Few practices have a single success metric they follow, and many that articulate one (i.e., assets per client) often don't adhere to their own guidelines for a long-enough period of measurement. Our experience tells us that the most effective success metric for a wealth management practice is profit per client. When advisors begin to focus on the quality of their book of clients, and by this we mean their profit per client, their businesses and lives begin to change dramatically, as do ideas about their potential legacies.

The great firms have those characteristics, but they don't just happen. The difference between a firm that doesn't have them but will get there someday and the firm that doesn't have all of those characteristics and will never get there, is the admission that one or more of the characteristics is missing and the commitment to correct it. When that admission happens, it is generally because the principals of the firm are dissatisfied in some way. They feel they're spending too much time on their work, or they can't spend enough time with their family, or they're not making as much money as they think they should, or they are not delivering enough value to their clients, or whatever the dissatisfaction might be. When the dissatisfaction is high enough, they become willing to change their focus and behavior in a way to correct the deficits, whatever they may be.

We have had the great fortune to work with Steve Moore for many years. Steve taught us many lessons, two of which Tim Noonan wrote about in his Foreword to Steve's recent book: *Ineffective Habits of Financial Advisors: And the Discipline to Break Them*. Tim wrote of the two lessons:

> *The first is the immense value—I would even use the word power—that arises from understanding how to convert your dissatisfactions into deliberate behavior that creates advantages for you. Second, I firmly believe that you will discover, as I did, that whatever it is that you think is holding you back from excellence as an advisor—gloomy economic climate, dipping markets, punitive regulators, narrow-minded bosses, skeptical or mistrusting clients, complex technological changes, whatever that list includes—it is not true. It is a falsehood. What holds you back is yourself. Excellence is there for you, within reach. So reach out and grab it.*

CHARACTERISTICS OF GOOD ADVICE

We posit that those are the characteristics of a successful advisory firm. Now let's turn to the next category, the characteristics of good advice. The first is that the advice is suitable to the client's need. Suitability is inseparable from a genuine understanding of the client's situation. One advisor who we interviewed for this book told us that he tape records his client discovery meetings (with the client's permission, of course) so he can go back and listen to what his client told him about their goals. Another advisor, Charlene Carter, in Eugene, Oregon, when asked her opinion on what makes a good advisor, responded succinctly, "Listening and understanding a client's point of view *before* giving advice."

There are many aspects of suitability including whether the advice is objective, authentic, and well researched, but any of these requires powerful listening skills. When advising on retirement income, does the advice provide potential for sustaining the client's desired lifestyle, does it result in a reasonable risk of failure, and is it flexible enough to allow the client a level of control they associate with their financial independence? In short, suitable advice should lead to a more precise specification of the client's desired outcome, together with a higher chance of reaching it. Together with empathy in the conversation.

Wealth management does not focus on one aspect of an individual's financial life. It looks at the entire "ecosystem" of the individual's financial needs, as one of America's foremost wealth managers, Russ Hill, likes to say. Good advice is, in this sense, *holistic.* It's not enough to know isolated pieces of the client's financial puzzle. Good advice means knowing as many of the parts as the client will share and coordinating how those pieces fit together. It is a fallacy that this requires being an expert in all financial areas. It is more important for advisors today to *know* a long-term-care expert than to *be* a long-term-care expert. As we will discuss in the second part of this chapter, some advisory firms work together to form a network of expertise in order to cover all the needs of their clients. These expert networks also serve as a prime marketing channel and a source of new referrals. You will increase your credibility by enfranchising other experts, and devising creative ways to work together on client dilemmas.

Why don't advisors do this more, when it's such an obviously powerful way to signal to the community that they are committed to being their client's best problem solver? The reason may be that many advisors started in the business at a time when splitting commissions, or worse still, losing a commission to a rival was a thing of fear and dread. So the idea of sharing a client takes some getting used to. If you put yourself in your client's shoes, you will see that, again to quote Russ Hill, "clients just want great service, not necessarily all of it from you."

In addition to being holistic, good advice is able to anticipate or accommodate potential *contingencies.* Going back to the idea that stimulated this book (why Zeus's plan failed) it failed to take into consideration the ways plans are disrupted. There is a tendency for clients' goals or problems to be expressed overconfidently when they do not bring to the table all the possible scenarios of what might change. The advisor's job in this sense is to act as a journalist. The advisor must question the sources of information, understand the accuracy of what's being said, evaluate whether the statements are plausible: All the things that a good journalist does. If you want to learn how to do this, read Gretchen Morgenson or Joe Nocera for a month. The other skill advisors must have is the ability to foresee the willingness or ability of their clients to do or not to do certain actions that could improve their situation. The most obvious example is the client's commitment to saving. Advisors must discern their clients' actual capacities to defer consumption now (or encourage others in clients' families to do so) in order to create security later. For the vast majority of clients, this is the difference between success and failure. In addition, the advisors' ability to communicate with their clients in ways that are empathic is also important. It's so important we dedicated Chapter 8 to this topic.

The next characteristic is the ability to *implement* advice in a reasonable and efficient way, such that the dependencies, the products, and services the advisor uses, don't perform in a way that are so at variance with the plan that they jeopardize its success. An obvious example of this is the implementation of an asset allocation in such a way that a part of the portfolio so underperforms the expectations that it causes a loss in confidence in the portfolio as a whole. In other words, there is so much slippage in the implementation of one slice of the pie that the client tosses out the entire pie. Advisors must have the ability to control the amount of slippage in the implementation stage so they can prevent circumstances from threatening the integrity of the overall plan.

The final characteristic in this category we call *attentiveness*. In a consulting sense you might call this stewardship; you are always looking at what is happening. It is surveillance. What you are being attentive to is not just whether the implementation is on track but whether the plan continues to be satisfactorily addressing clients' anxiety about sustaining their envisioned lifestyle. At the simplest, it comes down to one thing: Is the funded status greater than or less than 100 percent?

As an example, consider the scenario where an advisor starts out with a 35-year-old client, a doctor who has enormous earning potential but is at the beginning of her career and has no assets (but plenty of debt). This doctor is in the early phases of family formation, with a lot on her mind about establishing her practice and her own role in the community. This doctor, who's making decisions about her financial future at age 35, is a very different person 15 years later when she has accumulated wealth (so she has a lot to lose) and has her own experience with dissatisfied patients. At this later stage, she has a whole new set of considerations, so attentiveness isn't determining whether the plan is intact but whether the way you deliver advice to her has evolved to match her new situation. Your clients have a financial lifecycle, which must be incorporated into your client engagement roadmap, which we discuss later in this chapter.

Attentiveness is something that is measurable, and the way it can be measured is through client defections. Why do clients fire advisors and go to other advisors? Is it really because they are disappointed in a particular product? That could happen, but it generally is not the reason that we observe. More often than not, it is because the advisors they were with didn't understand what those clients were trying to do; they didn't get the clients or they were just unresponsive. They began looking for advisors who could get them. That sentiment often is inseparable from a disappointing investment experience, but the disappointing investment experience is merely the catalyst for dismissal. What really causes the breakup of the advisor-client relationship is the client's conviction that the advisor didn't see them.

EXTERNAL FACTORS

With all these things being valid about the nature of good advisory practices and good advice, there are some major externalities that must also be considered. One of them is the *economic climate* during the period of time the advice is being given. If you, as an advisor were doing all the things we just talked about in 1933 you would have gotten very different outcomes than if you were doing them in 1997. So there is a relationship between how robust the external environment is in terms of market rewards and what you are doing to build a successful firm and deliver quality advice.

Another factor relates to our earlier comments about regionality. The *conditions and trends of local environment* greatly influence the success of advisory practices. For example, a practice in a high new-industry growth area such as Orange County might have a completely different mode of operation than one in a mature market like Cleveland, Detroit, or Pittsburgh. You might have all the qualities of a good advisory practice and good advice but you might be working in a region in which there is either insufficient wealth or insufficient growth of affluence for you to be rewarded. This is a particularly important observation for younger advisors who might be operating in economic zones in which they have everything it takes to be successful, but they are just working in the wrong place.

The next factor relates to the *technical expertise* related to the environment in which the advisor is working. As an example, let's say you're an advisor in Edina, Minnesota and many of your clients work for 3M Corporation. There is a whole set of things you might want to know about that company: maybe the regulations that relate to people who work in that industry, the technicalities of their stock plan for executives, and so on. Where they join at a common root is in the advisor's commitment to an ongoing absorption of the technical details that affect the economic well-being of the people who work in that vicinity. In doing so, the advisor is able to quickly offer very specific and informed advice on what clients should do in a particular situation. For instance, let's say the client has to decide on whether to exercise options in their corporate plan in this calendar year versus several calendar years hence. If the advisor happens to know of a specific tax regulation affecting this industry that might influence the client's decision, that would be an illustration of an advisor who is on his game with respect to how to guide this homogeneous set of clients.

Some advisors demonstrate this technical expertise offensively and some do it defensively. By defensively, we mean they do it because they feel that it is an occupational hazard not to. However, the advisors who do these things offensively understand that, by knowing these things, they become particularly valued as advocates by their clients and known in their communities as a source of insight. This latter type is invariably more successful in our experience. They are more receptive to things that are going on in their external environment and they develop an ability to translate those events and contingencies into advice for their clients; they create "bridges of loyalty", as Howard Schultz of Starbucks would say.

These are the three external factors: the economic environment, the regional environment, and the technical expertise related to the unique aspects of the advisor's book of clients.

INTEGRITY

A final characteristic that sits atop all of what we've discussed so far in this chapter is that of *integrity*. Integrity is more than truthfulness and fee transparency, although those are very important. It's about threading a needle through all the characteristics discussed in this chapter in order to create not only the impression of high integrity but also its reality in the experience of the client. It is not an additional characteristic; it is something that is achieved through having all the characteristics discussed here. Integrity cannot be asserted; it must be demonstrated and it must be tailored.

Although most people think of integrity as basic honesty, we think it is at least as much about competence. Dan Baker described it to us this way:

> *I think the willingness (for the client) to be led comes from a deep level of trust. It's born out of the confidence in the advisor's competence and their ability to take the client where they want to go. Without that it would be a tragedy, it would be a very sad thing if somebody surrendered to their advisor and was led down the*

wrong path. We've had some clients who by nature are naturally trusting, they want to put their faith in an advisor, and they've been led down the wrong path or not served well in the past. So, they feel burned and less confident. I think a high level of competence is a big piece of this puzzle because when we're working with bright, afflu-ent people they want to know that if they follow our advice they're going to be taken somewhere where they want to go and it would be very meaningful for them to get there. Those are the elements (of a successful advisor/client relationship), **the client's willingness to be led, a high trust in the advisor and the advisor's ability to lead them to the right place.**

FROM EFFICIENT FRONTIER TO CLIENT ENGAGEMENT

To be successful in the business of giving good advice requires, we think, the characteristics we just discussed. It also requires clients **engaged** in the process of managing their wealth. To have a growing and successful prac-tice does not demand acquiring large numbers of new clients; it requires transforming your relationships with your current high-net-worth clients. These clients are the epicenter of your future firm. However, they will not consolidate their assets with you or refer their family, friends, and associates until they understand what they will accomplish by doing so. The first step is to shift the focus of your client engagements from issues concerning the markets to your clients' goals. The goals you should focus on are the ones that require planning, money, time, and ongoing coordination to accom-plish, in particular, helping clients achieve the standard of living they desire after they stop working. The fundamental question they are looking for you to help answer is, "Will my wealth enable me to continue my lifestyle for the rest of my life?"

When your clients understand that helping them achieve their financial goals is what keeps you up at night, they will disclose their most pressing needs and create opportunities for you to advise them. Our experience in-dicates that, when this happens, your clients are more likely to consolidate their assets with you and recommend you to others.

In the next section, we introduce the client engagement roadmap. The roadmap can be used as the central device for articulating the value you bring to your clients: how you currently bring them value and how you will be assisting them in the future. Delivering value to your clients and always making sure they are aware of it is a powerful guiding principle to follow.

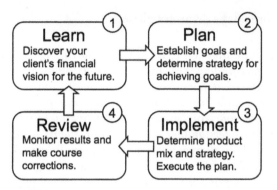

FIGURE 7.1   Learn, Plan, Implement, Review

The roadmap ensures that you are working on the right things for your clients and they know about it

Learn, Plan, Implement, Review

One formula of successful consulting is the Learn/Plan/Implement/Review cycle. In the **learning** step you discover information about your client needed to formulate a financial plan. The **planning** step involves establishing and prioritizing goals, and determining a strategy for achieving those goals. In the third step you **implement** the plan by executing agreed upon actions. Finally, in the fourth step, results are **reviewed** regularly and compared against the expected results, so course corrections can be made when necessary. The client engagement roadmap is an adaptation of this formula. Next we discuss the first step; the discovery phase.

Discovery: Rediscovering Your Client

At the beginning of a new client relationship you gather information about your client. Some of this information is quantitative (fact-facts), such as name, address, assets and liabilities, and so on, and some is qualitative (feeling-facts), such as the client's vision of retirement or their feelings about bequests.

Fact-finding ought not to be limited to new clients. Now is a good time to look at your most valued clients and go back through the fact-finding process with them. If you're apprehensive about going back to the fact-finding step with your long-time clients, don't be. Your clients will appreciate your efforts to better understand their financial goals and evolve your relationship to meet their needs, as they perceive their goals now.

Steve Moore on the discovery phase:

Using a consultative approach allows you to engage clients with qualitative fact-finding. Research from Dow Jones and CEG World-wide indicates that fewer than 7 percent of advisors use a consultative approach. Just asking good questions puts you ahead of 93 percent of your competition. Qualitative fact-finding provides you with an understanding of what your clients want, why they want it, and how they make their decisions. When you move beyond numbers on a page, you have the chance to gain insight into what is really important to a client. Ninety percent of your face-to-face fact-finding time should be focused on listening to the answers to your qualitative questions. Taking a consultative approach is about asking better questions and letting the client talk.

Winning advisors ask open-ended questions. The broader the question, the more talking room it provides for the client.[1]

As Steve says, qualitative questions should be open-ended. A simple question like, "I'd like to get to know you better, would you please tell me your story?" can cause a person to open up and tell you things about themselves you might never gather from a questionnaire. "What is your vision for retirement?" is another open-ended question that leads you down the road to understanding your client's desired future lifestyle.

Again, according to Steve Moore:

Your job is to listen, take notes and nod your head. When they (the client) articulate what they want, ask open-ended follow-up questions to find out why they want it and how they made the decision.

When you are done gathering your qualitative facts, simply thank the client for the opportunity to hear their story and their vision of their future. Tell them you have some thoughts but don't want to answer off the cuff. Inform them that you would like to think about their goals and how they can be accomplished.

As mentioned earlier, one of the advisors we interviewed for this book told us he audio records his fact-finding sessions with his clients. (Always ask your client's permission before recording them.) He told us he is always surprised at how many details he would have missed if he had to rely on his handwritten notes.

Marlene Shalton told us this about client discovery:

The Financial Planner can influence hugely the success or failure of the effort (of defining their financial vision). This is governed largely, I believe, by how deftly a Planner can employ those soft skills, necessary to guide, coach, educate and encourage the client, to look honestly at their lives and how they want to lead them. Putting the client at ease, asking open-ended questions, listening and hearing, providing empathy and structuring the sessions in a trusting and confidential manner are crucial to the Discovery meeting. How successfully the Planner employs those skills from the very beginning will have an enormous impact on the eventual outcome.

Once you have your client's information, create a document that summarizes what you heard. For the purposes of this description, we call this document a discovery agreement, Steve Moore refers to it as a financial vision document, which is probably a much more engaging way to characterize it with your clients. Whatever you call the document, be as clear and concise as possible in its detail. At the next meeting, present the discovery agreement to your client and have them *verify that you heard them correctly*. This accomplishes several things. First, you build rapport with your client by demonstrating your ability to listen to them and that you have made the effort to memorialize what you heard so you can help them reach their goals. Second, it allows the client to make adjustments if any are needed before you move to the next step of making a plan. This is not merely an exercise so you can put something in your file to show you've documented their investment objectives. You are showing evidence of your commitment to a thorough and disciplined approach to accomplishing their goals.

SAMPLE DISCOVERY AGREEMENT

The following text is an example of a discovery agreement...

You said you would like to be financially independent by the time you turn 62. To you, financial independence means you would be able to live at the level you have grown accustomed to without needing to work for income.

You believe the college education your children received provided them with tremendous opportunities. You now want to ensure that your grandchildren, Stacy and Max, also have an opportunity to receive a college education. You both take great pride in having put yourselves through college and want

> to give your grandchildren the sense that they have to work hard for this opportunity. To this end, you feel that they should participate in the funding of their own education.
>
> You are planning to move into a condo here in Cleveland because your children are spread throughout the country and you love to travel. You love London and Paris and want the freedom to travel without the concerns of home upkeep.
>
> You feel blessed by the opportunities you have been given throughout life. In particular, you are grateful for the opportunities that have come to you by way of your Stanford University degrees. You have passion for providing this same opportunity for success to other young people and want to continue to contribute to Stanford University scholarship funds.
>
> Ed has turned green. In this next phase of life he plans to do part-time management consulting work in the alternative fuel area. Sally plans to continue her volunteer work as a CASA (court appointed special advocate).

Source: Steve Moore, *Ineffective Habits of Financial Advisors* (Hoboken, NJ: John Wiley & Sons, 2010).

THE ROADMAP

To be effective, the steps we described in the personal asset liability model chapters must fit practically into the way you interact with your clients. For this, you need a roadmap. Over an extended period of doing strategic planning work with financial advisors, Steve Moore and subsequently others at Russell developed a tool to give his financial advisors client's a track to run on. The result was the client engagement roadmap, which generates a clear, concise, single-page depiction of what the client and advisor were working on together and where they were going to focus next.

You work hard for your clients and they don't always know about the hard work you do for them, but they are well aware of the fees they are paying you. The client engagement roadmap is a professional and succinct way of reminding your client at each review meeting of the value you are delivering.

One of your biggest challenges as a financial professional is to help your clients stay focused on the future; and *it is a future you know they apprehend.* Despite your best efforts, they sometimes struggle to remember your guidance. No matter how strong the message, we are all easily distracted. We are inclined to make emotional, sometimes rash, decisions based on what is happening at the moment in the news, losing sight of where they have been or where it is they desire to go.

A solution to this common problem is to fashion your client service experience around the client engagement roadmap. Clients need guidance in orchestrating their affairs. The roadmap positions you as the coordinator. Figure 7.2 is a sample of a client engagement roadmap. This sample shows what a roadmap might look like for a new client. You'll notice that the first couple of quarters have orientation topics listed that would not normally be included for a long-time client. As we will discuss later, the roadmap should be adapted to each client's specific needs. The topics listed in the sample are merely examples of topics that might be covered in a client review meeting.

Bob Bishopp, an exceptional advisor in Spokane, Washington, who is familiar with using the client engagement roadmap talked to us about how he uses it with his clients:

In meeting with clients we try to get a sense of how much and what kind of communication they need or want. When we know that, we try to plot that out on a systematic basis. We start out using calendar quarters and meeting with them four times a year. There are certain topics we like to cover in every meeting such as status of accounts, but we also introduce other items that might be relevant; educational sessions on specific topics. We also have a staff member call them prior to the meeting to see if there is anything in particular that they want to discuss, any topics they want to dig into more deeply. That is how we create the agenda. The key thing is always looking forward at the end of these meetings. We plan the next meeting before we end the current meeting, setting the agenda for the next meeting. We also agree on the things that could or should take place in between this meeting and the next. The roadmap isn't something that we give our clients, it's something that we show them. From their perspective they know that we are thinking ahead, always bringing up things to talk about as it relates to their situation.

We asked Bob Bishopp how he determines what information his clients want or need. His response:

We simply ask them. For instance if somebody brings in a 30-page brokerage statement, we ask them what it is about the information in that report that is of interest to them. We ask them to tell us

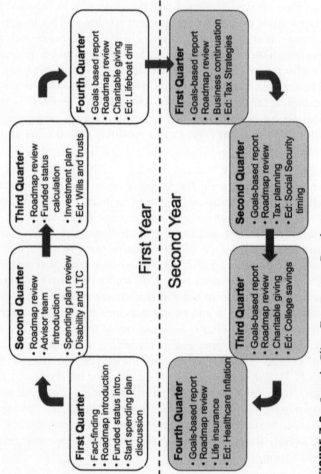

First Year

First Quarter
- Fact-finding
- Roadmap introduction
- Funded status intro.
- Start spending plan discussion

Second Quarter
- Roadmap review
- Advisor team introduction
- Spending plan review
- Disability and LTC

Third Quarter
- Roadmap review
- Funded status calculation
- Investment plan
- Ed: Wills and trusts

Fourth Quarter
- Goals based report
- Roadmap review
- Charitable giving
- Ed: Lifeboat drill

Second Year

First Quarter
- Goals-based report
- Roadmap review
- Business continuation
- Ed: Tax Strategies

Second Quarter
- Goals-based report
- Roadmap review
- Tax planning
- Ed: Social Security timing

Third Quarter
- Goals-based report
- Roadmap review
- Charitable giving
- Ed: College savings

Fourth Quarter
- Goals-based report
- Roadmap review
- Life insurance
- Ed: Healthcare Inflation

FIGURE 7.2 Sample Client Engagement Roadmap

about their experience with their previous advisor, what did they like what did they not. We ask what is of value to them. Most likely our new clients have left another advisor, and we would like to know why they left. With some of our best clients, we don't have to ask what they're looking for, they tell us what they're looking for.

*Interestingly enough, some of our best client relationships are not about the investment experience, it's about the people experience, about the relationship. They come from advisors with whom they did not have a relationship and **didn't feel like their opinions mattered.***

In the section that follows we describe how to get started using the roadmap. We discuss the topics that you should consider using, including how to adapt the roadmap to your client's specific outcome preferences. Then we suggest you practice using the roadmap on yourself and staff members before taking the final step and trying it out on your clients.

Roadmap Topics

The first step in familiarizing yourself with the roadmap is to understand the categories of topics that populate the roadmap and the dialogue that goes along with each of them.

Goals-Based Report   We suggest that the goals-based report be one of the first topic of business addressed in a client-review meeting. By doing this, you are emphasizing to your client the importance of their goals and their progress toward them. There will be times when there are other topics that you need to address in your client meeting, but the goals-based review should never be skipped. A client not interested in knowing how they are doing relative to their goals is a signal that you should dig deeper into understanding their lack of interest. This is an opportunity to learn your clients' levels of satisfaction with their plans, (and maybe with you). Take advantage of this opportunity.

Funded status should be the primary goal reviewed at each client meeting. Because funded status is a snapshot in time, changing throughout time, it is critical that your clients receive regular feedback.

Regular feedback has several advantages. It builds your client's confidence in the wealth-management process; it increases your client's commitment to their goals and allows for earlier course correction if or when it's needed. It's also important to review progress toward any other goals that your clients have set. Then there is the main benefit: It proves to your client that their desired outcome is your focus. It removes any confusion about what the central goal is. How many of your clients today could answer "Yes" if asked the question: "Does your advisor know what your central goal is and what would constitute failure?"

Roadmap Review The professional relationship with the client, for which you receive your fee, is "the engagement." The roadmap is the template for tailoring that engagement in a manner transparent to, and hopefully engaging for, the client. It addresses topics discussed in the previous quarters and provides an update of what was added on the basis of those discussions. The roadmap review is used to highlight and draw attention to the steps in the planning process. For example, if a client's long-term plan includes creation of an estate plan, steps in the process may include the referral to a qualified estate planning attorney and drafting of documents. These are items that you review and highlight in the roadmap review. Often clients have a vague understanding of the process and timelines associated with planning. This is unsurprising given, as we have noted, how disengaged clients are with the conventional financial planning discussion. The roadmap is a superior tool for helping to increase their awareness of how much work you are doing for them behind the scenes.

The roadmap review, as one of the first agenda items for your client review meeting, enables you to establish control of the client dialogue. It allows you to revisit past topics and close any open loops, to set the agenda for today's review meeting, and to advertise the value you are delivering to your client. Finally, reviewing the roadmap at every client meeting reinforces its status as the central tool around which the client engagement operates. It serves to establish your clients' expectations toward a consistent and professional process. As soon as clients can articulate that, they can tell their friends and associates about it.

Client's Research Agenda After the goals-based report and roadmap review, comes your opportunity to place items on the agenda based on the needs you uncovered in your fact finding or from subsequent conversations with your client. As an example, suppose your client has just changed jobs and has a large 401(k) balance that should be rolled over into their IRA account (for you to manage along with his other retirement assets). However, this quarter, you are focusing your client's attention on finalizing his estate plan that has not been updated in many years. Because the 401(k) rollover is less urgent than the estate planning, you place the 401(k) rollover item on the next quarter's roadmap. This way, you show your client that you are aware of the issue and that you will be prepared to discuss the topic in detail at next quarter's review meeting, even if the market happened to move in the interim. Next quarter you will not only be prepared for the discussion, you will also be able to focus all your attention on this issue without the distraction of the estate planning tasks.

Education Topics Education topics are less urgent than those on the client's research agenda. These items may relate directly to a need your client has expressed to you, a topic you feel your client should learn more about, or an item that is currently in the news or popular media that you feel should be addressed. As an example of how to prepare for these items, if you put college savings on the roadmap as an education topic, it may be helpful to prepare a brief overview of the issues surrounding education expenses as well an overview of available savings strategies. In advance of that conversation, you might alert an assistant to confirm birth dates of children and grandchildren.

Adapting the Roadmap

The client research agenda and education topics are examples of how you are able to *tailor* the roadmap to adapt to your client's circumstances. During the fact finding you will uncover your client's most pressing concerns. These are the topics to begin with. You may, however, find that there are needs your clients have that they are unaware of or that they have not given the level of priority that they should. For instance, if you were to discover your midcareer, high-income client has no disability insurance (and says they have no interest in disability insurance) you might still place this topic on next quarter's agenda because you suspect they need further education on the risk disability poses to their financial security (see Chapter 9: Tripping Over the Finish Line).

Roadmaps should encapsulate your clients' outcome objectives. They do not imply that you provide all the services related to each agenda item. An effective way to address this is to team up with other leading professionals in areas beyond the scope of your expertise. By referring clients to experts, you are creating a viral network of specialists that can address more of your client's financial needs. In the process, you may also find that these other experts are a good referral source of new business for your practice once they discover the evidence of the depth of your approach. These expert networks can be very elaborate. Mine (Tim Noonan's) include physicians, nutritionalists, and physical therapists (reflecting that my community includes people interested in long distance running and nutrition), as well as financial experts, insurance specialists, lawyers, art appraisers, real-estate brokers, even an expert in varnishing antique yachts. Your network is a manifestation of your reach into your regional economy.

TABLE 7.1　Possible Planning Topics

Creating a Spending Budget	Wills and trusts
Estate planning	College savings
Business planning	Life insurance
Health insurance	Long-term care insurance
Disability income planning	Tax planning
Aging parent needs	Employee benefits
Charitable giving	Business continuation
Beneficiary review	

Table 7.1 is a brief list of planning topics that might be appropriate for inclusion on your client's roadmap.

Prioritize and Tailor　There are a couple of things you can do that will bring the roadmap to life in the eyes of your client. The first is to prioritize the items on the basis of the insights you gained in the fact-finding process. Make sure that you begin with what your client said was most important and then move to what you know to be other critical items.

The second is to tailor the roadmap. Wherever possible, include the names of your clients, along with the names of their children and/or grandchildren. Instead of listing an item as simply a trust, list it as "Trust for Maddy" or "College Funding for Gigi." Doing so is a simple demonstration of your grasp of what is significant to them. In an age when your cell phone can tell you how many restaurants there are in a ten block radius that have tables available for you for dinner tonight, personalization is not just a nice touch, it's an expectation.

Figure 7.3 is an example of a tailored roadmap. Shown here is Tim Noonan's roadmap as prepared by his financial advisor Peter Rekstad.

Practice Using the Roadmap on Yourself

We've just talked about the topics that populate the roadmap and how to adapt the roadmap to your client's desired outcomes. Before using the roadmap on your clients, consider using it for yourself. Beginning with the first quarter, complete the roadmap as if you were the client. Start by including the review topics referenced in step one and then begin adapting the roadmap to your situation.

An interesting thing happened to me (Tim Noonan) when I did that for myself. I had never thought about my life broken down into quarterly increments. Being a distance runner for most of my life, I find long races much easier if I know the mileposts along the way. From the time I retire

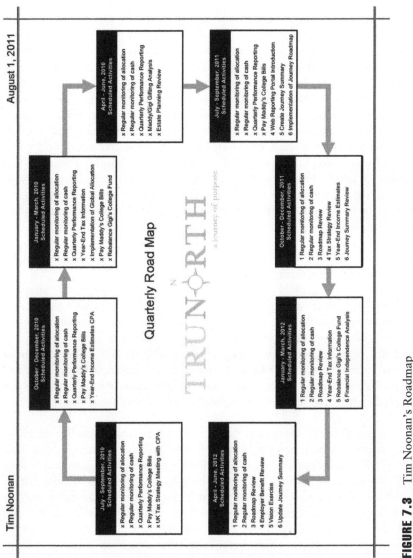

FIGURE 7.3 Tim Noonan's Roadmap

(I hope I don't retire until I'm 70) to the age my oldest grandparent died, 95 (this is my best guess at my own longevity, assuming I don't start riding motorcycles), that's 25 years. That's 100 meetings with my advisor throughout my retired life.

Say each meeting lasts an hour and a half, and assume a half-hour travel time. Add it all up and you get 200 hours. That's a little more than a week, just over eight days. I went one step further: I then calculated the ratio of time I might spend in totally useless and counterproductive worry about my financial future in proportion to the 200 hours during which I would be meaningfully engaged in accomplishing sustainable financial security. I figure that I spend about two hours every week ruminating (on account balances, potential rebalancing strategies, wishing I had over or under weighted small caps or whatever, I especially like to second guess whether my bond durations are too short). Those stupid, wasted hours add up to 2,600. Finally, reducing this to a ratio of pointless worry to constructive engagement, I came up with 13:1. Thirteen pointless, stupid, wasted, never-to-be-recovered hours of rumination for every one hour of purposeful work. So I came to the following conclusions.

1. I'm not willing to waste 2,600 hours of my life on anything especially pointless ruminations.
2. Given how much I ruminate over sustainable financial security, 200 hours with my advisor even double that, even triple that, is an investment I will make eagerly—especially if it helps to reclaim some of the 2,600 hours otherwise lost on my own foolishness.
3. I will be a different guy toward the end of those 100 meetings than at the start. I will be as old as I remember my grandpa before he died, probably as frail, maybe even frailer (he was a pretty tough guy). So I'm glad that I have selected an advisor a few years younger than me.

The moral of this story, and the point of our advice to practice the client engagement roadmap first on yourself is this: It doesn't seem obvious until you actually do it, but the act of envisioning your own engagement breaks the trance of the hyperbolic discount—by which I mean it brings the distant future into the immediate present, and it does so in a reassuring way. It makes it possible to concretely visualize how the messy, unpredictable, and complex challenge of creating your sustainable financial security will actually come about. And above all, it drives home the point that my advisor helps me navigate a tricky curve, and ensures that I will land at the exact spot.

Consider the sample topics we listed earlier as a starting point for adding items to your roadmap. After you have constructed your personal roadmap, have one or more members of your staff go through the same exercise in order to gain familiarity with the tool. When integrating the roadmap into your practice, you may wish to deliver the roadmap first to a select group of clients, learning how to effectively implement it before moving on to additional clients.

Introducing Your Clients to the Roadmap

Now you are ready to start using the roadmap with your clients. The roadmap provides you and your team with a clear plan and work agenda. The roadmap serves as a guide not only for your clients, but for your staff as well. With minimal effort, they will be in tune with current planning issues and items that need action or follow-up.

Once you have the initial roadmap completed, you can update it as your client's circumstances change and keep it in their file so that, at all times, you have a documented history of their goals and planning issues. You can also use the roadmap in meeting preparation or for follow-up on outstanding items that may have been referred out of your office. (Your compliance team will love it.)

It's important to make sure that each item on the roadmap is completed or addressed. The roadmap will become part of your permanent client file, so you need to make sure items on the roadmap are completed. If items are not completed, they must be advanced to the next quarter. Avoid the temptation to over commit yourself. With rigorous implementation and follow-up on the roadmap milestones, you will demonstrate tangible evidence of the value you provide in trade for your fee. We know of clients who report to their advisor that they keep a copy of their roadmap on their refrigerators. When you get to the point that clients are putting it on their refrigerators, you know you have applied it successfully. Visit my kitchen: mine is on display!

We've been asked how frequently an advisor should meet with their wealth-management clients. Review frequency is influenced by client personality, complexity of the client's financial life, and their level of wealth and in the future, we earnestly hope, their funded status. Some tasks need to be performed on a quarterly basis regardless of whether a face-to-face meeting takes place between you and your client, such as goal-based reporting, portfolio rebalancing, and account-statement generation. The roadmap should be populated with the tasks you perform on behalf of your client, even for the quarters when you do not meet in person. This way, at the next client review meeting you have documentation of the work you've done. By doing this you are able to demonstrate the behind-the-scenes value you've been delivering to your client since your last meeting.

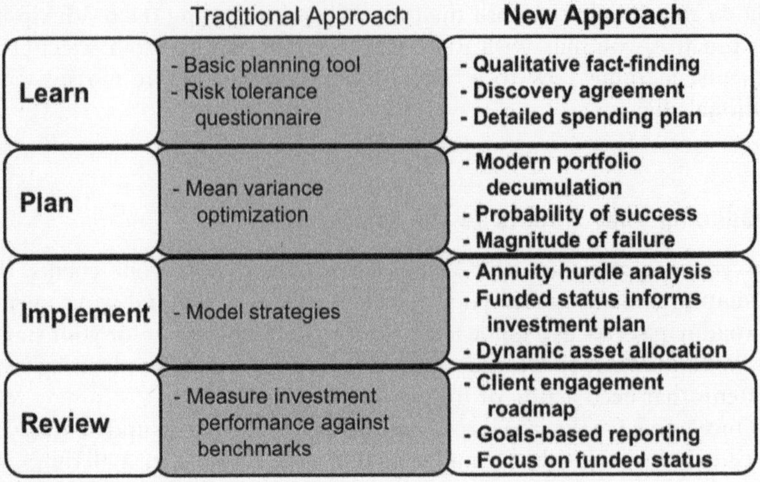

	Traditional Approach	**New Approach**
Learn	- Basic planning tool - Risk tolerance questionnaire	- Qualitative fact-finding - Discovery agreement - Detailed spending plan

Plan	- Mean variance
	  optimization
		- Modern portfolio
		  decumulation
		- Probability of success
		- Magnitude of failure

Implement	- Model strategies	- Annuity hurdle analysis - Funded status informs investment plan - Dynamic asset allocation

Review	- Measure investment
	  performance against
	  benchmarks
		- Client engagement
		  roadmap
		- Goals-based reporting
		- Focus on funded status

FIGURE 7.4   The New Approach

A LOOK AT THE NEW APPROACH

Taking the suggestions we've proposed from this and previous chapters, we've updated the learn/plan/implement/review cycle. In Figure 7.4 we show a comparison of the traditional approach to client management versus the new approach we suggest for clients in or near retirement.

BENEFITS OF USING THE ROADMAP

Using the client engagement roadmap with your clients has several benefits:

- The whole point of this book is that it is not just about investment performance anymore. By making the roadmap the focal point of client meetings, emphasis is placed on the processes required to ensure your client's financial security rather than on short-term investment performance. It shows your client, quarter after quarter, the value you deliver for the fee you are paid.
- It puts clients and advisors on the same page. It's clear to advisors that the use of the roadmap has caused them to dig deeper into their client's situation and gain better insight into their issues. The advisor and the client are in sync about what needs to be addressed and in what priority.

- Additional revenue opportunities. By using the roadmap to educate your clients about other financial topics, you may be finding opportunities to provide them with additional products or services. This increases your chances of having your client consolidate their wealth with you as opposed to another advisor.
- The roadmap is a marketing tool. Advisors who use the roadmap deliver a concise and compelling snapshot of their service and capabilities. Clients can show the roadmap to friends, family, or associates and the viral marketing effect from this can generate new clients through referrals.
- The roadmap is scalable and adaptable. Once you're accustomed to using the roadmap, you will find that it is easily replicated for use with many clients and flexible enough to be adapted to each client's specific needs. You are able to provide a service experience to your clients that is personalized yet scalable for you and your staff. It's a standardized routine that makes an ideal training opportunity for new members of your team.

The client engagement roadmap is a tool to transform the engagement between you and your clients, putting them at the center of the universe, positioning you as their advocate in organizing the activities prerequisite to maintaining their sustainable wealth and confidence. In the next chapter we discuss how client personalities differ and ways you can adapt your communication style to match their unique personality temperaments.

NOTE

1. Steve Moore, *Ineffective Habits of Financial Advisors* (Hoboken, NJ: John Wiley & Sons, 2011).

CHAPTER 8

Investor Archetypes

To be effective, engaged financial planning must become empathic, moving away from just addressing the technical aspects and seek to better engage clients. Understanding the psychology of planning is vital because if you can't get your clients to come to the decisions and behaviors that are necessary to achieve their financial security, the advice and strategies in the personal asset liability model are useless.

In Chapter 4 we introduced Meir Statman who helped us see the advisor/client relationship from a new perspective. The new perspective taught us a couple of important lessons. First, that individual personality type affects the way clients think about and plan for their financial security. The bulk of this chapter is dedicated to this insight. The second lesson we learned was that investors want more than economic utility from their investments.

In his recent book, *What Investors Really Want*, Statman elaborates on the benefits we want from our money:

> *Investments offer three kinds of benefits: utilitarian, expressive, and emotional, and we face trade-offs as we choose among them. Utilitarian benefits of investments center on what they do for our pocketbooks. Profits are utilitarian benefits. The expressive benefits of investments are in what they convey to us and to others about our values, tastes, and status. Some express their values by investing in companies that treat their employees well. Others express their status by investing in hedge funds. And the emotional benefits of investments are in how they make us feel. Bonds make us feel safe and stocks give us hope.*

PERSONALITY TEMPERAMENTS

Your client's personality temperament is the cognitive and emotional lens through which they see the world. Temperament can be thought of as a mix of observable personality traits, as well as characteristic attitudes, values, and talents. It has nothing to do with someone's financial goals or risk tolerance in the conventional sense. Temperaments are abiding, as opposed to moods, which are mercurial. They also encompass personal needs, career choices, the kinds of contributions that individuals make in their jobs, and the roles they play in society. For example, people who value downside protection are likely to gravitate toward professions that offer secure income even if they offer little chance for riches; those who value upside potential gravitate toward professions that offer better chances for riches, even if they do not offer secure income. Temperament affects investing goals and styles, as well as responses to setbacks to these goals.

Craig Cross, an advisor in California, explained it to us like this:

> *Sometimes you have to paint a picture (for your client), not everyone is comfortable with numbers, they can interpret them but some people dream in color, some people understand a graphic more than they do the numbers. The idea of presenting information in a number of ways is important.*

We encourage you to consider adapting your planning and communication style to your client's unique personality temperament as a means to increase their level of engagement. We call these different personality temperaments *investor archetypes*. Professor Statman provided the descriptions and recommendations regarding investor archetypes that follow. His insights are an extension of the Keirsey temperament sorter that Dr. David Keirsey developed in the 1970s.[1] His temperament sorter classifies people into one of four basic groups: guardians, artisans, rationals, and idealists. Dr. Keirsey further subdivides each temperament into four more classifications (for a total of 16 unique types). For our purposes, we focus on the four basic temperament groups. Figure 8.1 shows the percentage breakdown of temperaments by men and women.[2]

Knowing your clients' temperament allows you to have deeper conversations with them. It allows you to move beyond discussions about their finances to discussions about their lives. Why did you choose your career path? What would you like to do next, after your current job? Temperament affects the way your clients interact with the world and the choices they make. It affects their goals, perceptions, strengths and weaknesses, and education.

We spoke with Professor Statman about how to apply the knowledge of personality temperaments to financial planning. He had this to say:

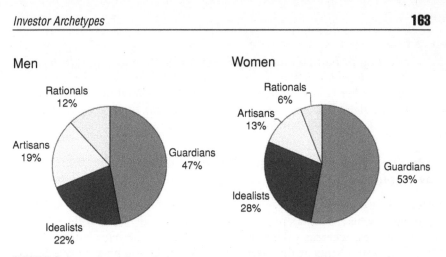

FIGURE 8.1 Proportions of Temperaments among Men and Women
Source: "Helping Advisors Help Investors: Insights from Behavioral Finance," by Meir Statman, presentation to Russell Investments.

*Rationals are usually smart, well-educated and independent thinkers, a bit overconfident about their investment abilities. I think they **need the advice of a planner more than they realize**. The Idealist would just like to leave it all to the advisor (they are delegators) whereas the Guardians would want to be heavily involved and make sure they understand all aspects of the plan. So, the question facing planners is what kind of detail and what kind of language are you going use with each personality? I think that you're going to bore Idealists with discussions of efficient frontiers and with Federal Reserve policy, so spare them. Guardians might be interested in well organized statements of investment policies, and Rationals might engage you in a discussion about abolishing the Federal Reserve. The question you must ask yourself is how are you going to take different personality types through a planning process. Are you going to do it step-by-step the long way (Guardians), or are you going to do it by drawing a picture and skipping the statistics (Idealists)?*

We asked Professor Statman if he felt that an advisor might adjust their asset allocation recommendation to a client based on their investor archetype.

He replied:

I think only in terms of how different temperaments are likely to interact with goals. Think of the two broad goals in life; one is freedom from the fear of poverty and the other is hope for riches.

Wanting to be rich and wanting not to be poor are two distinct desires. Both Idealists and Guardians want freedom from the fear of poverty, but Guardians care about riches more than Idealists. This means that planners can satisfy Idealists with more conservative portfolios than the portfolios of Guardians.

Adjusting Your Communication Based on Investor Archetype

Depending on their temperament, some clients may prefer plain language and facts, whereas others prefer anecdotes. Some clients want the numbers and statistics, whereas others just want to know the big picture. Understanding your clients at this deeper level will help you be a more effective communicator.

It may also be useful to determine your own temperament as it affects your communication style. Recognize that your temperament shapes the way you communicate and consider adjusting your style to your client's temperament. What follows is a discussion of the four investor archetypes, including a cheat sheet for each type that provides advice on how to tailor your communication and planning approach to each temperament.

Guardians   Guardians live by a plan, and, accordingly, they might be curious about contingency plans, such as strategies for downside protection in times of market volatility. Credentials are important to them. Guardians are managerial, logistical, factual, disciplined, conventional, traditional, frugal, and cautious. They are good at managing operations and skilled at planning and handling details of scheduling, shipping, billing, and regulatory compliance. They are concrete and more interested in solid facts than in abstract ideas. Guardians are steady and can be counted on to fulfill their responsibilities. They respect authority, whether the authority of bosses or that of financial experts.

Careers that appeal to guardians include those that involve administration; regulation; services and supplies; and safeguarding property, physical health, and welfare.

Guardians handle money conservatively, to construct solid financial foundations. They set goals and exercise the self-control and discipline necessary to reach them. Guardians associate money with security, success, and peace of mind, not just for themselves, but also for their families. However, guardians are rattled by uncertainty and disruption of order. Roadmaps appeal to them.

Guardians need detailed step-by-step plans about goals, procedures, and responsibilities. They respond well to orderly and linear presentations supported by facts and authorities (academics, successful investors).

TABLE 8.1 Communication and planning suggestions when working with Guardians

Individual's Behavior	Losses in their portfolio will shake their trust in their financial plan and advisor. Their level of anxiety about the future will be based on their funded status. When underfunded, they will be highly anxious due to an uncertain future. When underfunded, they may desire to reduce portfolio risk to bolster their sense of security.
Advisor's Challenge	When overfunded, dissuading them from making unnecessary changes to their portfolio. When underfunded, keeping them from becoming too conservative in their recovery plan.
Planning Approach	Use an orderly and linear presentation format. Clearly outline goals, procedures, and responsibilities—yours and theirs. Invite them to client events with industry experts to educate and reassure them. When changes are needed, use step-by-step plan modifications. When overfunded, congratulate them on a job well done. When slightly underfunded, alleviate their anxiety by showing them that their plans are still on track and need only modest modifications. When underfunded, restore their confidence in you by acting as a teacher of finance and human behavior. When underfunded, alleviate their anxiety by showing them how spending less, saving more, and working longer can help them get back on track.

A well-structured client engagement road map will help maintain their confidence, and they need time to process information. Allow consideration and decision to be separated in time. Guardians make for rational and cooperative clients. See Table 8.1.

Artisans Artisans do not live by a long-term plan, and so it's not likely that turmoil in the markets will be disruptive to them. This gives Artisans an advantage relative to other temperaments who might be frightened by the disruption of a long-term plan. Their resilience and ability to think tactically cushions the blow that the market has dealt to their financial situation.

Artisans are tactical, optimistic, playful, daring, adaptable, impulsive, and generous. They are enterprising and always looking for opportunities. They believe that all will turn out well and that the next roll of the dice will be the lucky one. Artisans resist being tied, confined, or obligated; they would rather not wait, or save for tomorrow. They adapt when they lose and are good at tolerating risk.

Artisans are not so good at self-control and the steadiness necessary to reach long-term goals. Goals-based reporting will be especially useful in this regard.

Careers that appeal to Artisans include those that involve, in a broad sense, marketing: salesperson, entrepreneur, lobbyist, and contract negotiator. Careers that involve tool work, such as carpenter, pilot, and surgeon appeal to artisans, as well as careers in entertainment and the arts.

Artisans are hands-on people and advisors should be ready to modify the plan in consultation with them. They are willing to take risk, even gamble. They might have heard of a creative way to make money quickly. Advisors should be ready to assess creative investments realistically so pyramid and similar schemes are avoided. Artisans know the value of saving and long-term planning, but their self-control is the weakest among all temperaments and they find it difficult to follow through on the plan. It is important to monitor artisans. See Table 8.2.

TABLE 8.2 Communication and planning suggestions when working with Artisans

Individual's Behavior	They are overconfident when overfunded. They may have a tendency to take on more risk to achieve higher returns.
	When underfunded, they may have a false sense that their financial predicament is not as severe as the numbers indicate. They may believe that no saving or spending modifications are needed.
	When underfunded, they may desire to increase risk without exploring prudent avenues to get back on track.
	When underfunded, they may feel that planning and saving are futile and it is better to live for today.
Advisor's Challenge	When overfunded, controlling their urge to take on more risk than required with their retirement assets.
	When underfunded, conveying to them the seriousness of their situation.
	When underfunded, encouraging them to alter their spending and savings habits. Creating a plan that would let both of you monitor spending and saving.
Planning Approach	Present different risk scenarios with examples to demonstrate potential negative impact to their future spending.
	Pause frequently to ask if they have any questions.
	Leverage their optimism but balance it with sober advice.
	Monitor their progress regularly using goals-based reporting.

Idealists Idealists are aware of the need to have a financial plan and receptive to the guidance by advisors but they are not interested in the details of the plan. They need extensive advisor help in financial planning and management and respond to education in plain language rich in analogies and metaphors rather than the language of statistics. (However, be cautious not to overuse analogies, metaphors, and similes. As we saw in the Maslansky study—Appendix B—individuals feel that the use of these devices indicates that you are not taking their financial plans seriously.)

Idealists are trustful, diplomatic, imaginative, empathetic, and compassionate. Their tendency to trust and see the best in everyone offers great joys but also opens them to exploitation. They're good at building and maintaining relationships and fostering harmony. They can easily place themselves in the shoes of others and offer help even when they have little themselves. They are as concerned about you as you are about them. They see money as a tool to improve their lives, the lives of others, and to support their causes. Idealists have little interest in the accumulation of wealth or the details of money management.

Idealists are naturally drawn to working with people, whether in education or counseling, in journalism or the ministry, often inspiring others to fulfill their potentials. Careers that appeal to idealists include those involved in guidance, advocacy, and public relations.

The self-sacrificing nature of idealists makes them vulnerable to requests for financial help from children, parents, and friends. Advisors can help by making themselves the "no" person. Idealists are also susceptible to affinity fraud and must be protected from them. They need sincerity and personalized relationships from advisors. See Table 8.3.

Rationals Rationals are systems oriented, likely to come up with ingenious and complex solutions, perhaps new kinds of derivatives they can analyze. You may struggle to convince them to keep financial plans and portfolios simple. They want to argue about whether a downturn in the market could have been foreseen and why you did not foresee it. Because of their facility for understanding models and their tendency toward overconfidence, it is vital that you educate them on the inherent limitations of models to represent reality.

Rationals are strategic, theoretical, analytical, skeptical, curious, and logical. They are good at planning, especially long-term planning. They analyze systems, identify flaws, and set up plans to correct them. Rationals are rigorously logical and fiercely independent in their thinking. They are skeptical of all accepted truths, authorities, and experts. They might seem standoffish and lacking in emotion. Rationals see financial markets and investments as systems, and they attempt to understand and control them, as they understand and control a machine. Rationals' ability to view the

TABLE 8.3 Communication and planning suggestions when working with Idealists

Individual's Behavior	They are bewildered about financial markets.
	They have a sense of imposition and prefer not to deal with financial issues.
	When overfunded, they have trust in their advisor and feel assurance that all will be well.
	When underfunded, they may have concerns about the effects on family and friends of changes in their financial circumstances.
	When underfunded, they have a need for rebuilding trust in their advisor and reassurance that all will be well.
Advisor's Challenge	Focusing their attention on the problems they face.
	Devising strategies to ensure that they understand and can engage in their plans, knowing that they have little interest in its details and are likely to rely on you.
	Guarding against their tendency to go out of their way to help others financially without evaluating its impact on their own financial situation.
Planning Approach	Use image tools (pictures) such as the client engagement roadmap and goals based reporting to help deepen advisor trust.
	When overfunded, convey in plain language that their plan is on track.
	When underfunded, create personalized communications that demonstrate sincerity.

market in the same way as they would a machine makes them overconfident in their ability to beat the market.

Rationals are drawn to careers in leadership such as CEO, military commander, or corporate team leader. Careers involving coordination, science and engineering, and systems design also appeal to rationals.

Rationals need demonstration of respect for their intellect and knowledge. They are likely to be persuaded by cogent arguments based on science. They tend to be stoical and unemotional. They are likely to accept the facts of their financial situation once explained (for instance, "the Monte Carlo simulation shows that you are less than 75 percent funded for your retirement goals"). See Table 8.4.

Determining Temperament

After reading this chapter it might be obvious to you which investor archetypes match each of your clients. If not, the questions that follow are useful in determining client temperament. For each question, the

TABLE 8.4 Communication and planning suggestions when working with Rationals

Individual's Behavior	They have a desire for extensive conversations about the cause of external events (such as market declines).
	They have a high level of skepticism and are likely to hold their advisors responsible for not foreseeing a crisis.
	They have a desire for ingenious and complex portfolio solutions.
	When underfunded, they desire to control their portfolios and substantially increase portfolio risk as a way to make up for an underfunded status.
Advisor's Challenge	Focusing them on the future without getting bogged down in analyzing the past.
	Controlling their tendency to increase portfolio risk.
	Overcoming their skepticism about advisors as well as economic and political leadership.
	Addressing their overconfidence and desire to run their own portfolio.
Planning Approach	Demonstrate respect for their intellect and knowledge. This is helpful in overcoming skepticism and creating a healthy dialogue.
	Lead with cogent arguments based on science, both the science of finance and the science of human behavior. This is useful in controlling their tendency to restructure their portfolio by increasing risk.

a. responses correspond to artisans, b. to idealists, c. to guardians, and d. to rationals. You may have your client read through the questionnaire and circle their responses, or you may wish to work these questions into your qualitative fact-finding discussions.

How would you complete the following statements?

I feel best about investments and myself when I . . .
  a. Act quickly on opportunities
  b. Help others as well as myself
  c. Have a solid financial plan
  d. Am successful at implementing a complex strategy

When the market and my stocks go up I feel . . .
  a. Excited and stimulated
  b. Enthusiastic and inspired
  c. Cautious and prudent
  d. Skeptical and calm

When it comes to my financial affairs, I tend to be ...
a. Practical and opportunistic
b. Compassionate and empathetic
c. Dutiful and diligent
d. Efficient and pragmatic

I most respect very successful investors when they ...
a. Are bold and adventurous
b. Use wealth to better society
c. Are frugal and responsible
d. Are independent minded

When evaluating a certain investment, I most trust ...
a. My gut
b. My friends
c. Bottom-line facts
d. Logic

When advising a friend who lost money on an investment, I would tell him:
a. "These things happen. It will turn around soon."
b. "It's best to stick with what you truly believe in."
c. "You should fully explore the risk before investing."
d. "If it seems too good to be true, it probably is."

The purpose of this chapter is to help you understand different personality temperaments and how those temperaments behave differently in dealing with financial planning. Knowing this allows you to adapt your planning and communication style to your client's temperament making for a more effective advisor/client relationship.

Throughout this book, we've talked about strategies to help your clients overcome the typical impediments they face trying to attain and sustain financial security. These known impediments include overspending, undersaving, investing badly, and failing to plan for a longer life than expected. There are other risks that you and your clients should be aware of and consider in your planning, risks often impossible to forecast. In Chapter 9, Tripping Over the Finish Line, we discuss these risks and how you might plan for them.

NOTES

1. Meir Statman, *What Investors Really Want* (New York: McGraw-Hill, 2011).
2. www.keirsey.com.

CHAPTER 9

Tripping Over the Finish Line

It is not enough to help your clients define the spending they will need to live their desired lifestyles and manage their wealth to sustain their financial security. As much work as that is, there are other risks we have not talked about that could endanger your client's financial security. We call this chapter Tripping Over the Finish Line because it would be a tragedy to get your client all the way to their place in the sun and have it all come apart because of an event that could have been protected against or planned for.

In this chapter, we first talk about the uncertainty of Social Security and how that affects the way you manage your client's wealth. It is not likely that Social Security will go away, but it would be wise to make conservative assumptions when planning for income from the system.

After Social Security, we discuss other insurable risks, namely, loss of life, healthcare expense, disability, and the potential need for long-term care. We discuss how to manage these risks and talk with an advisor who will give us his take on how to deal with these issues.

Finally, there is the risk of age-related cognitive decline. As we age, our mental functions decline, and for some that decline results in dementia. In the last section of this chapter, we discuss how this may affect the way you deal with your aging clients, what signs to look for to tell if your client is losing their capacity to make rational decisions, and what you can do to manage this risk.

RETIREMENT CONFIDENCE

To understand why your clients are so preoccupied with the prospect of less certain government benefits, let's start with some research about how Americans in general regard these issues. Each year, the Employee Benefit Research Institute (EBRI) along with Mathew Greenwald and Associates conducts a Retirement Confidence Survey (RCS) in the United States.[1] (This is the same Matt Greenwald you heard about earlier in the book.) They survey working-age individuals (workers) as well as individuals who have reached retirement age (retirees). In 2011 they conducted their twenty-first annual RCS. What follows are selected results on the topics of Social Security, Medicare, health-care expenses, long-term care expenses, and retirement.

These Confidence surveys have continually showed that in key areas American workers are not confident in their ability to maintain the lifestyle they want in retirement, the health care and long-term care they are likely to need, and the ability of the government to provide the benefits promised to them. Importantly, this action has not led most to increase their savings or their wealth. But it has led many to plan to work longer. Indeed, the delay in planned retirement age is the main trend revealed in the 21-year history of these surveys. But working longer does not usually allay the lack of confidence, thus advisors have to anticipate and deal with this underlying anxiety.

Confidence about Being Able to Pay Medical Expenses in Retirement

The share of workers *very confident* of having enough money to pay for medical expenses was 12 percent in 2011, the same as in 2010 and statistically equivalent to the 13 percent observed in 2009. Fifty percent said in 2011 that they were either *not too* or *not at all confident* about having enough money to pay medical expenses, compared with 51 percent in 2010 and 44 percent in 2009.

Confidence about Being Able to Pay Long-Term Care Expenses in Retirement

The share of workers *very confident* about having enough money to pay long-term care expenses was 9 percent in 2011, compared with 10 percent in 2009 and 2010. The share of workers *not confident* about being able to cover these expenses was 60 percent in 2011, compared with 61 percent in 2010 and 56 percent in 2009.

Confidence in Social Security

Seventy percent of workers were *not too* or *not at all* confident that Social Security will continue to provide benefits of at least equal value to the benefits retirees receive today. Skepticism about Social Security among them has fluctuated slightly, but it remained at about the same level for most of the past decade. It remains below the level measured in 1996, when 78 percent of workers were *not confident* that benefit levels would be preserved.

Three-quarters of workers express concern that the age at which they become eligible for Social Security retirement benefits will increase before they retire.

Confidence in Medicare

Seventy percent of workers were *not too* or *not at all* confident that Medicare will continue to provide benefits of at least equal value to the benefits retirees receive today. Although this proportion is below levels measured in the 1990s, it is higher than the levels measured in 2003–2009.

Confidence about Having Enough Money for Retirement

In 2011, half of American workers reported that they were *not too* or *not at all confident* that they will be able to live comfortably throughout their retirement. This is the lowest level of confidence recorded since this study began in the early 1990s. It is noteworthy that even after emerging from the recession, albeit to a weak economy, confidence in having a comfortable retirement did not recover, rather it dropped. This indicates that the Great Recession did have a marked impact on worker expectations for their financial security in retirement. It appears to have made them more realistic, which is good news for advisors. More clearly now understand they need help and therefore should be more receptive to professional advice.

"To me, these are positive findings: People are increasingly recognizing the level of savings realistically needed for a comfortable retirement. We know from previous surveys that far too many people had false confidence in the past," said Jack VanDerhei, EBRI research director and co-author of the report. "People's expectations need to come closer to reality so they will save more and delay retirement until it is financially feasible."

Survey co-author Matt Greenwald said, "Many people are planning to work longer and retire later because they know they simply can't afford to leave the work place—both for the paycheck and for the benefits." He added: "Unfortunately, many retirees also tell us they left the work force earlier than they planned, either because of health problems or layoffs. So it may not necessarily be a bad thing that those who can work longer choose to do so."

SOCIAL SECURITY UNCERTAINTY

In Chapter 2, we talked about the risk of insolvency to Social Security. Although the risk is real, it is fixable. However, according to the most recent EBRI data, people are clearly not confident in Social Security remaining intact in its current form. Many advisors have told us that people should only count on about 75 percent of their scheduled Social Security benefit for planning purposes. One expert said, "Anything more than that is gravy." The opinions we've gotten are age dependent. Younger people are less confident than older people about seeing full, if any, benefits from Social Security.

In the personal asset liability model we showed you how to calculate a funded status based on the present value of your client's assets and liabilities. The present-value-of-liabilities calculation only considers future spending beyond the individual's Social Security benefit and other annuitized wealth, such as an employer provided pension. Therefore, if your client's actual Social Security benefit turns out to be less than what was used in the liability calculation, the liability will be understated and the funded status overstated. **The degree to which your client's Social Security benefit is a meaningful percentage of their future spending will determine how big of a risk a Social Security reduction is to their financial security.** You should help your clients determine how significant (or not) this percentage is.

To quantify the potential size of this risk, we took one of the author's Social Security statements and calculated what a 25 percent reduction in benefits means in today's dollars.

Matt's projected benefit at age 70 (his normal retirement age under Social Security is 67) is $3,100. Matt's wife's benefit at age 70 (they are the same age) is projected to be half of Matt's or $1,550. Their total projected annual Social Security benefit (in today's dollar value) at age 70 is $55,800 ((3,100 + 1,550) × 12 = 55,800). If their benefit at age 70 ends up being reduced by 25 percent, then their annual benefit would be $41,850. The difference is $13,950 (55,800 − 41,850). If we assume that they could draw 4.5 percent from a portfolio starting at age 70 and have a high probability of not exhausting that portfolio during their lifetime, then a rough calculation of their present value of this benefit reduction would be $310,000 (13,950 ÷ 4.5 percent = 310,000).

This is one example of what a 25 percent reduction in Social Security would mean to one couple. Whether $310,000 of wealth at retirement is a meaningful amount is obviously based on each person's unique situation. However, here is the point to be made: given that we've stressed the importance of monitoring your client's funded status, a several hundred thousand dollar adjustment to their wealth could make a meaningful difference in their funded status and possibly warrant a change in the way they invest their retirement portfolio. This is the importance of having a precise estimate of Social Security and why it makes sense to use a conservative assumption when calculating your client's funded status.

Most experts we talk to do not feel that Social Security is at risk of collapse. They see the possibility of changes to the system, but they don't feel it is going to cease to exist as some fear. The possible changes in the future include increasing revenue to the system or a reduction in benefits.

Ideas for raising revenue that we've heard discussed are lifting the maximum wage base for which Social Security taxes are subject, beginning to tax certain benefits that are not currently taxed such as 401(k) contributions, or increasing the payroll tax rate as the trust gets closer to not being able to meet its obligations.

Another way to fix Social Security is to reduce benefits. Benefits could be reduced across the board for everyone, reduced progressively with age, or reduced progressively based on wealth (means testing). The most significant risk to your clients might very well be the introduction of means testing as a device to reduce benefits to the affluent in order to preserve them for the middle and lower classes. We don't believe (at the time of this writing) that any of these modifications to Social Security are imminent.

Another decision you may need to help your clients make is deciding when to begin claiming Social Security benefits. Claiming early (as early as 62) will result in a lower benefit than claiming later. Many people commence benefits as early as they can, but that usually is not the best decision. Claiming early because you believe Social Security is going to run out of money someday soon is (in our opinion) an irrational decision. The decision about when to claim should be based more on how long you think you will live. When in doubt, assume you will live longer than average. In most cases a person is better off claiming as late as possible (age 70). Exceptions to this would be people who are destitute and truly in need of the money or people with clear life-shortening health circumstances. That said, each person (or couple) should do their own analysis based on their unique circumstances before making a decision about when to commence Social Security benefits.

We asked Ilene Davis, "How do you advise your clients about when to take Social Security?" She said:

> *How I advise them is based on their health. It depends on the health of the client and their family history. I look at the client's life expectancy based on health and family history and then do the math to determine when's the best time to take Social Security. I have a client whose family history is that she will likely live beyond 100. I recommend to her to at least delay taking Social Security until she reaches full benefits. I have another client who is dealing*

with some real health issues, and may not live beyond 75, so he may be better off taking Social Security early, especially if he has enough resources to back up that income with personal savings. If clients plan on working longer, I generally tell them not to take Social Security unless they really have a family history of dying early.

For younger clients, I say let's not even count on Social Security. Let's create your entire retirement plan assuming that Social Security isn't there. Because, if I do my job as their advisor and they do their job, and we accumulate sufficient wealth, I can imagine the government saying, "You're rich, you have enough, you don't get any Social Security." We've already seen this starting to happen. Social Security was never supposed to be taxed, and now it's taxed if your income is above a certain level. The Social Security payroll tax was never supposed to be above 1 percent of your income, and now it is 6.2 percent. (In 2011 the Social Security payroll tax paid by employees is 4.2 percent as a result of a special tax relief act but is scheduled to return to 6.2 percent if no further relief is provided.) So, I ask my clients, "Do you expect the government to keep the promises they made in the past?" And most of them say. "No, I don't." So for younger clients we don't plan on benefits from the government.

OTHER INSURABLE RISKS

There are events that could happen in a person's life that could disrupt an otherwise well thought out and executed financial plan. The good news is these risks can be insured.

Loss of Future Income

If the success of your client's plan depends on savings from their future paychecks, and others are relying on their plan for their financial security (a spouse, children, aging parents) then events that may result in the loss of future income are risks they should consider protecting against. Loss of life or a disability that prevents them from working are the two events they should be most concerned about. Life insurance can protect against loss of life. It is beyond the scope of this book to discuss different types of life insurance policies or levels of appropriate coverage. However, we want to make the point that those who are counting on your client's income for their own financial security should be protected through some form of life insurance. Disability income insurance protects against loss of future income due to a disability on the part of the insured. Later in this chapter, we talk with an advisor about his approach to helping his clients protect against this risk.

Health-Care Expense

Large health expenses, such as those related to a major illness like cancer, can wipe out a person's financial assets if they are not properly insured. As health insurance laws in the United States have changed in recent years, fewer people are at risk of this happening, but it is still a risk to be aware of and to protect against through proper insurance coverage.

The cost of uncovered healthcare expenses in retirement can be huge. Medicare does not cover all medical expenses in retirement and with solvency concerns, it may cover less in the future. According to an EBRI brief, a *low risk*[2] couple, both age 65, would need $635,000 in savings (in 2008) to pay for their health-care costs not covered by Medicare for the remainder of their lives.[3]

Long-Term Care

A person who reaches age 65 today will need, on average, three years of assistance managing their daily living activities such as eating, bathing, getting dressed, and assistance due to incontinence.[4] Medicare and most health-care programs do not cover the cost of this assistance. A person who needs long-term care for many years, (e.g., as in the case of an Alzheimer's patient who lives many years with the disease), may deplete their financial assets well before they planned if the cost of care exceeds the spending level in their original plan. Long-term care insurance can protect against this risk.

Long-term care insurance premiums are lower for younger people. However, younger people are also less likely to see long-term care as a real risk in their future. Advisors have told us that their experience is most long-term care insurance policies are bought by people who have had to take care of a family member. That experience has caused them to see the risk as something that is real and they don't want to burden their family with having to take care of them if they should need long-term care later in life.

Perspective: Interview with a Wealth Management Advisor

We wanted to include here the advisor's perspective on how to deal with these risks in real life with real clients. What follows is an edited transcript of a conversation Matt Smith had with Tom Weilert, CLU, ChFC. Tom is a wealth-management advisor in Texas with a long history of helping his clients understand and manage these risks.

Matt: Tom, how do you help your clients understand and protect against disability risk?

Tom: You really have two types of disability risk, one during the accumulation or preretirement phase and the other after retirement, during the decumulation phase. Before retirement the need is for income replacement due to a disability. I've asked people for 30 years the question, "Do you have enough assets today that you can quit working, not change your lifestyle, and not ill-advisedly liquidate those assets?" And, if you can answer that question "yes," then you probably don't need disability income insurance. But, if you cannot answer that question "yes," then you need disability income insurance. Sometimes people have a lot of assets but they are illiquid, or there are tax issues with liquidating them, or there would be other complications if they had to actually call upon them for cash immediately.

        The second half of the disability question goes under the name of long-term care; the possibility that you might have a chronic medical condition where you need assistance with the activity of daily living. Depending on the statistics you look at, there's a likelihood that between 40 percent and 60 percent of us will need some level of long-term care in our lives.

        Occasionally a person will drop the disability income insurance when they pick up the long-term care coverage. They might do this if they feel they have just about enough assets to make it but they want to make sure they protect against a long-term care event. Long-term care insurance in retirement sometimes becomes a portfolio protection strategy. You want to protect the portfolio that you've built up, it's large enough to produce the income you're going to need, but you want to protect against a long-term care claim that might jeopardize that.

        As an example of how expensive a long-term event can be, I know of a woman whose husband just passed away at age 77 but was diagnosed with Alzheimer's at 57. He required 20 years of care. Alzheimer units typically run anywhere from $6,000 to $12,000 per month depending on the geographic location, and that is after-tax expense. That can destroy a financial plan.

The same thing would happen on the disability side if you didn't have a chance to build up your assets to a sufficient level. From a risk management point of view, I discuss both disability and long-term care with all my clients. We have a fair number of clients who have reached the point that they are self-insured from a disability income standpoint, but the government gives them such tremendous tax advantages for purchasing long-term care. Through an employer a good percentage of long-term care premiums could be tax deductible. Additionally, with provisions of the Pension Protection Act that went into effect in 2010, a person might be able to make distributions from annuities on a very tax favored basis to pay for long-term care premiums or out of life insurance contracts. The government is trying to encourage people to purchase long-term care insurance. I have clients who can, without question, pay for their long-term care expenses out of assets, but they use long-term care insurance as a risk-management tool.

Matt: Is there a risk that a couple may actually lose two incomes when one of them becomes disabled, because the spouse has to quit their job in order to take care of the disabled spouse?

Tom: Thirty-two years ago I was a licensed physical therapist. And, the reality is that the divorce rate of people who become disabled is very high. Sometimes the spouse can't quit their job because they need the income. That becomes an ugly situation. When we are doing planning for someone, risk-based planning, I talk about four areas that need to be addressed; health insurance, disability-income insurance, long-term care insurance, and life insurance. We need to address those four areas before addressing their asset allocation. In my opinion, all the questions about what to do with the client's portfolio are secondary to the risk-management questions I just mentioned.

Matt: Do you find it difficult to get people to understand the long-term care risk?

Tom: Yes, I do. **I typically have to ask someone three to five times before they really pay attention.** I have to see them and repeatedly ask them, and it's usually the third or fourth or fifth time that I've raised the issue that they finally realize they need to address it. What happens is they will start to see examples, personal experiences of a friend or a family member, and suddenly realize it's a potential problem for them. The people who walk in the door and are ready to buy (long-term care insurance) are the people who have had to help take care of their parents. They say, "I'm not going to do this to my children, because I know what it cost me to take care of my parents."

In our client reviews, I add long-term care to the list of items to review every time. It's a subject line on every client review, until the client tells me don't ask again. And, I've had two clients in my career tell me not to ask him again.

Matt: Is there an ideal age for the long-term care discussion with your clients?

Tom: We find that it's between age 45 and 55. We usually have to initiate the discussion. They're not coming through the door saying they want to buy long-term care insurance. First we have to get the disability in place. Then, at a point, they may have both disability and long-term care insurance. And usually between 55 and 60, if they've been financially successful, they drop the disability coverage, and they keep or add the long-term care insurance.

Now, I've heard other advisors say that you shouldn't buy long-term care insurance before the age of 60 because between the ages of 50 and 60 the chances of making a long-term care claim is between one and three percent. And, that sounds about right. But, the point that is being missed is the chance of someone between the ages of 50 and 60 becoming uninsurable and unable to buy a long-term care policy is much higher, I believe it is over 30 percent. So, if I have 100 clients (50 couples) above the age of 50, of those hundred people who say they are going to wait until they're 60 to buy long-term care insurance, over 30 percent of those folks won't be able to buy it when they're 60 because something has happened to cause them to be uninsurable. And, the people who are most likely to go on long-term-care claim early are those same people who became uninsurable.

Life, health, disability income, and long-term-care insurance all play an important role in protecting your client from events that could derail their financial plan. In the next section we discuss the risk your clients face caused by the potential for their mental facilities to decline as they age.

AGE-RELATED COGNITIVE DECLINE

Long-term-care insurance can protect your clients' portfolios from being wiped out if their need for assistance exceeds their budgeted spending. It is common for older people to need assistance due to a decline in their mental capabilities. Help with scheduling and taking their medications is one example of a need that arises from age-related cognitive decline.

As your aging clients' mental functions slow, you may need to adjust how you interact with them. At the very least, you should to be aware of the signs of mental decline and be prepared to deal with it, such as using more repetition with clients when introducing new ideas or giving them more time than before to think about and absorb new ideas. In extreme situations, you (and your clients) need to be able to deal with a loss of mental function that renders them unable to make financial decisions for themselves.

Absent dementia, older people have the ability to retain knowledge quite well but the speed at which they are able to access their stored knowledge slows with age. Complexity risk is an issue with older clients. Having a financial plan that requires the client to make frequent and complex decisions may be fine for the 65-year-old who enjoys the challenge but is inappropriate for the same client when she is 85 and uninterested or unable to deal with such complexity.

This section talks about the different types of intelligence, quantifies the decline of cognitive function as people age, and provides some practical advice about how to deal with age related cognitive decline.

There are two types of cognitive function: fluid intelligence and crystallized intelligence. Both types are involved in making financial decisions. The following is an excerpt from *What Is the Age of Reason?* a brief prepared by the Center for Retirement Research at Boston College that discusses cognitive decline:[5]

> *Fluid intelligence (i.e., performance on novel tasks) can be measured along many dimensions, including working memory, reasoning, spatial visualization, and cognitive processing speed. Fluid intelligence shows a clear age pattern ... suggesting a (consistent) decline of about 1 percentile per year after age 20.*
>
> *The prevalence of both dementia and cognitive impairment without dementia rises rapidly with age. [Figure 9.1] shows that dementia in the United States increases from an estimated 5 percent of the population at ages 71–79 to 37 percent at ages 90 and above. Similarly, the estimate for a less severe form of cognitive impairment that does not involve dementia rises from 16 percent at ages 71–79 to 39 percent at ages 90 and above. All told, about half of adults in their 80s suffer from either dementia or cognitive impairment without dementia.*
>
> *Age-driven declines in fluid intelligence, however, are partly offset by age-related increases in crystallized intelligence—sometimes called experience or knowledge. Most day-to-day tasks, such as*

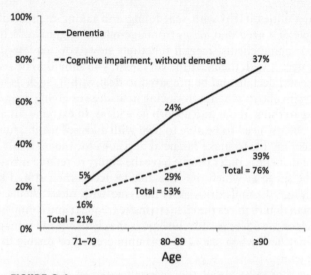

FIGURE 9.1   Prevalence of Dementia and Cognitive Impairment without Dementia in the United States (2002)
Source: Plassman et al. (2007); Plassman et al. (2008).

buying the right amount of milk at the grocery store, rely on both fluid and crystallized intelligence.

The researchers hypothesize that cognitive performance improves from youth to middle age, at which point it peaks before beginning a steady decline. Consequently, middle-age adults may represent the peak of the financial decision-making distribution.

In our discussion with Craig Cross about how he keeps his clients on their agreed-upon spending and investment plans he had this to say:

It involves being age sensitive and understanding the client's circumstances deeply. It may be a situation where a health issue has changed the plan or someone has inherited some money. We do a lot of conversation up front under the banner of behavioral finance; we can demonstrate that somewhere in your late 50s people start to lose cognitive ability and ability to make good financial decisions. When someone's in their 80s they better have a plan in place so their kids don't have to make these decisions for them. Having said all that, those 70 and 80-year-olds have wisdom that their kids don't.

Perspective: Interview with an Expert on Longevity

In May 2011, Matt Smith had a conversation with Dr. Laura L. Carstensen, PhD about what advice she would give financial advisors who may need to deal with the mental decline of their aging clients. Dr. Carstensen is the founding director of the Stanford Center on Longevity and author of *A Long Bright Future* (Broadway, 2009). What follows is an edited transcript of that conversation.

Matt: What advice do you have for financial advisors working with clients whose mental facilities may decline during the course of their relationship?

Laura: I don't know if there are any perfect answers to this but it's clearly an issue. I get this question a lot and I believe that the earlier in the relationship the topic is raised, the better. It's tough to raise this issue with a client who is cognitively fit and sharp. But, if the advisor waits to the point where she is questioning whether someone is making good decisions or worried about forgetfulness or what might appear to be an irrational choice, by that time clients have often lost the ability to monitor themselves. Clients may not see the kind of changes that the advisor sees in them and, therefore, they may be very offended at the suggestion that they are slipping mentally. If you can have this kind of conversation early on in a relationship, you can have it in a more objective and less emotional way.

About 38 percent of people over 85 have Alzheimer's disease or some form of dementia. Given these levels, everybody should think about this risk, both advisors and clients. They should consider what to do ahead of time and determine what safeguards should be put in place. One safeguard is to have the conversation early with your client about what to do if they should become unable to make sound decisions. This allows the advisor get the client's informed and active input, as opposed to trying to address the problem later on, after the mental decline has become a serious hindrance to their decision making.

Matt: What other safeguards do you recommend?

Laura: Another approach would be to involve an adult child or some other person who is close to the client—I would say a spouse but spouses are usually close to the same age and are exposed to the same risk. Advisors could have their clients begin to involve other people they trust in their decision making. That would be another way to do it. Advisors are extremely important in this kind of a situation because, unlike family members, loved ones, and friends, they can be dispassionate. In that sense, they can be especially helpful because they can be more objective.

Matt: Research shows that older people retain "crystallized knowledge" as well as younger people but their access to this knowledge is slower. How would this affect the way advisors should interact with older clients?

Laura: Absent dementia, there isn't anything about normal aging that prevents our ability to retrieve stored knowledge from memory. That is, we don't lose access to knowledge we've stored even though we might not retrieve it quite as quickly. To the extent that clients are informed and understand certain financial principles, there is good reason to expect they will continue to be able to access that knowledge base.

Again, let me make the point that, absent dementia, there isn't anything about aging that prohibits learning. We may be slower but it doesn't mean that we don't continue to learn. That is why knowledge bases continue to grow into advanced ages. It just might be that the advisor needs to use more repetition when introducing new ideas.

Matt: Is this an important distinction to make for advisors, that there are two different issues they may be faced with, dementia and normal age-related cognitive decline?

Laura: Exactly. There is normal age-related decline, which involves primarily information processing. This involves our ability to take in, process, and act on new information. However, other aspects of cognitive processing change very little with age. Automatic processing or procedural memory is what we call it in psychology. Those are abilities like being able to type on the keyboard or drive a car. Clearly, there is memory involved in those tasks, but it's as if it's in our fingertips more than our brains.

There is also almost no decline in emotional abilities, including our intuitions. If anything, there is some evidence that people get better at sizing up many situations with age so it is not that cognitive processing simply declines in broad strokes. There are certain areas in which decrements occur more consistently, and other processes that don't show much decline at all. And, I think it's important for advisors to know what skills their clients have maintained just as much as what has declined, because it points them in a direction where they might use those preserved areas to help their clients compensate for losses.

Matt: I'm curious about your opinion about how shortened retention periods for negative information in older people may influence their financial decisions.

Laura: We know from research in my laboratory and elsewhere that older people remember negative information more poorly than younger people do. Older people retain positive information just as well as younger people. So, there is a shift in the emotional tone of memories. We believe that this may cause people to become more vulnerable to financial fraud. We have just submitted a grant application to use neural imaging and other methods to see if we can test these hypotheses. Right now, we know that older people are less likely to remember negative information in laboratory studies. It's not clear yet how that translates into everyday life and financial investment, but there is good reason to be concerned given these basic findings.

Matt: It's clear that there are two issues here that the advisor should be aware of with their aging clients. The first is the decline of mental processing speed and the second is the issue of dementia. Is there advice you would give a financial advisor regarding what to look for to determine if their client is slipping into dementia?

Laura: I can give some tips, but you should know that this is not a neural psychological assessment. Things that I would look for if I were trying to make this kind of judgment would be if clients were forgetting information from a past meeting. I'm not talking about a meeting from years ago but let's say a meeting last month when you reviewed information about a product and now a month later they don't remember anything you told them about the product. I would be concerned about that kind of forgetfulness. Or, if they couldn't remember anything at all about the meeting I would be concerned.

Now, if they remember the meeting but they couldn't remember the name of a product you discussed, I would not be concerned at all. Naming problems, word-finding problems where somebody is talking and is struggling for a word; those are part of normal aging. However, when people are completely forgetting events or information you've already talked about, where the information just wasn't retained, that's a concern. With normal aging, the problem is more with retrieval of information, not that the information was never stored. Whereas with dementia, information is just not being stored at all.

I would be concerned if clients regularly missed appointments, especially those who didn't miss appointments in the past. That is an early telltale sign, missing appointments. These are the types of signs that I would be worried about.

Matt: If an advisor sees those signs what should they do?

Laura: I cannot answer that question from a legal or regulatory point of view of course. However, if I saw that behavior in a client I would hope that there was someone in that person's life who could be invited into the next meeting. If there is a spouse, you could see both of them together, or an adult child. In some ways when you get to the point where you're concerned, as we were talking earlier in our conversation, it is kind of too late. You want to have a conversation about what to do in this situation before the person gets to that stage. It would be better to be able to say, "remember when we talked about this before and we agreed if I ever became worried about your memory to talk to Charlie? Well, I think it's time to talk to Charlie." If you have already had that conversation with your client, and you have identified the person you are going to bring into the conversation, it's easy to say in a friendly way, let's just bring them in. I think you're in a much better position than if you try to raise for the first time this issue when somebody is showing signs of concern like not remembering things.

Matt: Is there anything else that you want to share with advisors on this topic?

Laura: I'm glad you are writing about this topic. We've entered an era of very long life very rapidly, in historic terms. In a blink of an eye we are living decades longer. Therefore, we need to build social structures, norms, and customs throughout our lives and certainly in the area of financial planning so that we can help people prepare for these long periods of relative uncertainty—uncertainty about their ability to finance their long lives and uncertainty about their capacity to make these kinds of decisions. The worst thing right now is that we are not talking about this enough. To me that is the biggest risk factor. Once we begin to have these conversations and it becomes part of the process of advising over the years, advisors will know what their clients wanted when they were at their fittest cognitively. I think it's very important to begin these conversations and start talking about this with clients.

Our friend and colleague, Don Ezra, (author of Chapter 11) has been an inspiration to us during our careers; because of his brilliance, of course, but also because of his generosity in using himself as an example when illustrating life-planning lessons. Don, now in his mid-60s, shares his insights on what it's like to be on the cusp of retirement. In Spring 2011, Don gave a speech in which he talked about preparing for the day when he may no longer have the cognitive skills to make financial decisions for himself. Here is a brief excerpt from his speech:

In my family, I was very startled by the experience of my father, a rigorously logical man if I ever met one, who called me one day, in his late 80s, to say that he had won the Spanish lottery—millions of euros. And the nicest part was that he had never bought a ticket; someone else had done that for him, and he was about to collect the money. My father had actually called and had been sent a form for the purpose. You can guess that the form required all his banking details. Let's just say he was not grateful that I convinced him it was a con, a scam.

Add to this the fact that my mother has Alzheimer's. My father-in-law died of Alzheimer's. And, both my wife and I come from long-lived families. I think there's more than a fair chance that one or both of us will go ga-ga some time before our estate events (an "estate-event" is what insurance companies call death).

So here's what we've done, earlier this year. We have written out a document (nine pages long, for what the information is worth) explaining our (financial) goals and plans. And we've given it to our kids.

It's partly so that they'll know about things in much more detail, and partly an appeal to them, that as we update it every year, as soon as they see incipient signs of my going ga-ga in particular, they'll feel confident enough to say, "You know, Mum, Dad doesn't sound right; he's always said . . . etc."

I want them to be confident that they know the plans well enough to quote them at me, when the time comes, and carry them out. I am totally confident that they'll recognize when the time comes, because they warn me about it constantly, already, although today I think it's in jest. These are kids who know me well, and they're not afraid to point out characteristics they think are odd.

The point we are trying to get across is that all of the hard work you do for your client—helping them determine a level of spending that is sustainable, coaching them to save and invest properly, keeping them on track by showing them quarter after quarter where they are relative to their goals—can all be undone if in their old age, they make irrational decisions. As we saw in the statistics earlier, over half the people over age 80 are experiencing either dementia or some other cognitive impairment. It is important to talk to your clients about the possibility of them not being able to make sound financial decisions as they age. Our advice on this topic is simple: discuss the issue with your clients early, have a plan in place for what to do if the time comes, and know the warning signs so you know when to take action.

* * *

We covered in this chapter many of the other risks facing you and your client's financial security. The first nine chapters of this book build on each other giving you the entire picture of how to help your clients build and sustain their surplus: We've made the case for having real conversations with your clients about sustaining their financial security, illustrated the extent of the retirement crisis in America, talked about how to find the right clients for your practice, discussed the people and events that influenced the personal asset liability model, took you step by step through the model, showed how the model fits into the business of giving good advice, and provided you with a language and psychology framework for adapting your communication to your client's temperament. The following chapters stand alone as they are in-depth essays on individual topics.

NOTES

1. Full details of the 2011 Retirement Confidence Survey are in the March 2011 *EBRI Issue Brief* and online at www.ebri.org/surveys/rcs/2011/. The RCS is conducted by the nonpartisan Employee Benefit Research Institute (EBRI) and Mathew Greenwald & Associates. The RCS is the longest-running annual retirement survey of its kind in the nation. EBRI is a private, nonprofit research institute based in Washington, DC, that focuses on health, savings, retirement, and economic security issues. EBRI does not lobby and does not take policy positions.
2. *Low-risk* is defined as willing to accept no less than a 90 percent chance of having enough money to pay for retiree health expenses as specified earlier (or only a 10 percent chance of *not* having enough money). Low-risk individuals must purchase all supplemental health insurance coverage to traditional Medicare individually on their own through a combination of Medigap coverage and Medicare Part D (prescription drug coverage), and be prepared in case they become very high users of prescription drugs. This last point is critical: Assume

you are only going to be at the midpoint in terms of drug use, you would need roughly half as much money. Are you *not* low-risk and willing to accept a 50 percent chance of not having enough money? Cut the numbers in half again if you are single, multiply by two-thirds if you are married. Bottom line: nothing in life or financial planning for retirement is simple.

3. "Retiree Health Savings: How Much Is Enough?" Fast Facts from EBRI #85, June 3, 2008.

4. "Understanding Long-Term Care," National Clearinghouse for Long-Term Care Information, U.S. Department of Health and Human Services, www.longterm care.gov/LTC/Main_Site/Undertanding_Long_Term_Care/Services/Services.aspx.

5. Sumit Agarwal, John C. Driscoll, Xavier Gabaix, and David Laibson, "What Is the Age of Reason?" (Center for Retirement Research at Boston College, July 2010), Number 10–12.

CHAPTER 10

On Shaping One's Future

Albert Bandura

Authors' note: In the fall of 2008 Steve Moore, Kevin Bishopp, and Tim Noonan were conducting a practice management seminar for a group of financial advisors in Arizona. It was during the apex of the global financial meltdown, and the advisors in attendance were at the center of the storm. Even so, they had made commitments months in advance to attend the seminar, and so they were there. One of the speakers at the seminar was Albert Bandura. Here we've provided an edited transcript of his presentation.

Albert Bandura is the David Starr Jordan Professor of Social Science in Psychology at Stanford University and past president of the American Psychological Association. In a 2002 study, Bandura was ranked the fourth most eminent psychologist of the twentieth century just after B.F. Skinner, Jean Piaget, and Sigmund Freud.[1] His book *Self-Efficacy: The Exercise of Control* is the definitive text on the topic.[2] Self-efficacy is the belief in one's capabilities to organize and execute the courses of actions required to produce desired results.

Why is this presentation included in this book? There are a few reasons: First, the development of self-efficacy (confidence) is critical to success, the success of your advisory practice as well as the success of your client's financial plans. Second, we believe that excellent advisors are made, not born, and that learning to give excellent advice is an acquirable skill. The self-efficacy you cultivate for the skill to give excellent advice is vital to your success as an advisor. Finally, it is a rare thing to find such timely, plain spoken, and distilled wisdom as Professor Bandura delivered that day to the advisors in Arizona, and we wanted to share his brilliance with you.

PROFESSOR BANDURA'S PRESENTATION

This morning I will share with you our knowledge on how people can exert control over their motivation, way of thinking, emotional well-being, and accomplishments.

Among the sources of self-management, none is more central or pervasive than peoples' beliefs in their capabilities. I call this belief self-efficacy. This core belief is the foundation of human motivation and accomplishments. **Unless people believe they can produce desired results by their actions, they have little incentive to act or to persevere in the face of difficulties.** Whatever other factors serve as guides and motivators, they are rooted in the core belief that one has the causative power to shape one's future.

Human well-being and accomplishments require an optimistic and resilient efficacy. This is because the usual daily realities are strewn with difficulties. They are full of frustrations, conflicts, impediments, adversities, failures, setbacks, and inequities. To succeed, one cannot afford to be derailed by these types of frustrations. A resilient sense of efficacy enables one to override troublesome experiences.

I share with you one example of resilience to the demoralizing effects of repeated failure. Consider the following life conditions replete with adversities and grim risk factors. Born out of wedlock on a tiny island in the Caribbean. His mother's first husband imprisons her for adultery and deserts the family. Mother dies. Guardian commits suicide. Left destitute in childhood with the death of his aunt, uncle, and grandfather. His meager belongings are sold off leaving him penniless.

A key enablement factor overrides this grim catalogue of risk factors. A clergyman raised funds from local merchants to educate him at King's College (now Columbia). Alexander Hamilton thrived in this new environment. He became a founding father of our nation, and left a staggering legacy of achievements that shaped our federal governmental systems.

Another oft-cited example of remarkable resilience to the demoralizing effects of repeated failure on the rough road to success is the story of a man who failed repeatedly for every public office he sought: at the local and state level, at the congressional House and Senate level, and selection for the vice presidency. At age 51, Abe Lincoln became the most distinguished president of the United States.

The road of success is through learning from mistakes, and failures. As the saying, "If you want the rainbow, you must put up with the rain."

The functional belief system in difficult undertakings combines realism about tough odds with optimism that one can beat those odds through self-development and perseverant effort. In his delightful book titled, *Rejection*,

John White reports that the prominent characteristic of people who achieve success in challenging pursuits is an unshakable sense of efficacy and a firm belief in the worth of what they are doing. Resilient efficacy provides the needed staying power.

Virtually every innovation that has touched our lives was repeatedly rejected:

- Mr. Warner, of Warner Brothers, said of talking movies, "Who the hell wants to hear actors talk?"
- E.E. Cummings had one of his books rejected by 15 publishers. When he finally got it published, by his mother, the dedication read WITH NO THANKS TO . . . followed by the list of publishers who had rejected his prized offspring.
- David Sarnoff's associates to his urging to invest in the radio, "The wireless music box has no imaginable commercial value. Who would pay for a message sent to nobody in particular?"
- Ken Olson, founder of Digital Equipment, rejecting the home computer, "There is no reason anyone would want a computer in their home."
- A Yale professor explaining to Fred Smith, who went on to found Federal Express, why he gave him a C grade for his thesis proposing an overnight delivery service, "The concept is interesting and well-formed, but in order to earn better than a "C" the idea must be feasible."
- MGM's evaluation of Fred Astaire in a screen test, "Can't act. Can't sing. Slightly Bald. Can dance a little."
- Vince Lombardi was rejected for a coaching job because, "He possesses minimal football knowledge and lacks motivation."
- Decca records rejected the Beatles with the nonprophetic evaluation, "We don't like their sound. Groups of guitars are on their way out." After Decca discarded them, Columbia records followed suit.

And the rejection list goes on.

Innovation requires resilience to unmerciful rejection. The people who are successful, innovative, nonanxious, nondespondent, and tenacious social reformers take an optimistic view of their efficacy to influence events that affect their lives. George Bernard Shaw put it well when he said: "Reasonable people adapt to the world. Unreasonable ones try to change it. Human progress depends on the unreasonable ones."

Don't despair if you suffer rejection and setbacks. Those who have gained fame and fortune have suffered mightily in the hands of rejectors lacking foresight.

We are currently facing a financial crisis of overwhelming proportions. This places severe strains on maintaining productive self-management. Unpredictability and uncontrollability breed stress and despondency. The present is chaotic, with complex financial arrangements operating through global networks that are difficult to unravel. To predict and correct them is a daunting challenge, but the course is predictable and eventually correctable. The market will rebound, as it always has.

There are two antidotes to loss of coping efficacy and demoralization. The first is to focus on what is within one's control, rather than dwell on what is personally unmanageable. That only makes things worse. The second is to view the present in a broader time perspective. One can find some solace in the fact that the adverse financial conditions will eventually improve. But recovery from this financial crisis will take longer, requiring sustained resilience.

These coping strategies help to support one's staying power in these difficult times. The challenge is to maintain a proactive orientation until the early signs of restored confidence in the financial systems begin to appear.

Because of the centrality of efficacy beliefs in people's lives, we studied how to enable them to shape their course of life. People's beliefs in their efficacy can be developed in four ways.

The most effective way of instilling strong efficacy is through *mastery experiences*. Performance successes build a robust belief in one's personal efficacy. If people experience only easy successes, they come to expect quick results, and are easily discouraged by failure. **Resilient efficacy requires experience in overcoming obstacles through perseverant effort. Resilience is also built by training in how to manage failure so it becomes informative, rather than demoralizing.** Motivation gurus tell us how to succeed, but they do not tell us how to manage failure. The path to success is through learning from mistakes and setbacks.

The second way of developing efficacy is by *social modeling*. Competent models convey knowledge, skills, and the strategies for managing task demands. By their example in pursuing challenges, models foster aspirations and interest in activities. Seeing people similar to oneself succeed by perseverant effort raises the observers' beliefs in their own abilities.

Social persuasion is the third mode of influence. If people are persuaded to believe in themselves, they will exert more effort. This increases their chances of success. Credible persuaders must be knowledgeable and practice what they preach. Effective efficacy builders do more than convey faith in others. They arrange situations for others in ways that bring success. They avoid placing them prematurely in situations where they are likely to fail. They measure success by self-improvement, rather than by triumphs over others. Pep talks without enabling guidelines achieve little.

Finally, people rely partly on their *physical and emotional states* in judging their efficacy. They read tension, anxiety, and weariness as signs of personal deficiencies. Mood also affects how people judge their efficacy. Positive mood enhances a sense of efficacy, depressed mood diminishes it. People often misread their fatigue, windedness, aches and pains, as evidence of declining physical efficacy. These physical conditions are often due to a sedentary lifestyle. Efficacy beliefs are strengthened by reducing anxiety and depression, building physical strength and stamina, and changing misreading of physical states.

We know how efficacy beliefs work. They regulate human motivation and performance accomplishments in four major ways. They affect whether individuals *think* pessimistically or optimistically, in self-enhancing or self-debilitating ways, how well they *motivate* themselves and persevere in the face of difficulties, the quality of their *emotional well-being* and their vulnerability to stress and depression, and the *life choices* we make. These choices set the course of life paths.

How People Think

Efficacy beliefs affect how people think, especially when they run into difficulties. Those of high efficacy visualize success scenarios that provide positive guides for performance. Those of low efficacy visualize failure scenarios and dwell on the many things that can go wrong. This impairs their motivation and performance.

How people view intelligence affects how they read and manage their successes and failures. Some people view intelligence as an inborn aptitude. Others view intelligence as an acquirable skill. The more you work at it, the smarter you get.

Viewing ability as an acquirable skill is a highly functional orientation for personal development. Mistakes are instructive rather than threatening. Such individuals seek challenges that provide opportunities to expand their knowledge and competencies. They regard errors as a natural part of learning. One learns from mistakes. Therefore, they are not easily rattled by difficulties. They focus on the task at hand, and how best to solve problems. They judge their capabilities more in terms of personal improvement, than by comparison against the achievement of others. They seek evaluation of their performance for improvement. They welcome the help of others to improve their knowledge and skills.

For those who view ability as an inborn aptitude, achievement tasks carry high threat. Poor performance shows they lack intelligence. They view mistakes as threats because they imply a lack of basic intelligence. Therefore, they prefer safe activities they can do well in at the expense of expanding their knowledge and competencies. They regard high effort as a threat, because it suggests they are not smart. They focus on themselves, whether they are up to the task, and the consequences of poor performance, rather than concentrate on how to solve the problem. They judge their capabilities against the achievements of others. The successes of others belittle their own perceived ability and undermine their functioning. They avoid evaluation and take evaluation personally. They are reluctant to seek help from others because it suggests they are less smart.

We gave bright business graduates the task of managing a complex simulation of a company. They made managerial decisions for a series of projects and got feedback in how well their organization performed. At periodic intervals, we measured their perceived managerial efficacy, their organizational aspirations, and the quality of their analytical thinking in learning how to run the organization.

Before they began, we instilled beliefs about the nature of intelligence. Half of the managers were led to believe that the simulation measured their inborn aptitude for complex decision making. The other half was told that it involved an acquirable skill. This is a beneficial view of ability. They were given tough productivity goals to fulfill. We measured the quality of their functioning, over many production projects.

This was a bright group of folks, MBA red-hots with managerial experience! But what a difference a belief makes. Viewing ability as an acquirable skill fostered resilient efficacy. Managers remained resolute in their efficacy. In the face of difficulties they set challenging organizational goals and they used efficient analytic strategies. This view of ability paid off in high performance attainments.

For those who viewed intellectual ability as an inborn aptitude, their perceived efficacy plummeted as they encountered problems. They lowered their organizational aspirations for the group, they became more and more erratic in their analytic thinking, and they exhibited progressive deterioration in performance.

One of my students, who was on the Stanford rowing team, wondered whether beliefs about ability affect learning of physical skills as well. We tested it experimentally. Students were given the task of learning a physical skill. Some were told it measured their innate physical aptitude. Others were told it measured an acquirable skill. Initial practice raised efficacy and skill in both groups, but thereafter, those in the innate group showed no further gains in efficacy or skill. They acted as though they had reached the limits of their ability. Their innate view left them discontented with their performance, disinterested in the activity, and plateaued at a low level of skill development.

Those in the acquirable group continued to increase their efficacy and skill. They also found the activity more self-satisfying. They developed a higher interest in it. At the end of the study, they were told that there was some free time. They could quit, or continue the activity. Seventy percent of the acquirable skill group chose to continue to perfect their skill. The inborn ones made a hasty retreat.

How People Motivate Themselves

Efficacy beliefs play a key role in motivation. People motivate themselves and guide their behavior by the goals and challenges they set for themselves. You don't hop into a taxi and say, "Take me somewhere."

Goals, by themselves, are not motivating. It is the personal investment in them that is the driving force. You care about the goals you adopt, and invest your self-evaluation in how well you do. Once people commit themselves to certain goals, they seek self-satisfaction from achieving them. They intensify their efforts by discontent with substandard performance.

Without commitment to something they feel is worth doing, people are unmotivated, bored, apathetic, and cynical. They seek diversions to escape from boredom.

Self-motivation through goal setting requires feedback of how one is doing. People enhance their motivation when they adopt challenging goals, and get performance feedback. Neither goals, without knowing how one is doing, nor knowing how one is doing without any goals, is motivating.

Most public policies are doomed to failure, because they focus solely on goals without any feedback system.

Feedback for the same performance can be enabling or demoralizing depending on how it is presented. Let's revisit our MBAs managing the simulated organization. Consider an instance in which their goal attainment is at 75 percent of their productivity goal. For half the managers, the feedback focuses on their 25 percent shortfall. For the other half, the feedback focuses on their 75 percent progress toward the goal. It is the same performance level, but one type of feedback accents the negative. The other accents the positive.

What a difference feedback framing makes. Under the progress feedback, the managers were resilient in their efficacy. They set progressively higher goals, increased the quality of their decision making, were more satisfied with their performance, and achieved higher organizational productivity. Under the shortfall feedback, their efficacy plummeted. They lowered their goals. Their decision making got more erratic. They were dissatisfied and achieved lower organizational productivity.

Self-efficacy and self-evaluation act in concert in predicting motivation in the face of failures and setbacks. High efficacy and discontent over substandard performance heightens motivation. Either high discontent or high efficacy alone, result in a small increase in motivation. People who distrust their efficacy and couldn't care less about mediocre performances slacken their efforts and just coast along apathetically.

People perfect skills for subverting their efforts to do what is difficult, or unpleasant. Here are the top subverters of self-management. People put off what needs to be done under the illusion that they will have more time tomorrow. This strategy is captured well in the Spanish proverb: "Mañana is the busiest day of the week." They distract themselves with trifling matters that waste time. They do other things first. These detours take time away from what needs to be done. Computers and wireless devices provide a handy, limitless source of detours. The author of a recent best seller was asked about his writing schedule. "I check the e-mails first," he replied. "Then I get down to writing. But before long, I am back in the e-mails." Shakespeare would have a tough time in this electronic era. People find excuses in the pressure of more immediate demands, unfavorable circumstances, and situational impediments to put off what needs to be done.

Goals are not automatically motivating. In fact, most good intentions end in failure because they are too general, too distant, and noncommitting. The goals that are motivating are the ones that activate self-investment in the activity. They include explicitness, temporal proximity, and level of challenge.

> *Explicit*—Explicit goals motivate because they specify the type and amount of effort needed to succeed. In her stage show, Lily Tomlin provides a familiar example of the ineffectiveness of vague, noncommitting goals. Her character, Crissy, never quite manages to get her act together. She says, "I vowed to make something of myself when I grew up." Then she says, "I guess I should have been more specific."

> *Temporal proximity*—The effectiveness of goals in regulating motivation depends on how far into the future they are projected. Long-range goals provide the vision of a desired future. But they are too distant to serve as current motivators. There are too many competing influences for distant futures to regulate current behavior. It is too easy to put off matters in the present to the tomorrows of each day. Short-term goals provide guides, strategies, and motivators to get to where one is going. Seemingly overwhelming activities are mastered by breaking them into smaller manageable steps.

Level of challenge—Self-motivation is best sustained by attainable sub-goal challenges. Subgoals focus attention on what one has to do in the here and now to turn a distal (distant) vision into reality. Under distal goals, people put off matters in the present until looming deadlines spur them into a flurry of activity. I had planned to write an article on the deadline control of behavior, but, without a deadline, I never got around to it.

> Bandura's comments about temporal proximity relate to our proposed model for managing your client's financial security in that your clients' beliefs in the importance of their funded status helps them overcome the tug of hyperbolic discounting of a temporally distant goal. The funded status converts future liabilities, which are otherwise easy to ignore, into a present-day measurement that can steer immediate decisions and trade-offs.

Mastering challenging subgoals builds efficacy, interest, and satisfaction where they are lacking. There are several ways that subgoals achieve these positive effects: subgoals sustain effort that builds competencies. Subgoal attainments also provide clear markers of increasing mastery. Evidence of mastery builds efficacy. Subgoal attainments bring self-satisfaction. Satisfying experiences build interest in activities.

The benefits of stepwise mastery are illustrated in a project designed to turn students who were disinterested and failing in academic activities into academically engaged and competent ones. The students pursued enabling instruction with either a long-range goal, a series of subgoals leading to the long-range one, with no goals, or with no instruction. Those with subgoals

> Sustainable financial security may be the ultimate goal for your clients, but it can seem to be a difficult and distant goal. Reaching a desired funded status, even if it requires future savings, can be a subgoal that helps motivate them to action. Breaking this down further, creating a spending plan is a component of the funded status subgoal. This is a task that your client can begin working on right away. This is an example of how you can create smaller steps that your client can take immediate action on, which lead up to their overarching goal of creating sustainable financial security.

developed strong efficacy in the activity. Those with long-range goals alone had little effect. Those with subgoals also produced higher achievement. Distal goals had little impact. Subgoal successes also built interest where it was lacking.

Subgoal motivators and guides are especially important for individuals who distrust their abilities. They need proximal markers of progress and enabling and supporting guidance that confirms their growing efficacy.

Emotional Well-Being

People's beliefs in their efficacy to cope with threats and stressors affect their emotional well-being and vulnerability to anxiety and depression.

> Consider that managing your clients' funded status may make them more confident and optimistic about their future.

There are several ways in which perceived efficacy regulates emotional states.

Coping efficacy affects how people view their environment. Those who believe that threats are unmanageable see their environment as fraught with danger. They dwell on their coping deficiencies, magnify the severity of possible threats, and worry about things that rarely happen.

People live with psychological environments largely of their own making. Control over ruminative, disturbing thoughts is a second way in which efficacy beliefs regulate stress and depression. The exercise of control over one's own consciousness is summed up well in the proverb: "You cannot prevent the birds of worry and care from flying over your head. But you can stop them from building a nest in your hair." It is not the sheer frequency of disturbing thoughts, but the perceived helplessness to turn them off that is the major distressor. Belief in one's coping efficacy takes anxiety out of taxing and stressful situations.

Tough work demands are stressful for individuals who believe they lack the efficacy to meet them but not for those who are assured in their capabilities. Stress is especially prevalent when individuals are held accountable, but not given sufficient resources and control over how the work is done.

Chronic exposure to stressors produces burnout. This is characterized by: emotional exhaustion, depersonalization that treats clients like faceless objects, lack of any sense of personal accomplishment, and cynicism about one's work.

There are three remedies to work-related stress. Change the workplace by giving employees greater control over how the work is done. Responsibility without personal control is demoralizing. Develop employees' self-efficacy and skills in ways that enable them to manage their work life better, and gain a sense of accomplishment and pride in their work. Develop their efficacy for stress management. This includes how to achieve recuperative breaks from emotionally taxing work through leisure activities. Not bringing work-related problems home, either in homework or rumination about the job.

This is toughest to do in this electronic era. Wireless devices serve as an electronic leash that respects neither time nor place. Worklife increasingly intrudes on familial, social, and recreational life.

Don't lose sight of what people discover, retrospectively, as truly important in one's life. Remember the insightful words of the late Senator Tsongas, "No one on their death bed ever expressed regret for not having spent more time in the office."

Low efficacy to control over what one values gives rise to depression. It does so in at least three ways.

One route is through *unfulfilled aspirations*. People who impose on themselves standards of self-worth they judge they cannot attain drive themselves to bouts of depression.

A second route to depression is through a *low sense of social efficacy*, to develop social relationships that bring satisfaction to one's life, and cushion the adverse effects of chronic stressors. Social support reduces stress, depression, and improves health. However, social support is not a self-forming entity waiting around to buffer us. People have to find supportive relationships, cultivate, and maintain them. It requires social efficacy to do so.

The third route to depression is through efficacy to control one's *ruminative thinking*. Much human depression is generated by dejecting, ruminative thought. Low efficacy to regulate ruminative thought contributes to the occurrence, duration, and recurrence of depressive episodes. Ruminating about one's adverse life condition only drives one into deeper despondency. The best antidote to depression is active engagement in activities. It shuts down the depressing rumination.

Life Choices

There is much we do designedly to shape our future. However, sometimes the direction our lives take is determined by the most trivial of circumstances. People's marital partnerships, occupational careers, and other aspects of their life courses, are sometimes formed by chance events.

As a graduate student, my friend and I were late for golf start time. We were bumped to a later time slot. There were two women ahead of us. They were slowing down. We were speeding up. Before long we became a jovial quartet. I met my wife-to-be in the sand trap!

Some years later, I delivered a presidential address at the Western Psychological Convention, on the psychology of chance encounters and life paths. A short time later, an editor from one of the publishing houses called me. He explained that he had entered the lecture hall as it was rapidly filling up. He seized an empty chair near the entrance. In the coming week he would be marrying the woman who happened to be seated next to him. With only a momentary change in time of entry, seating constellations would have altered, and they would not have met. A marital partnership was fortuitously formed at a talk devoted to fortuitous determinants of life paths!

Psychologists avoid chance like the plague. They are in the business of explaining, predicting, and modifying behavior. Chance is a troublesome nuisance.

Most fortuitous events leave us untouched, others exert some influence, and still others can branch us into new directions of life. Fortuity does not mean uncontrollability of its effects. You can exercise some influence over the fortuitous character of life. You can make chance happen by pursuing an active life. Chance favors the inquisitive and venturesome, who go places, do things, and explore new activities.

You can also make chance work for you by cultivating your interests, enabling beliefs and competencies. These personal resources allow you to make the most of opportunities that arise unexpectedly. Pasteur put it well when he noted, "Chance favors only the prepared mind."

Self-development and active engagement in life gives people a hand in shaping the courses their lives take. So, as you navigate your life course with its many trials and tribulations, may the Efficacy Force be with you.

NOTES

1. Steven Haggbloom, et al., "The 100 Most Eminent Psychologists of the 20th Century," *Review of General Psychology* 6, no. 2 (2002), 139–152.
2. Albert Bandura, *Self–Efficacy: The Exercise of Control* (New York: W. H. Freeman, 1997).

Building a Simple and Powerful Solution for Retirement Saving—Russell's Approach to Target Date Funds

Grant W. Gardner, PhD and Yuan-An Fan, PhD

Authors' note: In August 2006, Grant and Yuan-An authored this white paper on the design of target date funds. The framework they lay out in this paper establishes two foundational ideas that are reflected in the personal asset liability model. First, it incorporates human capital into the asset-allocation decisions for individuals accumulating wealth for retirement. Second, it uses for its definition of success a wealth target sufficient for the individual at retirement to purchase an annuity equal to their targeted replacement income. They create rules for an intelligent way for individuals to balance the value of their human capital with a basket of financial assets throughout the course of their career.

Target-date funds are designed to provide a simple investment solution for participants in defined contribution plans and others who contribute regularly to retirement savings plans. In this paper, we outline the Russell methodology for designing target-date funds. Russell's target-date funds have distinguishing features that work to improve the odds for successful investment for retirement. Although there is no certainty that this objective will be met, the funds should appeal to investors who would like to know their fund is explicitly designed to overcome the uncertainty found on the long path to financial independence in retirement.

TARGET-DATE FUND BASICS

Although many investment managers with varying investment philosophies offer target-date funds, they share common features. The investors choose funds targeted to an expected year of retirement—say, target-date fund 2040. The investors make regular contributions, and the fund manager selects appropriate asset classes, allocates the fund among them, and devises the best investment strategy within each asset class.

The strategy evolves over time in a way considered appropriate for a typical investor planning to retire at the target date. However, the managers of these funds are unable to exercise full discretion over investment decisions because target-date funds come with a full specification of the way in which aspects of the investment strategy should evolve over time. In particular, the asset allocation among the major asset classes is mapped out by date through the life of the fund. This industry convention is a response to concerns of investors who would be hesitant to pour their life savings into black-box investment strategies. Moreover, the sponsors of defined contribution plans that offer these funds would feel uncomfortable allowing their participants to handle investments without such guidelines.

The path of asset allocation over time is the primary determinant of the risk-and-return characteristics of a target-date fund. More specifically, because the bulk of assets held in these funds are equities and bonds, the evolution of the total equity/total bond split over time determines the essential risk and return nature of such funds. Although diversification across equities and bonds and the investment performance within these categories can affect fund performance, it is critical to the fund's success that the manager gets right the glide path of the equity/bond split over time.

Regardless of the provider, the glide paths of target-date funds have a common feature: the allocation to equity declines as the fund approaches the target date. Younger investors in funds with distant target dates, therefore, will have higher allocations to equity than older investors in funds with nearby target dates. This characteristic is reflected in Figure 11.1, which shows a typical glide path for a 40-year target-date fund.

THE HUMAN-CAPITAL MODEL AND GLIDE PATH

A good explanation for this common characteristic is found in a human-capital model of lifetime saving and investing.[1] The essence of this approach is to view an investor's stream of future savings as the cash flows from an asset whose present value can be calculated.[2] Thus, at any age before

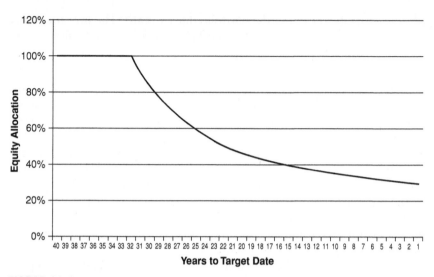

FIGURE 11.1 Typical Target Date Glide Path
Source: Russell Investments.

retirement, the investor's wealth has two components: financial wealth in the form of equity, bonds, and other financial assets, and human capital, which is the present value of remaining savings flows discounted at an appropriate risk-adjusted discount rate.

To help explain this approach, we outline a make-believe case in which this human capital is liquid. Investors can sell their human capital, in effect swapping the stream of future savings for an immediate cash payment, and invest that cash in financial assets. An investor, say a 25-year-old who plans to retire at 65, must choose an investment strategy to manage this wealth until age 65. In the spirit of target-date funds, the portfolio should change over time, but the glide path of the equity/bond mix must be fully specified in advance.

The investor's wealth at retirement is the sum of (liquidated) human capital, plus any other wealth, compounded by the rate of return on the portfolio over the next 40 years. In notation:

$$W_{64} = [W_{24} + H_{24}](1 + r_{25})(1 + r_{26})(1 + r_{27}) \ldots L(1 + r_{64})$$

where W_{64} is financial wealth at the end of the investor's 64th year (that is, 65th birthday),

W_{24} is financial wealth at the end of the 24th year,

H_{24} is the value of human capital at the end of the 24th year, and

r_t is the return on the portfolio during year t. The investor wants
an investment strategy that balances reward and risk over the
entire investment horizon.

It is clear that each period's return has the same influence on final wealth
as any other. The ordering of the returns makes no difference. If we assume,
therefore, the same behavior of asset returns in all periods, the only type of
strategy that makes any sense is to hold the same portfolio in all periods.
If all periods have the same impact on final wealth, why would an investor
do different things in different periods? This result is confirmed by formal
mathematical optimization. Thus, in this make-believe case in which human
capital is immediately liquidated and invested in financial markets, the glide
path is flat. The precise mix of stocks and bonds depends on the investor's
ending wealth target and attitude about risk, but for every case the glide
path will be flat.[3]

Now we return to the real world in which human capital is illiquid.
This human capital can still be thought of as an asset with a present value,
but it is an asset that cannot be sold. The solution to the investor's glide-
path problem is to find the best mix of stocks and bonds *given that he or
she is stuck with an allocation of human capital.* Figure 11.2 illustrates the
situation. At age 25, the investor's wealth is mostly in the form of human

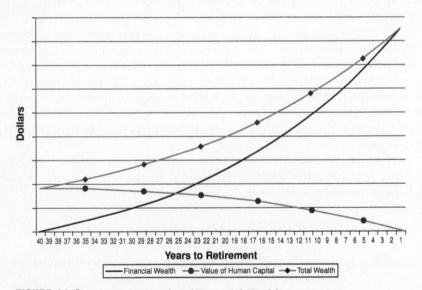

FIGURE 11.2 Human Capital and Financial Wealth
Source: Russell Investments.

capital. As time passes and this human capital is liquidated in the form of savings, financial wealth begins to grow and human capital depletes. At retirement, human capital is depleted and all wealth is in the form of financial assets.

What will the glide path look like in this situation? From the discussion of the make-believe case, we know that the optimal solution is a flat glide path in which there is complete liquidity of human capital. Without liquidity, the investor will allocate the available financial wealth in a way that comes as close as possible to optimal risk/return trade-off of the flat glide path of the liquid case. If human capital is more like a bond than a stock, then young investors will typically want to hold most or all of their financial wealth in equity to offset their illiquid bond position. As time passes, human capital depletes and financial wealth grows. To maintain the same risk/return exposure, the investor will want to move out of equity into bonds. At retirement, when all human capital is depleted, the glide path will be at the same level as the flat glide path of the liquid case. This path is shown in Figure 11.3.

Two more aspects of the human-capital approach are important. First, the declining equity allocation in the glide path depends on the assumption that savings risk is similar to that of bonds. If savings were more like equity, which might be the case for an investment banker or equity manager, the same logic we have used here would suggest a glide path that starts with a

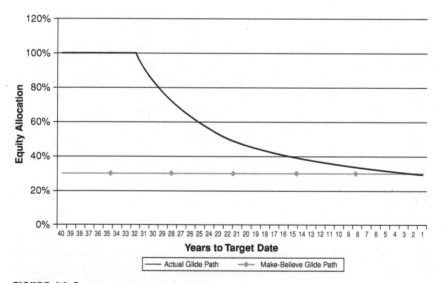

FIGURE 11.3 Target Date Glide Paths
Source: Russell Investments.

high exposure to bonds early in life. The presumption of bondlike behavior in savings seems sensible for investors with income based mostly on salary and not directly driven by the equity market. Second, because the human-capital approach casts the glide-path problem as a conventional asset-allocation problem, the intuition developed over decades of use of this conventional paradigm can be used as a reality check.

DETAILS OF RUSSELL'S GLIDE PATH

Although the human-capital approach explains the basic shape of the equity glide path, more information is needed to construct a sound strategy. The essential nature of a target-date fund is to provide a sound investment strategy for an individual saving for retirement at a specific date. To create a sound strategy, we need to know the target date, initial wealth and savings over time, the wealth goal at the target date, and the investor's attitude toward risk and return. In addition, constraints on the strategy are imposed by the need for *simplicity, transparency,* and *consistency*.

Simplicity

Although each individual should have a unique investment solution because each is unique in terms of wealth, savings behavior, and attitude toward risk, practicality demands one fund, or, at most, a handful of funds, that will work for almost all investors with a given target date. In designing a fund strategy to meet the needs of such investors, the manager must define a typical investor who epitomizes the bulk of the likely investors. We assume this investor is a participant in a defined contribution retirement plan. In this chapter we specify what we see as typical. This information should give investors insight into judging whether this strategy fits their circumstances. Moreover, we demonstrate how the strategy will work for an investor who is not typical. We believe an investor or defined-contribution-plan sponsor should demand this type of information when evaluating a target-date fund.

Transparency

The need for transparency also constrains the design of target-date strategies. Because target-date funds are long-run strategies that are meant to be put in place and allowed to run their course, industry convention requires that the basic investment strategy, including the glide path, be specified in advance. Although discretionary management or even prespecified rules for changing asset allocation in response to market behavior could potentially improve the investment performance of the strategy, this potential is declined for the sake of transparency.

Consistency

The requirements of simplicity and transparency lead to an additional constraint on the design of the glide path—*consistency*. The concept of consistency is that a single glide path must be used for all target dates. That is, the glide path for a 10-year target-date fund started today will be the same as the glide path of the final 10 years of a 40-year fund. The internal logic behind this requirement is that the investment strategy is designed for the same typical investor whether retirement is 10 or 40 years away. This requirement is an industry norm, and we will follow it. It is important to understand, however, that this requirement implies that someone just entering a 10-year target-date fund has spent the past 30 years saving and investing in a way similar to that of the typical investor and has current wealth and future savings plans consistent with that individual. Common sense demands an evaluation of whether the glide path actually works well for someone who is atypical when entering the strategy.

Russell seeks to build funds with target dates out to a maximum of 40 years. Consequently, our typical investor in a 40-year fund must start out 40 years from retirement. We assume the investor starts with no wealth.

Modeling Uncertainty

The investor faces uncertainty about asset returns, inflation, and the level of savings on the path to reaching the retirement goals. Moreover, the investor must cope with the difficult question of how much wealth will be needed to fund retirement.

In constructing a glide path, we address this uncertainty. We generate 20,000 scenarios of savings, interest rates, inflation, and asset returns, and we find the glide path that, when averaged over these scenarios, does the best job of balancing the desire to have as much wealth as possible at retirement against the risk of falling below a wealth target needed to finance a comfortable retirement. The assumed behavior of the returns on equity and bonds as well as inflation is shown in Table 11.1.

Investor Income

We explicitly model the growth of an investor's income over a 40-year working life. We assume that income, which determines annual savings and target wealth, grows at the rate of inflation plus the rate of real income

TABLE 11.1 Asset Class Return and Inflation Assumptions

Asset Classes	Expected Return (%)	Standard Deviation (%)	U.S. Equity	Non-U.S. Equity	Fixed Income	Inflation
U.S. Equity	8.9	18	1			
Non-U.S. Equity	8.9	19.1	.54	1		
Fixed Income	6.3	2.9	.26	.21	1	
Inflation	3.2	4	.14	.16	.64	1

Note: Russell's methodology for forecasting asset-class returns and inflation for the purpose of asset allocation produces forecasts that differ by time horizon. The forecasts in Table 11.1 are Russell forecasts at a 20-year horizon, as of December, 2005.

The "equity" portfolio used in the construction of the glide path is a 67 percent/ 33 percent mix of U.S. equity and non-U.S. equity.

All information shown in Table 11.1 is based on assumptions. Expected returns employ proprietary projections of the returns of each asset class. We estimate the performance of an asset class or strategy by analyzing current economic and market conditions and historical market trends. It is likely that actual returns will vary considerably from these assumptions, even for a number of years. References to future returns for either asset-allocation strategies or asset classes are not promises or even estimates of actual returns a client portfolio may achieve. Asset classes are broad general categories that may or may not correspond well to specific products.

Opinions and estimates offered constitute our judgment and are subject to change without notice, as are statements of financial market trends, which are based on current market conditions. This material is not intended as an offer or solicitation for the purchase or sale of any financial instrument. The views and strategies described may not be suitable for all investors.

growth. In our model, inflation is a stochastic variable with a mean of 3.2 percent a year and a standard deviation of 4 percent. The correlation of inflation with the returns of equities and bonds is shown in Table 11.1. We assume real wages grow at 1.5 percent a year. Because the level of savings and target wealth are both linked to income, the starting level of income has no effect on the glide path. We pick an arbitrary value of $1,000 a year.

Savings Behavior

Annual savings are the product of the investor's income and a savings rate. Our assumed yearly savings rates are shown in Figure 11.4. These rates represent the recommended individual contributions to a defined contribution plan plus typical company matching policies and are based on Russell research and industry sources.

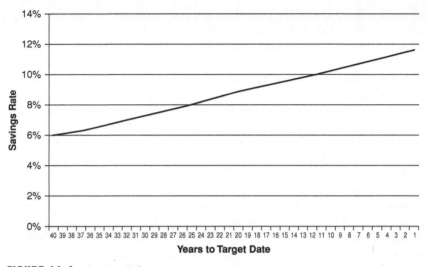

FIGURE 11.4 Savings Behavior
Source: Russell Investments.

The pattern is clear. The savings rate for younger workers is low but increases each year. Although we assume the savings rate is predictable, we treat savings income as a stochastic variable due to the uncertainty of inflation. Thus the amount of savings each period is a stochastic variable. Our modeling takes account of this uncertainty in savings.

Target Wealth

To create a sound investment strategy, we must be clear about the goal. The goal is to have as much wealth as possible at retirement, but to avoid having wealth fall below a target level. What should that target be? The quick answer is "enough to allow the investor to retire comfortably," but what does that mean? Our definition of the target wealth level is the amount of final wealth it takes to purchase an immediate annuity that replaces a given percentage of the investor's income in his or her final year of work. This concept can be broken down into its component pieces:

Target Wealth = Final Year Income

× Income Replacement Ratio × Annuity Factor

Retirees typically do not need as much income as they did before retirement to maintain their standard of living. They stop saving and do not need to replace that part of their income. Also, taxes decline because they may be living off wealth rather than taxable income. In addition, most retirees in the United States will draw Social Security benefits. Because of the way Social Security is structured, the fraction of final-year income replaced by benefits declines as income increases.

Taking these factors into consideration, Aon Consulting and Georgia State University studied replacement rates for a variety of income levels. Based on their research, we use a replacement rate of 42 percent.[4]

How much wealth does the investor need to provide that income? One easily quantifiable answer to that question is that the investor needs enough wealth to purchase an immediate life annuity that delivers that amount of income. The annuity factor is the cost of a $1 annuity and thus translates the investor's income target into a wealth target. The value of the annuity factor depends on age, sex, and the level of interest rates. For our modeling purposes, we calculate the annuity factor for a 65-year-old male.[5] The interest rate is a stochastic variable generated in our model. Thus, each of our 20,000 scenarios has a different target wealth that depends on the investor's final-year income and the level of interest rate that prevails at retirement.

Attitude toward Risk

In the model we use to construct the glide path, risk is the danger of falling below target wealth at retirement. Our measure of risk is the "shortfall penalty function" shown in Figure 11.5. The horizontal axis shows wealth at retirement. If wealth at retirement is greater than the target, the penalty is zero. If wealth falls below the target, there is a shortfall. The greater the shortfall in wealth, the greater the penalty. Moreover, the curvature of the function means the penalty grows in increasing proportion to the shortfall. In other words, if the shortfall doubles, the shortfall penalty more than doubles. This aspect of the shortfall penalty function means that we heavily penalize large shortfalls. In using mathematical optimization to search for the best glide path, we reward candidate paths for producing a high level of wealth at retirement, and we penalize paths for falling below the wealth target.

We derive our glide path by finding the mix of equity and bonds in each of the 40 years that maximizes:

Expected Value of Wealth at Retirement

− (Risk Aversion Parameter × Expected Shortfall Penalty)

The size of this risk-aversion parameter reflects the investor's attitude about the trade-off between risk and reward. In principle, there is a different

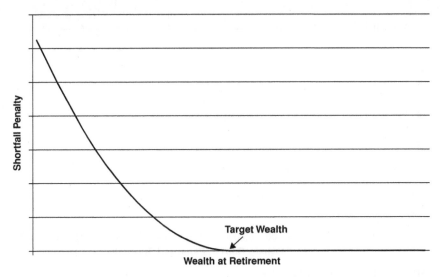

FIGURE 11.5 Shortfall Penalty Function
Source: Russell Investments.

optimal glide path for each possible value of this parameter. Thus, in order to decide on a glide path of a typical investor, we must choose this parameter value for a typical investor. Unlike the savings rate and income-replacement rate, this parameter cannot be directly observed or estimated from data.

To choose the value of the risk parameter and thus the single glide path from the possibilities on the efficient frontier, we let the marketplace define typical. First, we find the optimal glide paths for a wide range of values of the risk aversion parameter. Associated with each optimal glide path is an expected ending wealth at retirement and a value of penalized shortfall. We can graph these combinations of expected ending wealth and penalized shortfall to get a sort of efficient frontier of risk (square root of penalized shortfall) and reward (expected ending wealth) that is available with various optimal glide paths. This is shown in Figure 11.6. Each point represents the expected result of a glide path that is optimal for a particular value of the risk-aversion parameter. The dollar amounts shown for expected ending wealth and the square root of penalized shortfall are based on an assumption of a $1,000 initial income.

Next, we take the glide paths of major providers of target-date funds, simulate their performance using our assumptions about savings behavior and our definition of risk, and plot them on the efficient frontier. Because our paths are optimal given our assumptions, these competitor funds will fall on or below the efficient frontier. Not surprisingly, most of them cluster

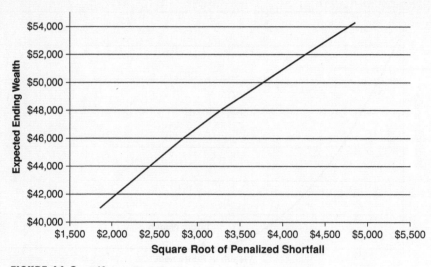

FIGURE 11.6   Efficient Frontier
Source: Russell Investments.

in a fairly narrow range below the efficient frontier. We take this as evidence that a typical investor exists and a competitive marketplace is trying to meet that investor's needs. We choose a point on the efficient frontier that is near this competitive cluster. Thus, at least according to our assumptions, our glide path meets the needs of the typical investor, but it does it a little better than the glide paths used by others.

Figure 11.7 shows our glide path. It has the general shape suggested by the human-capital approach. It is aggressive in the early years, maintaining a 100 percent equity allocation through year 11. At retirement, the equity allocation is down to 32 percent. Other Russell research shows this level of equity exposure is consistent with funding lifetime income at the level assumed in the construction of our wealth target. In other words, if the investor meets or exceeds the wealth target, this 32 percent equity portfolio is a prudent portfolio in retirement.

EVALUATING THE GLIDE PATH

In evaluating how well this glide path should perform, we need appropriate performance measures. Although conventional performance measures, such as expected return and standard deviation of return, can be calculated under certain assumptions, they provide little useful information for target-date funds. The reason is that these time-weighted performance measures are

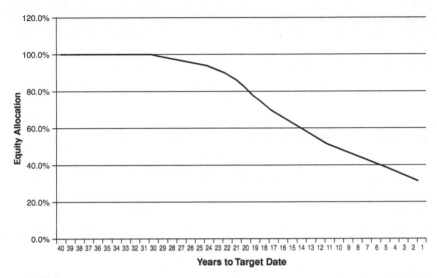

FIGURE 11.7   Russell Target Date Glide Path
Source: Russell Investments.

designed to measure how well a strategy does at growing an initial level of wealth over a given time period. By design, they ignore the pattern of cash flows during the investment period. Although this aspect of their design is appropriate for evaluating managers who have no control over cash flows into and out of a portfolio, they ignore the essence of what a target-date fund is supposed to do: Manage around an assumed stream of savings to build wealth at the target date. We need performance measures that evaluate a target-date fund in the context of what it is designed to do.

To generate meaningful performance measures that have intuitive appeal and are useful for comparing one fund against another, the best procedure is to specify a typical investor, as we did earlier, and then simulate the investment results for a given glide path. The measures we suggest are specified in the following sections:

The Expected Value of Ending Wealth

This is a fundamental measure of the fund's ability to build wealth. Its magnitude depends on assumptions about the level of savings. The absolute magnitude of this measure is unimportant for comparisons among funds simulated on the same set of assumptions. For that purpose only the relative size of ending wealth matters. To get an absolute measure that might have meaning to the investor, we can scale by the first year's income level. For example, our recommended glide path has an expected ending wealth of $44,800 for each $1,000 of initial (age 25) income. Thus, an investor who begins saving according to our assumptions at the beginning of the 40-year glide path should expect to have wealth at retirement equal to 44.8 times his or her current income. Adjusted for inflation, expected retirement wealth should be about 12.2 times current income.

Probability of Failing to Achieve the Wealth Target

This is the first of two measures of risk. Recall that the wealth target is the cost of an annuity to replace 42 percent of final year income. For our assumptions, the average value of this wealth target is $30,200 for each $1,000 of initial income. The probability of not achieving this target wealth is 0.188 for our glide path. In other words, there is less than a 19 percent chance that the investor will not meet the goal of a comfortable retirement.

Shortfall Measure

The probability of failing to achieve the wealth target, while informative, is flawed as a risk measure. The reason is clear: Under this measure of risk, failing to make the wealth target by $1 is considered just as bad as failing to make it by $1,000. Obviously, the first case is not nearly as bad as the second. The measure of risk used to construct our glide path takes the magnitude of failure into account, and so, too, should a performance measure of risk. A well-specified measure is the expected shortfall penalty, or its square root, which is used as the risk measure in Figure 11.6. By design, the square root of the shortfall penalty is expressed in units of dollars. However, this measure has no simple intuitive meaning. An alternative measure of the magnitude of shortfall is its expected value when there is a failure to achieve the wealth target. Note that this is a conditional expected value of shortfall. It is different from the simple expected value of shortfall because it does not average in all the zero values of shortfall that occur in those scenarios where the wealth target is satisfied. Obviously, the smaller this number, the less the risk. For our glide path, this measure of risk is $4,630, which can be compared with the expected target wealth of $30,200.

These recommendations on measuring performance have been made in the context of forecasting the future performance of the glide path. However, the concepts also apply to performance evaluation of existing funds over historical time periods. Sensible comparisons of historical fund performance should, of course, take into account the target date. However, even if comparisons are among funds with similar target dates, there can be a serious problem if funds are compared using typical time-weighted returns. The equity/bond mix will primarily drive the relative performance among funds. The fact that Fund A has a glide path with more equity than that of Fund B over a period in which equity outperforms bonds really says nothing about the relative merits of the glide paths in terms of these investments doing their job of building wealth. The glide path does not reflect a manager's judgment on whether stocks will outperform bonds over a given horizon. It is just an aspect of a predetermined, long-range strategy aimed at building wealth.

In order to evaluate funds in the context of their intended purpose of building wealth, we need some measure of how a fund transforms savings into wealth. One approach is to assume a flow of savings over a period of a few years and then calculate the ending wealth generated by investing this savings flow into a fund.[6] This approach is not perfect, but it is an improvement over time-weighted return calculations.

Clearly, performance evaluation of target-date funds is a difficult issue. Investors and plan sponsors should consider these difficulties and not jump to conclusions when comparing funds based on historical performance.

PROVIDING FOR THE ATYPICAL INVESTOR

In order to design a glide path, we need assumptions about the savings behavior, the wealth target, and the attitude toward risk of a typical investor. Otherwise, there is no way to quantify the glide path and evaluate its performance. Through the use of the methodology we have described, we can have confidence in a good outcome for the typical investor. However, what happens if the investor is atypical? Is our glide path robust enough to provide a good investment solution for a variety of investors with different circumstances?

Probably the most common and important case of an atypical investor is one that is approaching middle age and has saved very little.[7] In our glide path model, we assume a 45-year-old new entrant into a 20-year target-date fund has been saving and investing for the past 20 years in a manner consistent with the first 20 years of our typical investor. If that is the case, the investor has accumulated significant wealth, and picking up in the "middle" of our glide path is the right strategy. However, what if the new entrant has materially less wealth? Will our glide path provide a good investment solution?

This question must be evaluated in realistic terms. A person who has not saved much at age 45 is unlikely to have as much at retirement as someone who has been following a disciplined savings and investment program since age 25. An example will provide some insight. Suppose that the low saver enters year 21 of our glide path with accumulated wealth that is only

60 percent of the expected wealth of the typical investor at that stage of life. As Figure 11.7 shows, such an investor's initial equity allocation will be 83 percent and will begin declining significantly each year. If this investor begins to save according to our assumptions, the chance of meeting the fund's wealth target is 53 percent. The expected shortfall when the target wealth is not achieved is around $5,060, which can be compared with an expected target wealth of $29,020.[8]

It is difficult to judge whether this is a good outcome for an investor in these circumstances. The attractiveness of this outcome compared with others available with alternative strategies depends on the investor's attitude toward risk. An alternative to our glide path is for the low saver to choose a riskier, more aggressive strategy with a high equity allocation that lasts for a number of years. For example, suppose the investor chooses an all-equity portfolio and holds it to retirement. The probability of success in meeting the fund's wealth target increases from 53 percent to 57 percent. However, the expected shortfall when the target is not achieved increases from $5,060 to $8,100. In sum, increasing investment risk above that implied by our recommended glide path slightly improves the odds of reaching the wealth target but increases the chances of a severe shortfall in retirement wealth.

Another alternative is to focus on our risk measures and follow a strategy that is more conservative than our recommended glide path, in effect accepting that achieving the wealth target is unlikely and trying to protect against a bad retirement outcome. What would such a conservative strategy look like? To answer this question, we designed an optimal target-date strategy specifically for the circumstances of this low saver, using the same risk criteria employed in designing our recommended glide path. This optimal strategy is more conservative, starting with an equity allocation of only 49 percent and ending with an equity allocation of only 8 percent. The probability of meeting the wealth target is only 36 percent, but the expected shortfall when the target is not reached is only $3,700.

Whether a low saver would prefer one of these alternatives to our recommended glide path depends on the person's willingness to take risk. We can say that our glide path provides a reasonable, middle-of-the-road solution for this atypical investor. It is by no reasonable standard a bad solution for someone in this situation, and, perhaps, this is the best that reasonably can be hoped for in a one-size-fits-all investment solution.

FROM GLIDE PATH TO TARGET-DATE FUND

Although the overall equity/fixed income mix embodied in the glide path is the single most important factor in determining the success of a target-date fund, other aspects of fund construction are also important. The first of these other aspects is the allocation of the portfolio among the various segments of the equity and bond markets. Sensible risk management and fundamental investment theory require broad diversification across these markets. In particular, the allocation should include exposure to all investable segments of both the U.S. and non-U.S. equity markets. Russell includes explicit exposure to small-cap U.S. stocks, real estate investment trusts, and emerging-markets equity through most of the glide path.[9] Likewise, Russell fixed-income exposure is broad, including most segments of the U.S. fixed income market. The precise allocation among asset-class segments for each point on the glide path is determined using standard portfolio optimization techniques that attempt to give the best risk/reward trade-off. In addition to constructing the best combination of currently available asset classes, Russell will continue to search for opportunities to extend exposure into other asset classes and additional segments of equity and fixed-income markets, and we will add them to the portfolios when they are viable in terms of accessibility and we believe they will serve to improve the risk/return characteristics of the portfolios.

The second aspect of Russell's portfolio construction is the intelligent use of active management in the asset classes. Russell's target-date funds invest in Russell's actively managed asset-class funds. For each of these underlying funds, Russell selects those whom it views as the best-of-breed managers from each category of manager investment style. It then combines these managers to produce fund returns intended to beat passive benchmarks with careful management of additional risk. The incremental return provided by active management—if successful—might have a meaningful impact on wealth at retirement in a long-term investment strategy, such as a target-date fund.

CONCLUSION

Target-date funds offer investors simple-to-use investment opportunities yet intelligent mechanisms for funding retirement. They provide them with an investment strategy designed to meet their needs. Although these funds cannot incorporate all the specifics of an individual's circumstances and desires in the way a customized financial plan can, they do provide a disciplined strategy that should work well in transforming consistent savings into wealth at retirement. Because of their simplicity and sound strategy, target-date funds can be particularly valuable as an option for defined contribution plans. They provide the best solution for investors who lack the knowledge to make complicated investment planning decisions or who do not want to take the time to manage their retirement investments.

Although target-date funds are attractive in concept, the details of the design and implementation of a fund determine its value as an investment strategy. The most important element of a fund's design is its equity glide path. A well-designed glide path should incorporate reasonable assumptions about savings, inflation, and capital market returns as well as a clearly specified investment target. This investment target should be linked in a clear way to the retirement spending needs of the fund owner. Investors and defined-contribution-plan sponsors should demand to know what assumptions stand behind glide paths. Otherwise, they are buying retirement savings black boxes that may be unsuitable for them or perhaps that are flawed in their basic design. In addition to a well-designed glide path, a target-date fund should have diversification across asset classes and sensible management within the asset classes.

ABOUT THE AUTHORS

Grant W. Gardner, PhD, received his doctorate in Economics from Harvard University in 1981. Prior to 1993, he was a university professor at the Fuqua School of Business at Duke University and at Southern Methodist University's Department of Economics. While at Duke for most of the 1980s, Grant was responsible for conducting research and teaching undergraduate, MBA, and executive-education courses in macroeconomics, international economics, international financial management, international business, and corporate finance.

Yuan-An Fan, PhD, received his doctorate in Operations Research from the University of Texas at Austin in 1985. Prior to 1992 he was a mathematical software designer with the Houston-based IMSL, Inc.

NOTES

1. The idea of incorporating human capital in portfolio decisions has a long tradition in the academic finance literature. The classic article is Robert Merton, "Optimum Consumption and Portfolio Rules in a Continuous-Time Model," *Journal of Economic Theory* 3, no. 4 (December 1971), 373–413. Other academic work in this area includes Z. Bodie, R. C. Merton, and W. F. Samuelson, "Labor Supply Flexibility and Portfolio Choice in a Life Cycle Model," *Journal of Economic Dynamics and Control* 16, nos. 3/4 (July/August 1992), 427–449 and R. Jagannathan and N. R. Kocherlakota, "Why Should Older People Invest

Less in Stocks Than Younger People?" *Federal Reserve Bank of Minneapolis Quarterly Review* 20, no. 3 (Summer 1996), 11–23. A recent application that includes life insurance as well as investment is P. Chen, R. G. Ibbotson, M. A. Milevsky, and Kevin X. Zhu, "Human Capital, Asset Allocation, and Life Insurance," *Financial Analysts Journal* 62, no. 1 (January/February 2006), 97–109. Thomas J. Fontaine, "Target-Date Retirement Funds: A Blueprint for Effective Portfolio Construction," Alliance Bernstein Global Investment Research (October 2005), applies the basic concepts of human capital to target-date glide-path design and recognizes the important effects of the timing of savings flow on the performance of a target-date fund glide path. This approach differs from our approach (and the approach generally used in incorporating human capital into investment decisions) in that it does not apply formal optimization techniques.

2. In the academic literature, human capital is typically defined as the present value of labor income rather than savings. In these models, consumption, saving, and investment strategy are determined simultaneously. In contrast, Russell's model is limited to investment strategy alone, implicitly taking saving and consumption as predetermined. In this framework that considers only portfolio construction, it is more appropriate to define human capital as the present value of the savings flows into the portfolio.

3. This result sheds light on some muddled thinking that often passes for conventional wisdom. It is sometimes stated that investors should hold more equity when they are young. Then, as they age, they should plan to switch to a more conservative portfolio. The reasoning is that when the investor is young, he or she has the opportunity to wait out the ups and downs of the equity market. However, as this example illustrates, the age of an investor in and of itself should not influence the mix of equity in the portfolio. The reason that young people should typically hold a lot of equity is not because they can afford to wait for market ups and downs, it is because their future savings will be available to make up for any early market losses. This logic will be explained shortly. For details on good and bad explanations of why young people should hold equity see Jagannathan and Kocherlakota (see note 1).

4. See the Aon Consulting/Georgia State University, "Replacement Ratio Study: A Measurement Tool for Retirement Planning," Aon Consulting (2004), 10. The 42 percent replacement rate corresponds to a preretirement income of $80,000.

5. The annuity factor varies by age and sex. For a given age, the annuity factor is greater for women than for men. For individuals of the same sex, the annuity factor declines with age. The choice of a 65-year-old male gives an annuity factor that is in the middle of the range of annuity factors for individuals of both sexes between ages 60 and 70. In that sense, it represents the typical retiree.

6. An interesting initial attempt in measuring performance this way is described in Mark Labovitz, "Targeting Target Maturity Funds," Lipper Fund Industry Insight Report (2006).

7. We use the word *atypical* to designate an investor who does not behave in a manner consistent with the assumptions of our model. Sadly, demographic evidence suggests that this case is all too typical in the United States.

8. This expected target wealth is slightly different from that given earlier for the glide path. The reason for this difference is that, in calculating the results for the 20-year glide path we had to choose a beginning level of income, in effect resetting the income path. We chose to reset at the mean value of income at the beginning of the 21st year of the 40-year glide path.

9. Emerging markets equity is excluded from the asset allocation in the later years of the glide path when the overall allocation is primarily in fixed income and intended to have low volatility.

CHAPTER 12

Investment Aspects of Longevity Risk

Don Ezra, Co-chair, Global Consulting, Russell Investments

Authors' note: In this white paper, Don identifies the disadvantages to the individual who is on his own versus being a member of a pension plan or owning an annuity. The key insight he provides is that once the individual has lost his ability to pool longevity risk, deferring annuitization as long as possible is crucial because the cost of annuitization is high, not only because of the expense, but also due to the loss of control and flexibility over one's assets. The individual's inability to pool their longevity risk is the seminal issue that led us to the development of the personal asset liability model discussed in Chapter 5.

This article first appeared as a Russell Research Viewpoint in February 2008, published by Russell Investments. It was written for those who, understanding investments fully, including swaps and derivatives, want to translate longevity risk into investment terms. The original article also contained a theoretical discussion of longevity derivatives that is not included in this version.

WHY LONGEVITY RISK NEEDS TO BE UNDERSTOOD

When I turned 60, I started to think about postretirement income. Until then, my financial planning thoughts were solely about building wealth. Now I'm wondering about life beyond work. Will I be able to afford to retire?

A wise colleague helped me to get my thinking process started. He explained that during one's working career, one's focus is on accumulating wealth. One's time horizon is the approximate number of years until one's projected retirement date. It isn't necessary to get the time horizon exactly right. The trade-off is between higher expected wealth (good news) and higher uncertainty of wealth (bad news, because it can result in low wealth).

After retirement, wealth is no longer the yardstick. Rather, income becomes the yardstick. The trade-off is now between higher expected income (good news) and higher uncertainty of income (bad news, because it can result in low income). However, now it is no longer acceptable to have an approximate time horizon for planning. The time horizon extends until one's death—and that is unpredictable. In fact, there are now two risks, as one draws down one's assets. How large will the return on the remaining assets be? How long will the assets be needed? Low returns are bad news, just as they were before retirement. However, now longevity is also bad news. (Not psychologically or from the perspective of enjoying life, of course; but financially, because paying for longevity is undoubtedly a drain on wealth.)

I found my colleague's framing of the problem very helpful. It has had the beneficial effect of changing my terminology. He contrasted *accumulation* before retirement with *decumulation* after retirement. *Decumulation* means drawing down accumulated wealth for the rest of your life. I like the word. In fact, because it focuses on the financial side only, it's going to become my word of choice when people ask me about retirement. I'm not planning to retire.[1] I intend to keep working; it's my hobby. However, when my income from work declines or stops, I'll need to decumulate.[2] Good, that's settled.

I understand the risk inherent in investing. I have an intuitive idea about different asset classes, and about expected returns and the approximately normal distributions of returns and standard deviations and correlations. However, I don't have the same intuitive feeling about this new risk, longevity.

I found an old mortality table[3] for retired people. It told me that the life expectancy of a 60-year-old male is approximately 19 more years. That's a good start, I thought. I can find a more up-to-date table, and check with my doctor, and so on; but at least I now have an order of magnitude for roughly how long I can expect to live. But ... that's just an expectation—like saying that one expects a return of 10 percent per annum on equities. How about the range of uncertainty? To my surprise, I found that the concept of the standard deviation of one's life expectancy is an unknown notion to most people, even financial planners. In fact, some people didn't even understand the concept. "How can you have a standard deviation? You're either dead or alive. When you die, that's it. That will tell you what your longevity is. It's just one number."

Yes, of course. In just the same way when one looks back, one has experienced only a single rate of return over one's lifetime of investing. However, when one looks forward, there's uncertainty. In the same way, looking forward, 19 years might be the average number of years that a group of 60-year-old males will continue to live; but they'll all live for different lengths of time. Their ages at death will form a distribution. How wide is that distribution? That's what the standard deviation of life expectancy measures.

So I did the calculation myself. I used the mortality table to project how many would die after living one year, how many after living two years, and so on. That produced the distribution. Then the standard deviation followed.

I asked five people what they thought the standard deviation might be, in round numbers. One year? Five years? Ten? Longer? Three of the five people thought 5 years, one thought 10, one 15. It turned out to be roughly 9 years. (One colleague, an actuary, clearly had the right mindset. He said: "A few will live to 100. Let's say that's a two-standard-deviation event. If the average age at death is 79, then 21 more years will be roughly two standard deviations. So, in round numbers, I'd say: 10 years is the standard deviation.")

Two things surprised me through all of this. One is that the distribution is extremely wide. Plot the proportion of deaths at each age and you get a distribution far wider and far less peaked than the typical equity distributions we are used to. That suggests that longevity could be a bigger risk than low returns. I have been unwilling to be 100 percent in equities, because I don't like the low end of the distribution. Logically, shouldn't I be much more risk-averse about longevity?

Another way to interpret the width of this particular longevity distribution is to note that its standard deviation is, in round numbers, about 45 percent of the expectancy. That's much more than twice as wide as the typical one-year equity distribution. Think of a 60-year-old male decumulator as starting off with a particular expectancy; he could lose 100 percent of it if he dies early, or gain an additional 100 percent of it if he outlives that expectancy by two standard deviations. Yes, this is a wider range of uncertainty than we're used to considering in traditional investment terms.

The other surprising thing is how wrong my admittedly small sample of friends turned out to be in their estimates of the standard deviation of longevity. One was right; three were 50 percent too low; one was 50 percent too high. Imagine the same range when considering the standard deviation of equity returns. Let's say it's roughly 16 percent per annum. Imagine thinking that it's only 8 percent (too low by half). Or that it's 24 percent (too high by half). We would make completely inappropriate asset-allocation decisions if our estimates of the standard deviation were 50 percent off the mark. Yet that may be the state of affairs with the uncertainty of longevity. If we don't have a rough, intuitive idea of how large the uncertainty is, we'll make decisions that are totally inappropriate.

I think financial planning for decumulation requires us to understand longevity risk just as deeply as we understand return risk.

LOOKING AT LONGEVITY DISTRIBUTIONS

Because a picture is purportedly worth a thousand words, let's start with a picture of a longevity distribution.

I replaced the out-of-date table I originally had with the most up-to-date one I could find: the RP-2000 table, required by the IRS for use in certain pension-fund calculations.[4] This table has a number of components. The survival rates I focused on are those for "healthy annuitants."

Figure 12.1 shows, for a large group of males of various ages, the proportions that are projected to die after one year, two years, and so on, according to RP-2000.

Several aspects of Figure 12.1 are worth noting.

- The curves look almost normally distributed, for those ages.
- There is a right-hand tail, because a very few are expected to survive to extreme old age. However, the distributions clearly don't have a left-hand tail, because at those starting ages a noticeable proportion of the group is expected to die within the first year. There would be a left-hand tail if the starting age were very young, because relatively few die young.

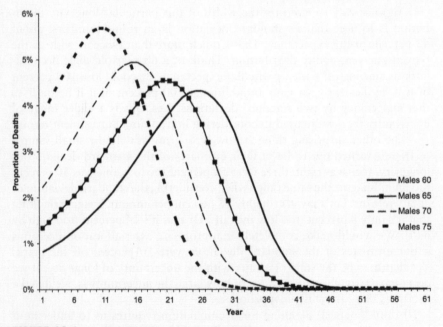

FIGURE 12.1 Longevity Distributions for Males

■ Although RP-2000 projects a few survivors to age 120, in reality virtually no males aged 60 are expected to survive for more than about 45 more years, nor males aged 75 for about 30 more years—that is, beyond age 105.

These curves are flatter than the one-year distributions we're accustomed to seeing for equity returns. Assuming a standard deviation of 16 percent per annum, the equity return distribution peaks at about a 10 percent proportion on the vertical axis; that is, it's much steeper than these longevity curves, implying a tighter distribution. Of course, a typical one-year bond-return distribution would be even tighter and more peaked than an equity-return distribution. (More about the comparison between investment uncertainty and longevity uncertainty in a moment.)

Figure 12.2 shows the patterns for women. The patterns are identical to those in Figure 12.1, although of course the careful reader will notice that the numbers are different.

Typically, financial planning for decumulation involves a couple rather than a single person, and has as its goal that the income is required to last (although perhaps at a lower level) as long as the second-to-die of the

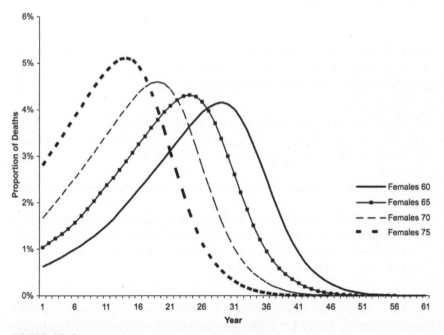

FIGURE 12.2 Longevity Distributions for Females

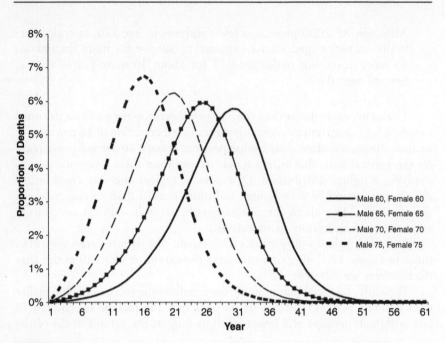

FIGURE 12.3   Longevity Distributions for Second Death, Males and Females

couple survives. So it might be interesting to see the longevity curves for the second-to-die of a couple. That's in Figure 12.3.

Observations on Figure 12.3:

- Once again the general shape of the curve is unaltered.
- This time the curves do seem to start very close to 0 percent on the left-hand side, because the chance that both partners will die early is small.
- The curves do stretch a little further to the right, the careful reader will notice.
- Because of the lower starting point on the left, the curves appear to be a little bit more concentrated in the middle than are the curves for males and females separately. This is confirmed in Table 12.1, which shows numerical summary statistics.

The standard deviations for second-to-die combinations are typically smaller than for single lives, because the curves are pushed closer to the right-hand end of the distributions; but the right-hand ends are all forced by

TABLE 12.1 Average Life Expectancies and Standard Deviations in Years*

Male Age	Expectancy	Std Dev
60	21.6	9.1
65	17.6	8.2
70	13.9	7.2
75	10.6	6.1

Female Age	Expectancy	Std Dev
60	24.2	9.9
65	20.1	9.0
70	16.2	8.1
75	12.7	7.1

Second-to-Die Combinations Male/Female Age	Expectancy	Std Dev
60/60	28.4	7.4
65/60	26.8	7.8
65/65	23.9	7.0
70/65	22.3	7.3
70/70	19.5	6.6
75/70	18.1	6.8
75/75	15.5	6.0

*Calculated from RP-2000 tables for healthy annuitants.

the RP-2000 tables to stop by age 120. Hence, the slight squashing affect, resulting in lower standard deviations.

Because the distributions aren't symmetrical, the standard deviations themselves are far from perfect representations of the width of the distributions—although their relative sizes do seem to capture the main characteristic of how wide the distributions are.

ANALYSIS OF THE RISK OF A FIXED IMMEDIATE ANNUITY

So far, I have let the impression remain that longevity distributions are typically wider than investment return outcome distributions. For example, in Table 12.1 the standard deviations range from roughly 25 percent to over 50 percent of the corresponding expectancies. However, it doesn't necessarily follow that longevity gives rise to more financial uncertainty than does investing in equities, for two reasons.

First, the equity distribution I've been referring to is a distribution of possible dollar outcomes if one holds equities for one year. We really need to use a multiyear distribution, because it's the rest of one's life that is relevant. That would be much wider, in dollar terms, than the one-year distribution. Second, the longevity curve shows the distribution of deaths, not a distribution of financial outcomes. Like life itself, longevity is a backdrop that frames a number of contingencies.[5] Longevity is uncertain, and its uncertainty leads to problems that can be at least partly solved by financial instruments (like insurance and annuity products). Those financial instruments give rise to outcomes, which, because the length of life is uncertain, are themselves uncertain. It is the uncertainty of the financial outcomes from longevity-related instruments that can be compared directly with the uncertainty of investment in equities over a period of several years.

The longevity-related financial instrument I considered is a fixed immediate annuity. Given the extension of the word *annuity* to cover a wide variety of products, let me define what I mean by a *fixed immediate annuity*. It's a contract under which you pay a lump sum to an insurance company, in exchange for which the insurance company pays you a regular fixed income for as long as you live.

Essentially, when you buy a fixed immediate annuity, you're doing a swap with the insurance company. You're swapping your longevity for the longevity built into whatever table the insurance company is using. You pay a lump sum to the insurance company equal to the present value of payments over the standard longevity, and you receive periodic (typically monthly) payments for the duration of your own longevity, whatever that turns out to be. Just as one can do an interest-rate swap, exchanging fixed interest rate payments for variable interest rate payments, so, too, one can do a longevity swap, exchanging fixed longevity for variable longevity.

(Because you pay your lump sum in advance and receive periodic payments later, you also expose yourself to counterparty risk, that is, the risk that the insurance company won't survive long enough to meet its obligations to you.)

Figure 12.4 shows this conceptually. You pay a lump sum equal to the present value of $100,000 per annum declining over time at the pace shown by the standard-longevity curve. You receive $100,000 per annum for as long as you live, which in Figure 12.4 is assumed to be another 22 years. If you live for a shorter period, the line labeled "your longevity" would fall to zero, further to the left. If you live for a longer period, that line would continue at $100,000 to some point further to the right, before again falling to zero.

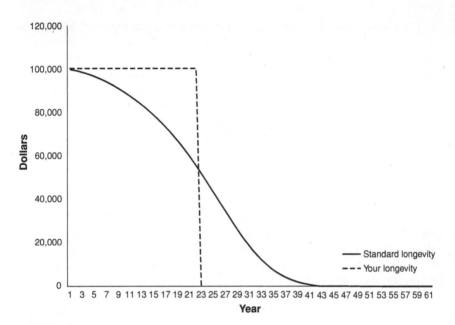

FIGURE 12.4   Immediate Annuity = Longevity Swap

The insurance company doesn't particularly care how long you survive. It expects that, with a sufficiently large group of purchasers of these contracts, and with the margin it has built into standard longevity by shifting the curve further to the right than it actually expects it to be, and with the expense and profit loadings it has built into the lump sum calculations, it will make a satisfactory profit over the long term. Those who die early effectively subsidize those who die late and generate profits for the insurance company.

Consider a lot of people (a cohort, as actuaries call them) who are all males aged 75. (I chose that age because their life expectancy is approximately 10 years.) How much would they pay for a fixed immediate annuity? To simplify my calculations, I ignored profit margins and expense loadings and discounted the RP-2000 longevity curve at an annualized interest rate of 6 percent. I made the further simplifying assumptions that annuity payments would be made at the start of each year, and that predicted deaths occurred at the end of each year, immediately before each policyholder received the annuity payment for the next year.

The purchase price for an annuity of $1 per annum then turned out to be $7.81.

Someone who dies after one year receives a payment of $1. By the end of the year (when death, for purposes of this discussion, is assumed to take place), it is worth $1.06, assuming that the annuity payments can be accumulated at 6 percent per annum (or, which is the same thing, that their utility has a time value of 6 percent per annum). Someone who dies after two years receives two annual payments of $1, and their combined value at the time of death (at the end of the second year) is $1.06^2 + 1.06 = 2.184$.

Similarly, someone who dies after n years has 1.06 an accumulated value (or utility) of $1.06^{(n)} + 1.06^{(n-1)} + \cdots + 1.06 = (1.06) \times [1.06^n - 1]/.06$.

In this way, I generated a distribution of cumulative amounts received, the probability or frequency associated with each of these amounts being given by the frequency distribution of deaths according to RP-2000.

The mean of this distribution is $18.31, and its standard deviation is $13.93. The "coefficient of variation" of the distribution is the ratio of the standard deviation to the mean. In this case it is $13.93/18.31 = 0.76$. (Essentially, this answers the question, "For each unit of mean reward, how uncertain was the outcome?")

Suppose, now, for comparative purposes, that this is one of two hypothetical worlds. In this world, returns are fixed (everyone gets 6 percent per annum) and longevity is variable. For my cohort of 75-year-old males, then, their longevity uncertainty generates a coefficient of variation of 0.76.

Consider, now, a second hypothetical world. In this world, longevity is fixed (the entire cohort lives for, say, 10 years), but investment returns are uncertain. For example, the cohort invests in fixed income and receives returns that, each year (and with no serial correlation across the years), come from a normal distribution with mean 6 percent and standard deviation 8 percent. In the second world, we have a distribution of amounts received at the end of 10 years. What is the coefficient of variation of this distribution? Answer: 0.24.[6]

This is much smaller than the 0.76 that resulted in the first hypothetical world. The interpretation, then, is that longevity uncertainty makes buying a fixed immediate annuity (for this group of 75-year-old males) a much riskier proposition than investing in fixed income for 10 years.

Suppose, in a variant of the second world, that the cohort invested instead in equities, characterized by an annual mean and standard deviation of 9 percent and 16 percent, respectively. What, then, is the 10-year coefficient of variation? Answer: 0.49.

This, too, is much smaller than the 0.76 that resulted in the first world. The interpretation is that longevity uncertainty makes buying a fixed immediate annuity (for these 75-year-old males) riskier than investing in equities for 10 years.

Experiments along these lines suggest that a coefficient of variation for equity investing has a high slope. It increases rapidly as the investment horizon increases. In contrast, the coefficient of variation for longevity uncertainty in a fixed immediate annuity has a smaller slope. For a cohort of males age 60, for example, 22 years of equity investing would be riskier than buying an annuity (if you accept my input assumptions, of course).

Here's another way of looking at this: the older you are, the riskier the annuity becomes, relative to 100 percent equity investing.[7,8] Yet, paradoxically, this can be interpreted in still another way: the older you are, the greater the value of the protection that the annuity gives you! In fact, this simply says that the older you are, the more the annuity is characterized by its long right-hand tail.

That says nothing about how valuable the right-hand tail is to you. A simple thought experiment allows us to see why this is so. Think of two people who have identical longevity distributions ahead of them but dramatically different amounts of wealth. Imagine, for example, that Warren Buffet has an identical twin with just enough money to be able to decumulate for a period equal to his remaining life expectancy. For Warren Buffet, the chance of outliving his wealth is essentially zero, so the right-hand-tail protection given by the annuity has virtually no utility. In fact, the chance of dying early and losing all his wealth, if he were to invest everything in a fixed immediate annuity, would presumably be a horrifying risk. For his imaginary twin, though, the fear of outliving his savings might be horrifying, and thus the longevity protection from the annuity might be enormously appealing.

Both twins face the same probability distribution from buying an annuity, but, clearly, the utilities attached to the presumed different outcomes vary enormously.

For most of us, investing all of our assets in equities is beyond our risk tolerance. The time-honored way to counter longevity risk is, of course, to buy a fixed immediate annuity. Should this also be beyond the risk tolerance of most of us? Or are there situations in which the favorable aspects of the annuity outweigh the risk? Let's look at this in a little more detail.

THE DESIRABLE FEATURE OF FIXED IMMEDIATE ANNUITIES

The desirable feature, of course, is the right-hand-tail protection. We can calculate roughly how big a benefit this is.

Suppose you live in a country with effectively no immediate annuity market.[9] Suppose you know how much you propose to spend each year for the rest of your life (and, to simplify the illustration, suppose your annual expenditures will stay constant forever). You can make a best estimate of the return you'll receive from, say, an investment in fixed income. Knowing your life expectancy, you can calculate the lump sum you would need to have today in order to decumulate over a period equal to your life expectancy. For example, for a hypothetical male age 60 (whom we'll call, without loss of generality, Don), an annual expenditure of $1 would require a lump sum of $12.04 to provide for decumulation over 22 years, if his annual fixed income return is 6 percent.

Of course, if $12.04 is all he has, it's pretty much a 50/50 proposition whether Don or his lump sum will expire first. That's not much comfort. Suppose, then, Don decides that he wants two standard deviations' worth of protection. Looking at Table 12.1, this means that Don needs enough to decumulate over a period of 21.6 + (2 x 9.1) = 40 years, roughly. Now Don needs $15.05 instead of $12.04. That's 25 percent more.

Obviously the additional amount varies with age and with fixed income returns assumed. For example, if Don wants to spend $1 each year in real rather than nominal terms, and if the fixed-income return provides a real annual return of 3 percent, then Don needs an additional 50 percent rather than 25 percent. And if Don wants enough for the money to last indefinitely and in real terms, invested in fixed income, then Don needs $33.33. That's almost 3 times as much as the initial estimate of $12.04.

It's clear that the ability to do a swap with an insurance company, and pay only enough to decumulate over your expectancy, is potentially a very valuable feature.[10]

HOW LARGE AN ANNUITY DO YOU NEED, AND ARE THERE OTHER SOLUTIONS?

As far as the left-hand tail of my longevity distribution is concerned, it's very important for me to avoid it. I don't want to lose (or want my heirs to lose) my capital once I lose my life, if I should happen to die early. How do I avoid this risk?

With market investments, if a risk is too big to tolerate, the response is simple: Diversify.

For example, I like the potential reward from equities. That's why I invest in them. However, I don't like the potential downside. It's important for me to cut out or, at any rate, reduce the chance of losing, say, 10 percent in a given year. So I reduce the potential downside by combining equity investments with fixed income investments.

What does diversification do? It greatly reduces the chance of a big downside. In exchange, of course, it also greatly reduces the chance of a big upside, but I'm happy with that trade-off. An unexpected *good* return is enough to keep me happy. I don't absolutely need an *extreme* upside. It's not essential to my purpose. So I sacrifice it and I'm happy with the downside reduction.

However, that's not how I view longevity risk. I can't say, "I don't mind giving up the extreme right-hand tail of the distribution, it's not part of my purpose." It is *precisely* my purpose! I can't say, "That's okay, I'm happy to decumulate until I'm 95 or 100, I don't need money beyond that age." If I live beyond that age, I *do* need financial protection; I *do* need money—right up to my last breath. Living with zero income is not just scary; it's a killer—literally.

One possibility, of course, is that a decumulator has so much wealth that there's no chance of outliving that accumulated wealth. In that case, longevity doesn't present a problem.

So let's consider that Don doesn't have that much wealth. He has enough to provide full decumulation for his desired lifestyle for some years, but not indefinitely. Then, longevity does present a potential problem.

Given that he doesn't want the extreme left-hand tail of the longevity distribution to take away his capital as well as his life but that he still needs the protection an annuity gives against the extreme right-hand tail, can he diversify?

Yes, if he is willing to tolerate the possibility that his investments won't fare well. He can estimate what he needs in order to live not his desired lifestyle, but a tolerable lifestyle in extreme old age. He can buy an annuity to protect his tolerable lifestyle. And he can then invest the rest of his wealth in whatever form he is comfortable with.

ACKNOWLEDGMENTS

I thank Craig Ansley, Robert Collie, Richard Fullmer, Michael Hall, Shailesh Kshatriya, Steven Murray, Steven Schubert, and Craig Wainscott for their extremely helpful input at many stages of my thinking.

NOTES

1. This pleases my wife. She doesn't want me at home all day long. She says, "I married you for better or for worse, but not for lunch."

2. Simple observation suggests that some start to decumulate long before their income starts to decline.

3. Actuaries talk about *mortality,* meaning "dying." Ever since I turned 60, I've greatly preferred the word *longevity,* meaning "living long." If actuaries were to talk of *longevity tables* and *longevity risk*, the profession could be associated with positive rather than negative concepts. It wouldn't go all the way to creating a warm and fuzzy image for the profession, but it would be a start. Also, I interpret the phrase *longevity improvement* as being positive, psychologically, but I'm much less sure about the ambiguous phrase *mortality improvement.*

4. And it added 2.6 years to my life expectancy!

5. For me, this notion is forever captured by the wonderful title of an actuarial textbook that sounds more like a philosopher's story: *Life and Other Contingencies*, by P.F. Hooker and L.H. Longley-Cook (Cambridge University Press, 1953).

6. I derived this number from Monte Carlo simulations. I used 5,000 runs, each run consisting of 10 independent draws from a normal distribution with mean 1.06 and standard deviation 0.08, and multiplied together the 10 draws to obtain the accumulated value of $1 at the end of 10 years. The 5,000 runs generated 5,000 outcomes; the coefficient of variation of these outcomes was 0.24.

7. A colleague points out that, instead of calculating the accumulated values of amounts received in the future, one could, alternatively, calculate their present values. Calculating present values has the intuitive appeal that all values are measured in the same units (today's dollars), and it results in expected values that are of the same order of magnitude as fixed annuity purchase prices. Of course, this does not change the conclusion that, the older you are, the riskier the annuity becomes, relative to equity investing.

8. Another colleague points out that I have chosen a specific concept of risk here, involving the uncertainty of the distribution of dollar payoffs. Other concepts are possible and sensible. For example, a retiree may think of risk as the inability to sustain a stream of cash flows. Such a retiree would probably consider the annuity distinctly less risky than investing in equities or even in fixed income.

9. Like Australia.

10. Here's another way to think about the value of longevity protection. If Don lives 40 more years and draws his annuity for 40 years after paying only $12.04, the realized annualized internal rate of return on his transaction is 7.91 percent, rather than 6 percent on which the 22-year purchase price is based. This means that survival for two additional standard deviations generates an additional annual return of 1.91 percent for Don. If you believe that the equity premium is worth roughly 3 percent per annum, the annuity pays long-lived Don the equivalent of a 64 percent exposure to equities, without the volatility.

CHAPTER 13

Mismeasurement of Risk in Financial Planning—A Lesson in Risk Decomposition

Richard K. Fullmer, CFA

Authors' note: In this chapter Fullmer discusses the pervasive mismeasurement of risk in financial planning. He argues that the risk that should be focused on when planning for retirement income should be the risk of income shortfall rather than volatility of portfolio return. The total risk measurement he proposes is the product of the probability of shortfall times the magnitude of shortfall. In real life, this means that missing by an inch may matter less than missing by a mile.

Financial planning is complex. Modeling tools have proliferated as a way to help wade through the complexity and facilitate sound decision-making processes. The selection of the risk measure in these tools is all-important. Poor decisions can result if the risk measure is faulty or incomplete.

A BRIEF HISTORY OF FINANCIAL PLANNING TOOLS

Early attempts at financial planning models asked the individual to specify values to assume for important variables such as the rate of return on the portfolio and the rate of inflation. These assumptions would then be used to project forward the portfolio balance, after accounting for withdrawals taken from it to fund the individual's spending plan. Planners quickly realized that these deterministic models were wholly inadequate.

One problem was that the individual may have little knowledge with regard to the values that were reasonable to assume. Another problem was that the inherent nature of the capital markets meant that, even if reasonable values were selected, the future could—and certainly would—turn out quite differently than assumed. Yet another problem was that the success or failure of the financial plan was subject to path dependency. Even if the capital markets did deliver the assumed average rate of return over the planning period, the plan could still fail if the returns came about unevenly rather than smoothly. If returns were poor early and good late, the investor might run out of money in the middle of the planning period, before the market had a chance to recover. Deterministic models were dangerous because they did not measure risk, at least not in any comprehensive and meaningful way.

To address these shortcomings, deterministic models were replaced by probabilistic models. These typically used a technique called Monte Carlo simulation, which projects out numerous (hundreds or thousands) potential paths that could unfold over time for variables such as portfolio returns and inflation. Dividing the number of paths under which the plan fails by the total number of paths simulated gives the probability of failure. This was a significant improvement that could address all three of the problems described earlier.[1]

BEWARE THE RISK MEASURE

Simulation models are wonderful tools if used properly. Unfortunately, that is not always the case. Think about the purpose for using such a model in the first place. In the case of financial planning, it is to help individuals assess a suitable saving rate, retirement date, spending budget, investment strategy, and so on. Of course, this requires an understanding of the investor's risk tolerance as well as the risk of ruin inherent in the investor's financial plan.

This leads us to consider exactly what *risk* means in this context. How is it defined? Well, many financial planning tools define it as the probability that the plan may fail (e.g., that the individual runs out of money). The conventional guidance is that investors should plan using a low (e.g., 5 to 10 percent) probability of failure, although the suitable probability threshold for any particular individual will depend on his or her risk tolerance.

The problem with this definition and treatment is that the probability of failure is not a complete measure of risk. Just as not measuring risk can be dangerous, so, too, can mismeasuring it.

A BRIEF HISTORY OF PROBABILITY THEORY

The seventeenth-century mathematicians Blaise Pascal and Pierre de Fermat are widely regarded as the founders of probability theory. One might think that such a discovery would encourage the inventors to further their work to see what other interesting and useful things they might discover next. The effect of the discovery on Pascal, however, was quite different. He began to turn away from mathematics and toward philosophy. Why?

Pascal began his work on probability theory after receiving a most interesting and challenging puzzle from Antoine Gombaud, the Chevalier de Méré. The challenge went something like this: Suppose two players are in the middle of a game and have to stop play early, before the game is finished. Given the current situation of each player at the time, how should they divide the stakes?

The answer depends on each player's probability of winning at the time the game prematurely ends. At the time, no one knew how to calculate this.

After he and Fermat solved the Chevalier's puzzle, Pascal soon realized that its solving led to a remarkably profound thought. As useful as probability theory might be, it was not so much what it said but what it didn't say. The probability that an event might occur was an exceedingly useful thing to know, but it was only half of the story. The other half was the consequence of the event, should it actually occur.

With that thought, Pascal began to turn his mind from the subject of probability measurement to the subject of risk measurement and what it means in the context of living one's life. He realized that the consequences matter—sometimes a little and sometimes a lot. In other words, the magnitude of the consequences is an important element of risk measurement.

RISK DECOMPOSITION

Having now established that the probability of an event occurring and the magnitude of the consequences of it occurring are both important, the natural next question is, "Which is more important?" The answer is neither.

To see why, let's decompose risk in terms of these two factors. The decomposition goes like this:

$$\text{Total Risk} = \text{Probability} \times \text{Magnitude}$$

Risk is simply the product of the two—their importance is equal. An event with high probability and low magnitude may have an equivalent overall risk exposure as an event with low probability and high magnitude.

Consider the following example. Insurance companies are in the business of risk transfer. They agree to accept certain risks in exchange for a premium payment. How much is the risk transfer worth?[2] The answer is revealed by the formula. It is a function of the probability of claims occurring and the potential magnitude of claims that occur. More specifically, it can be found by multiplying the frequency by which claims may occur (the probability) by the potential size of the claims that may occur (the magnitude).[3]

Here is another example. Say that the fine for a speeding ticket is $100 when the driver's speed is less than 15 miles per hour over the speed limit and $1,000 when the driver's speed is more than 15 miles per hour over the speed limit. You plan to drive on a road for which the posted speed limit is 50 miles per hour. Clearly, the risk to you of driving 67 miles per hour on this road is much greater than the risk of driving 63 miles an hour. This is true even if the probability of getting caught is exactly the same.

Getting back to the topic of financial planning, models that measure only the probability of failure ignore one side of the risk equation completely. This is not to say that Monte Carlo simulation should be scrapped. Simulation models actually lend themselves very well to proper risk measurement—if only the modeler takes care to measure both the probability of failure and the magnitude of the failure cases that occur. In this context, the magnitude is the total amount of desired spending and bequeathing that does not occur because the portfolio ran out of money—often referred to as shortfall.

Just as the insurer/insured both need to understand the total amount at risk when pricing/purchasing an insurance policy, so, too, does the individual investor need to understand the total amount at risk when making financial planning decisions. Thus, planning tools that use this type of risk measure . . .

Shortfall Risk = Probability of Shortfall

. . . have it wrong. A better risk measure is . . .

Shortfall Risk = Probability of Shortfall × Magnitude of Shortfall

Having said that, the probability statistic may be good enough as a quick check on whether a particular spending plan is reasonable. However, it is inadequate when it comes to actual decision making. In fact, the choice of risk measure can have a significant impact on financial-planning decisions, especially with regard to asset allocation.

ILLUSTRATIONS

The significance of the risk measure to financial planning can be illustrated by using Monte Carlo simulation and showing the results separately for each component of risk. The following hypothetical illustrations are for a retired investor planning at a 30-year horizon. Retirement spending is modeled as an inflation-indexed withdrawal rate from the portfolio. The horizontal axis displays selected withdrawal rates from 3 percent to 8 percent, in 0.25 percent increments. The vertical axis displays the risk measure. The risk of shortfall (running out of money) for five different asset allocations is then plotted. These allocations range from 20 percent equity to 100 percent equity, in 20 percent increments. The percentage of the portfolio not allocated to equity is invested in bonds. The magnitude of shortfall refers to the amount of desired spending that does not occur because the portfolio ran out of money.

Figure 13.1 plots the risk measure as the probability of shortfall. Notice the pattern of the asset allocation lines that cross over in the $4^{1}/_{2}$ to $5^{1}/_{2}$ percent range. Conservative portfolios have an unambiguously lower probability of failure at the lower withdrawal rates to the left of the crossover range. Aggressive portfolios have an unambiguously lower probability of failure at the higher withdrawal rates to the right of the crossover range—although,

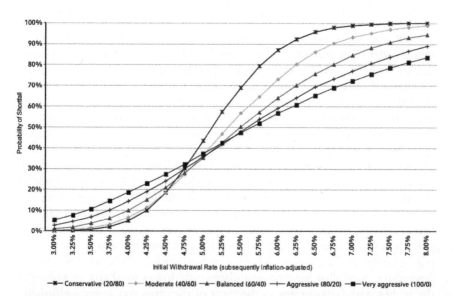

FIGURE 13.1   Probability of Failure (Shortfall), 30-Year Planning Horizon

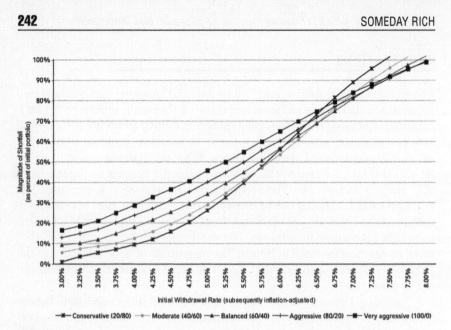

FIGURE 13.2   Magnitude of Failure (Shortfall), 30-Year Planning Horizon

at these withdrawal rates, the risk is quite high no matter what allocation is used.

Figure 13.2 plots the risk measure as the average magnitude of shortfall for cases in which a shortfall actually occurs. This chart reveals a similar pattern, but the crossover range occurs much further to the right and is much wider than under the probability-based measure. Here, the crossover occurs in the $5^3/_4$ to 8 percent range. Conservative portfolios have an unambiguously lower magnitude of failure at the lower withdrawal rates to the left of the crossover range. Aggressive portfolios have an unambiguously lower magnitude of failure at the higher withdrawal rates to the right of the crossover range—although, again, at these withdrawal rates, the risk is quite high no matter what allocation is used.

Figure 13.3 plots the risk measure as the holistic measure of total shortfall risk, computed as the probability of shortfall times the magnitude of shortfall.[4] Not surprisingly, this chart reveals the same type of pattern, and its crossover range occurs somewhere between the crossovers shown in Figures 13.1 and 13.2. Here, the crossover occurs in the 5 percent to $6^1/_2$ percent range. Conservative portfolios have an unambiguously lower total risk of failure at the lower withdrawal rates to the left of the crossover range. Aggressive portfolios have an unambiguously lower total risk of failure at the higher withdrawal rates to the right of the crossover range—although, as before, the risk is quite high no matter what allocation is used.

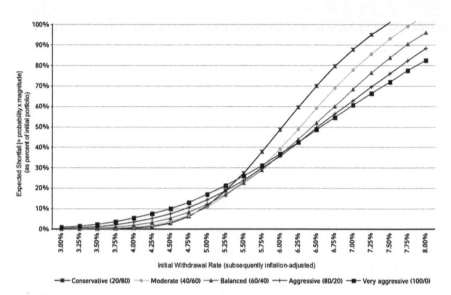

FIGURE 13.3 Total Failure Risk = Probability of Shortfall (×) Magnitude of Shortfall

Table 13.1 summarizes the data in these figures by showing the minimum-risk portfolio at each withdrawal rate under each risk measure. Here, *minimum risk* refers to the asset allocation (among the five allocations tested) with the lowest level of shortfall risk according to each risk measure.[5] At lower withdrawal rates, each risk measure points to the same conservative (20 percent equity) portfolio. At higher withdrawal rates, each risk measure points to the same aggressive (100 percent equity) portfolio. For the in-between withdrawal rates, however, different measures result in different portfolios.

For these in-between withdrawal rates, you can see that the probability measure can lead to an overly aggressive asset allocation decision because it does not consider the magnitude component of risk, which tends to be greater for more aggressive portfolios. On the other hand, the magnitude measure can lead to an overly conservative asset allocation decision because it does not consider the probability component of risk, which tends to be greater for more conservative portfolios (in this range of withdrawal rates). Only the total risk measure can help lend itself to an appropriate asset allocation decision.

For perspective, the last column in Table 13.1 shows the probability of failure for the portfolio identified as the minimum-risk portfolio under the total shortfall-risk measure. This shows that higher withdrawal rates are

TABLE 13.1 Minimum-Risk Portfolio by Withdrawal Rate and Risk Measure, in Percent

Initial Inflation— Adjusted Withdrawal Rate	Equity Allocation for the Portfolio That Has the Lowest . . .			Probability of Shortfall (PR) for Minimum Total-Risk (TS) Portfolio
	Probability of Shortfall (PR)	Magnitude of Conditional Shortfall (CM)	Expected Total Shortfall (TS) = PR × CM	
3	20	20	20	<1
3.25	20	20	20	<1
3.50	20	20	20	1
3.75	20	20	20	2
4	20	20	20	5
4.25	20	20	20	10
4.50	20	20	20	18
4.75	40	20	20	30
5	60	20	40	37
5.25	80	20	40	47
5.50	100	20	60	50
5.75	100	40	60	57
6	100	40	80	59
6.25	100	40	80	64
6.50	100	40	100	65
6.75	100	60	100	69
7	100	60	100	72
7.25	100	80	100	75
7.50	100	80	100	79
7.75	100	80	100	81
8	100	100	100	84

extremely risky, even under the minimum-risk portfolio. The risk level is also relatively high within the crossover range—the $4^3/_4$ percent withdrawal rate at the lowest end of the crossover range has a nearly 1-in-3 chance of failing.

IMPLICATIONS

By focusing solely on the probability component of risk, the full extent of the risk goes unmeasured. This is as true in financial planning as it is everywhere else in life. This mismeasurement of risk may lead the investor to select an inappropriate portfolio.

When measuring risk as the probability of failure, the asset allocation decision will typically err on the side of too aggressive. This is a direct result of ignoring the magnitude of failure. As in the speeding ticket example, if all risks (spending shortfalls or traffic fines) are treated the same regardless of their magnitude, then aggressive actions (higher equity allocations, higher driving speeds) will not appear as risky if the magnitude of the consequences is also considered.

This observation holds regardless of whether the investor is risk averse (and, therefore, interested in a low-risk portfolio/plan) or relatively risk tolerant (and, therefore, interested in a portfolio/plan with the potential to generate greater upside). It holds regardless of the investor's age, gender, marital status, retirement date, planning horizon. It holds regardless of whether the investor has bequest goals. It holds regardless of whether annuities and other insured products are considered in the asset-allocation decision. Getting the risk measure correct is vitally important.

METHODOLOGY DISCLOSURES

Figures 13.1–13.3 present data for a retired investor desiring a specific inflation-indexed annual rate of withdrawal for 30 years.

The risk of shortfall is shown using three different risk measures. *Shortfall* is defined as failing to achieve the desired withdrawals from the portfolio over the 30-year horizon.

Risk is defined in three ways:

1. Probability of shortfall (Figure 13.1): the number of failing scenarios divided by the total number of scenarios.
2. Average conditional magnitude of shortfall (Figure 13.2): the average of the shortfall amount for those scenarios that result in failure.
3. Expected total shortfall (Figure 13.3): the product of the probability of shortfall and the average conditional magnitude of shortfall.

A Monte Carlo simulation process is used to determine the probability and average conditional magnitude of shortfall by generating thousands of possible scenarios for portfolio returns, interest rates, and inflation. These simulations depicted in this article are created using the following broad-based asset-class return assumptions for equity returns, fixed-income returns, and inflation. They are hypothetical in nature and do not reflect

TABLE 13.2 Hypothetical Assumptions

	Expected Return, %	Standard Deviation, %	Correlations		
			Equity	Fixed Income	Inflation
Equity	8.5	15.4	1.00		
Fixed Income	6.0	5.5	0.25	1.00	
Inflation	3.0	4.0	0.16	0.15	1.00

actual investment results, and they are not guarantees of future results. The results may vary with use and over time. (See Table 13.2.)

It is important to remember that this process is based on assumptions that may not reflect the behavior of actual events. For example, Monte Carlo simulation may not fully account for certain rare and extreme market catastrophes that fall outside normal expectations.

A different set of assumptions would create a different probability distribution. Expert opinion regarding expected returns, volatility and market trends vary widely.

It is also important to note that the projections or other information generated by the Monte Carlo Simulator regarding the likelihood of various investment outcomes are hypothetical in nature, do not reflect actual investment results, and are not guarantees of future results. Other investments not considered may have characteristics similar or superior to those being analyzed.

Different methodologies will produce different results.

The portfolios were selected in increments of 20 percent exposure to equity, as follows:

Conservative: 20 percent allocation to equity 80 percent allocation to fixed income.

Moderate: 40 percent allocation to equity 60 percent allocation to fixed income.

Balanced: 60 percent allocation to equity 40 percent allocation to fixed income.

Aggressive: 80 percent allocation to equity 20 percent allocation to fixed income.

Very Aggressive: 100 percent allocation to equity.

The following asset classes are included in the Monte Carlo analysis:

■ **Equities:** Investment in stocks. Stock represents ownership and control in a corporation and may pay dividends as well as appreciate in value. The value of a stock will rise and fall in response to the activities of the company that issued them, general market conditions, and economic conditions.

■ **Fixed Income:** A government, municipal, or corporate bond that pays a fixed rate of interest until the bond matures; or a preferred stock that pays a fixed dividend. Bond investors should carefully consider risks such as interest rate risk, reinvestment risk, call risk, and default risk.

NOTES

1. Of course, no model of the future is perfect. Probabilistic models are still subject to forecasting error, sampling error, and so on.
2. In other words, "What is the actuarial price of the risk exposure?" For a variety of reasons, this price may be different than the premium actually charged by the insurance company—the need to also cover operating expenses is one reason.
3. Technically, the risk equation should consider the entire set of potential claim sizes along with the corresponding probability that each claim size may occur. The magnitude component of risk, then, is best measured as a probability distribution rather than a single average number. The magnitude component is, of course, conditional on a claim actually occurring. To be more accurate, then, we could write:

$$\text{Total Risk of Loss} = \text{Probability of Loss} \times \text{Conditional Probability}$$

$$- \text{Weighted Magnitude of Loss}$$

   Technicalities aside, the point being made here is simply that claim size is just as important as claim probability. The concept holds true of any situation in which risk is to be measured.
4. This value is also known as the expected shortfall, because it represents the mean probability-weighted amount of shortfall in the plan.
5. If all possible asset allocations were tested, the minimum-risk portfolio at the lowest withdrawal rates would be a 100 percent TIPS (Treasury Inflation-Protected Securities) portfolio that is duration matched to the required future cash flows.

CHAPTER 14.

Modern Portfolio Decumulation*

A New Strategy for Managing Retirement Income

Richard K. Fullmer, CFA

Author's note: This white paper by Fullmer is a logical extension of his mismeasurement of risk work from Chapter 13. The key thought here is that the conventional standard for accumulation of wealth is not optimal for decumulation. Besides just identifying that, he comes up with an alternative approach for investing in the decumulation phase, making the case for using a dynamic asset-allocation methodology in this phase of the investor's life.

EXECUTIVE SUMMARY

This chapter outlines a strategy to improve the ability to obtain a stable and steady stream of distributions for life from a retirement portfolio and at the same time fund future wealth goals, such as for gifts and bequests.

Typically, planners suggest managing longevity risk either by annuitization or in the spending plan (by reducing spending in the event of poor market performance or outliving the plan). This chapter proposes an alternative method for managing it in the investment portfolio.

---

*Reprinted with permission by the Financial Planning Association, *Journal of Financial Planning*, August 2007, Richard K. Fullmer, "Modern Portfolio Decumulation: A New Strategy for Managing Retirement Income." For more information on the Financial Planning Association, please visit www.fpanet.org or call 1–800–322–4237.

Conventional approaches often fail to properly define the investment problem. To be effective, it is important to fully address longevity risk and use appropriate and complete measures of risk and risk aversion. For this problem, modern portfolio theory is an inadequate framework for portfolio construction.

A new multiple-period, cash-flow-based investment framework is described that incorporates a dynamic asset allocation strategy and uses the cost of lifetime annuitization as a hurdlefor managing longevity risk in the portfolio.

By transforming longevity risk into investment risk and actively managing it in the investor's portfolio rather than in the spending plan, this approach is particularly useful for investors with a strong desire to maintain a given standard of living.

* * *

This chapter describes a new framework for efficient portfolio construction in the decumulation phase of the investment lifecycle, in which an investor who has accumulated assets over time wishes to use those assets to fund ongoing living expenses. It combines elements of both investment theory and actuarial science, introducing an effective way to manage longevity risk in the portfolio.

Most retirees have two financial goals: funding consumption and retaining wealth. Consumption goals may be specified in terms of purchasing power (monthly amounts to be adjusted for inflation). The amount needed from the portfolio to fund the consumption goal in any time period is equal to that period's consumption goal less the amount of income available from other sources, such as Social Security, pensions, and part-time work.

Wealth goals are amounts desired in the portfolio beyond those needed to fund consumption. Gifts and bequests are examples.

The consumption and wealth goals compete for the same resources in that the investor's portfolio must fund both. Once the demands of these goals and the degree of emphasis that the retiree places on them have been determined, the task is to determine how to allocate the portfolio to achieve them.

APPROACHES TO MANAGING LONGEVITY RISK

It is common to categorize approaches to managing longevity risk in terms of insured annuitization or self-annuitization. The former involves the transfer of risk to an insurance company, whereas the latter involves systematic withdrawals from an investment portfolio. Here, the term *annuitization* refers to insured-annuitization through the purchase of an immediate fixed (or inflation-adjusted) annuity. Annuitization essentially decumulates assets immediately by irrevocably exchanging them for a future stream of payments. Such an exchange means the assets are no longer available to fund wealth goals or unexpected expenditures that may occur.

Annuitization transfers longevity risk to a third party. However, a systematic withdrawal plan offers no such transfer. Thus, formulas are often suggested for reducing future spending in the event of poor markets or unexpectedly high inflation. This amounts to managing longevity risk through *spending* management. This approach sacrifices the investor's standard of living in the event of poor market returns.

Another approach is available, however: managing longevity risk through *portfolio* management. In this approach, it is the portfolio, rather than the investor's standard of living, that responds to market performance and economic conditions.

Understanding that annuitization offers insurance against living too long leads us to consider these classic guiding principles for making insurance decisions:

- Never risk more than you can afford to lose.
- Do not buy insurance that you do not need.

A logical conclusion is to annuitize when you need to, but not before. This concept plays an important role in the framework that follows. Before describing this framework, however, a review of conventional approaches highlights key issues that we must first address.

Conventional approaches to meeting a retiree's consumption and wealth goals are commonly derived from existing models for wealth accumulation, such as Harry Markowitz's breakthrough paper describing efficient portfolio construction using mean-variance optimization. Although modern portfolio theory may serve the industry well for those saving for the future, it falls short as a methodology for decumulation. The purpose of accumulation is to acquire wealth; the purpose of decumulation is to achieve lifetime cash flows from the portfolio. Traditionally, modern portfolio theory:

- Assumes no cash flows, which are the retiree's primary investment objective.
- Ignores the investor's risk aversion for failure to achieve the cash flows.
- Incorporates a single-period framework. However, decumulation is a multiple-period investment problem because the required cash flows are periodic and ongoing.
- Uses an inadequate definition and measure of risk (the standard deviation of return).
- Assumes a known time horizon, but the retiree's time horizon is unknown.

To achieve lifetime income from a portfolio, the financial planning methodology and the investment framework must address these shortcomings. Specifically, they must fully address longevity risk, avoid the fallacy of time diversification of risk, measure risk completely, and account for the investor's aversion to cash-flow risk.

A plan for systematic withdrawal from a portfolio cannot eliminate longevity risk. A common approach for dealing with this is to select a drop-dead date that the investor is statistically unlikely to reach. Then, a methodology such as Monte Carlo simulation is used to determine the likelihood that a spending and investing plan will last to that date.

Using this approach, longevity risk derives from two sources:

1. Running out of money during the selected time horizon (because the assumptions did not turn out in reality as planned).
2. Running out of money after the selected time horizon (because the investor outlived the drop-dead date).

If longevity risk is managed in the spending plan, the portfolio need not deal with it. However, if it is managed in the portfolio, the investment model must fully account for it.

A DIFFERENT MEASURE OF RISK

A common misunderstanding in financial planning is that time diversifies risk. It does not. When risky assets are included in a portfolio, risk always increases with time and this effect is magnified in decumulating portfolios.

Yet it is common to use either historic or projected portfolio returns over long time horizons to show how risky portfolios *appear* suitable over long holding periods. Figure 14.1 shows hypothetical average annualized real returns for a 60 percent equity/40 percent bond portfolio (see Table 14.1 for assumptions).

Because the range of outcomes narrows over time, Figure 14.1 seems to show that risk decreases with longer time horizons. However, this conclusion is wrong. The problem here is a flaw of averages. Figure 14.1, although interesting, does not convey the risk. It is not *average* return that matters but *cumulative* return. Cumulative returns directly measure changes in wealth.

Figure 14.2 shows cumulative real returns for the same scenario as Figure 14.1. Although the standard deviation of average returns decreases over time, the standard deviation of cumulative returns increases over time. Should there be no cash flow into or out of the portfolio over the time horizon, the asset balance will show the same pattern as the cumulative return, as shown in Figure 14.3.

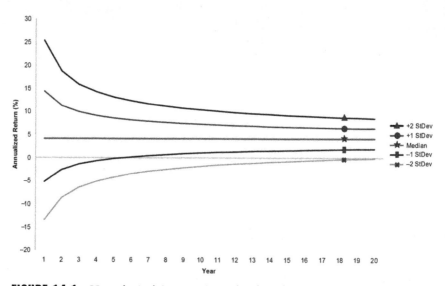

FIGURE 14.1 Hypothetical Average Annualized Real Returns

Figures 14.2 and 14.3 together show that the standard deviation of cumulative return is a suitable measure of risk for lump-sum investment portfolios (where no cash flows are involved). As shown in the two charts, the investor's level of wealth is directly tied to the cumulative return. This explains why traditional wealth-based portfolio construction models use the standard deviation of cumulative return to measure risk.

However, this is not the case with decumulating portfolios, where cash flows are the primary objective. If market returns are poor early in retirement, the portfolio may go broke before the markets recover. Figure 14.4 shows the projected asset balance for the same portfolio assuming a 5 percent withdrawal rate in the first year, subsequently adjusted for inflation. Clearly, the pattern shown in this chart has little resemblance to the cumulative return chart shown in Figure 14.2. It is evident that the standard deviation of return is not a suitable measure of risk for the retirement income problem. Thus, the investment model requires a different measure of risk that *is* suitable.

Probability alone does not risk make. History is littered with the wreckage of those who learned this lesson the hard way.

Monte Carlo simulation tools are popular, and their probabilistic methodology is an improvement over the deterministic methods of their predecessors. However, the *probability* of bad outcomes is not a complete measure of risk. Decomposing risk into its two primary components reveals that the *magnitude* of bad outcomes is as important as the probability.

TABLE 14.1 Asset-Class Forecasts and Weightings

Asset Classes	Expected Return, %	Standard Deviation, %	Correlations						60–40 Portfolio Weight, %
			U.S. Equity	Non-U.S. Equity	REITs	Bonds	Cash	Inflation	
U.S. Equity	8.63	18.26	1						39
Non-U.S. Equity	8.64	19.27	.61	1					16
REITs	7.45	15.31	.39	.36	1				5
Bonds	6.16	2.89	.28	.25	.49	1			40
Cash	4.44	3.39	.26	.27	.52	.81	1		0
Inflation	3.10	3.10	.15	.16	.39	.48	.82	1	n/a

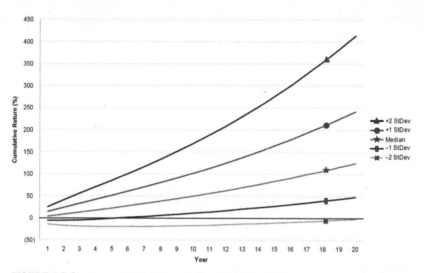

FIGURE 14.2 Hypothetical Cumulative Total Real Returns

Risk is measured as the product of these two components: Total Risk = Probability × Magnitude.

Actuaries and risk analysts will quickly recognize this equation. Even though the probability of a bad outcome may be small, if the magnitude is large, then the overall risk may be significant and, therefore, the investment model must account for it.

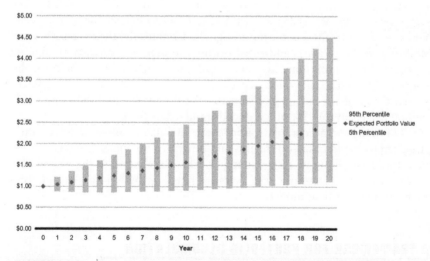

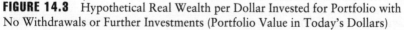

FIGURE 14.3 Hypothetical Real Wealth per Dollar Invested for Portfolio with No Withdrawals or Further Investments (Portfolio Value in Today's Dollars)

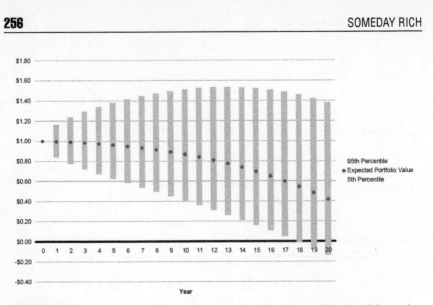

FIGURE 14.4   Hypothetical Real Wealth per Dollar Invested for Portfolio with 5 percent Initial Withdrawal Rate Annually Adjusted for Inflation (Portfolio Value in Today's Dollars)

Accounting for the Investor's Aversion to Cash-Flow Risk

A prevalent assumption in retirement planning is that, if the plan fails, the investor must either spend less or go back to work. The term *cash-flow risk* refers to the risk that the portfolio will fail to deliver the lifetime cash flows required to fund consumption goals. Commonly, the investor's aversion to cash-flow risk is addressed during the planning process by making conservative assumptions. Less commonly, it is factored into the portfolio construction model, in which case the implication to the portfolio manager is that the investor has no aversion to cash-flow risk at all but is perfectly willing to accept the risk of a reduced standard of living.

This may be acceptable for investors willing to raise or lower their standard of living based on the ups and downs of the market. However, for investors less willing to assign control of their livelihood to the vicissitudes of the markets, cash-flow risk aversion must be built into the portfolio manager's investment model.

A FRAMEWORK FOR PORTFOLIO DECUMULATION

Having identified shortcomings in the conventional approaches that must be overcome, the framework for decumulation follows.

Portfolio construction models are generally written as an objective function, which defines exactly what the portfolio manager is charged with accomplishing for the investor. The objective is to maximize wealth, subject to achieving the desired cash flows to fund a lifetime of consumption and the desired bequest and other wealth goals. Appendix 14A illustrates this objective function in mathematical terms, addressing the periodicity of the cash-flow goals and the investor's risk tolerance for achieving them. It also discusses the application of shortfall risk measures. *Shortfall* describes the risk that the portfolio may fail to meet the investor's ongoing objectives. This measures risk in terms that are readily meaningful to the investor while accounting for both the probability and magnitude components of risk.

A complication in the decumulation problem is that an uncertain lifetime makes the time horizon largely unknown. If the horizon is unknown, how can shortfall risk be measured? Furthermore, how can the objective function possibly be optimized?

One method is to use mortality statistics to model the time horizon as a probability density function and then incorporate it into a stochastic model for calculating a probability of success or ruin. In practice, this method is limited as a means for determining an optimal portfolio. The reason is subtle. The stochastic mortality approach models the paths of numerous potential lifespan horizons, which implies that retirees have many lives to live, even though, in reality, they have only one. Constructing a portfolio based on numerous phantom lives is problematic because, although longevity risk management is possible using multiple real lives, it is not possible using phantom lives.

This insight is a key point to resolving the dilemma. Let's return now to the guiding principle to insure (annuitize) when you need to, but not before. The logical inference is to construct the optimal investment portfolio of assets for the individual's goals and continually evaluating the option to annuitize those assets when (and only when) necessary to ensure continuing lifetime income. Rather than simply annuitizing assets early in retirement, the idea is to leverage the *option* to annuitize those assets later. As Milevsky and Young (2002) show, this is a real option with real value that can be quantified.[1]

Transforming Longevity Risk into Investment Risk

The key for leveraging this optionality is setting the projected cost to annuitize the investor's desired lifetime income stream as a *wealth* goal in the objective function. Doing so effectively transforms longevity risk into investment risk, because now it is the portfolio's job to preserve the ability to annuitize the desired lifetime income stream. By combining these separate but related types of risks, they can be managed holistically and, thus, more effectively. Although this method may not guarantee the ability to annuitize on any particular future date (unless an insurance company underwrites the guarantee), the investor is free to exercise the annuitization option at any time. By monitoring the investor's wealth relative to the current cost of annuitization, the decision to invest or annuitize can be continually evaluated by a financial advisor. To implement, a two-step process is used:

Step 1. Select a time horizon during which the investor (a) is willing and able to forecast a spending budget (define the cash-flow goals), and (b) strongly desires to avoid relinquishing liquidity and control of financial assets.

This liquidity horizon may be of any length. Because it is not an assumed drop-dead date, however, it does not necessarily have to extend beyond life expectancy as a means of mitigating longevity risk. Having been transformed into investment risk, longevity risk is now actively managed inside the portfolio rather than in the selection of a drop-dead date.

Step 2. Set the wealth target at the end of this horizon as the amount needed to fund a lifetime annuity. Ideally, this target will be exceeded and the annuitization decision can be deferred indefinitely, but this is the minimum requirement. The annuitization cost calculation uses simple and well-established formulas (see Appendix 14B for an example that applies this methodology).

Visualizing the Framework

Figure 14.5 illustrates a hypothetical scenario. An initial $1 million investment is shown as the column above year 0, the cash-flow goals are shown as the short columns above years 1–23, and the wealth goal is shown as the taller column above year 20. A box drawn around the chart area for years 1–20 indicates a 20-year liquidity horizon. A 5 percent initial withdrawal rate is used ($50,000 in the first year). Inflation-adjusted spending is desired to maintain the investor's standard of living, so the chart shows real values (today's dollars).

In the event that the investor is still living after 20 years, ongoing cash flows continue to be needed. These are accommodated by the taller column above year 20, indicating the minimum amount required in the portfolio to fund the purchase of a lifetime annuity at the end of year 20. Other wealth goals are indicated by the patterned area of the column above year 20. As long as the portfolio achieves the cash flow and wealth goals, it will have met its purpose of providing for lifetime income.

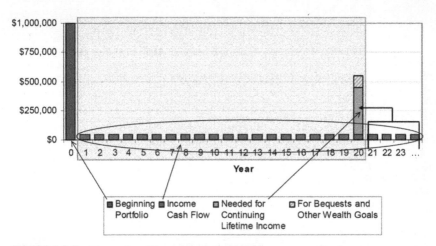

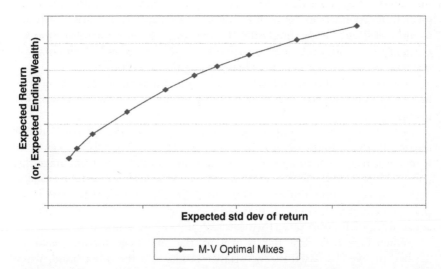

FIGURE 14.5 Example of Framework Showing Investment Goals (Portfolio Objectives)

Illustrating the Investment Strategy

Figure 14.6 shows various points on the efficient frontier for hypothetical mean-variance (M-V) optimal portfolios using the traditional definition of risk for wealth accumulation.

FIGURE 14.6 Wealth Accumulation Efficient Frontier (Mean-Variance Optimal Mixes)

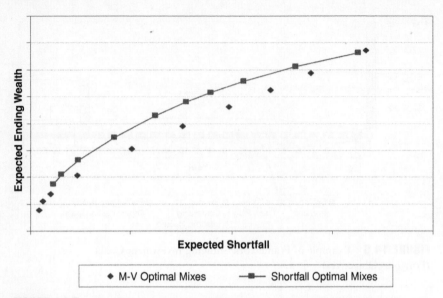

FIGURE 14.7 Wealth Decumulation Efficient Frontier (Static Allocations)

Figure 14.7 illustrates these same portfolios in the context of the decumulation framework as described in Appendix 14A. Notice that risk is now measured not by standard deviation of return, but in terms of shortfall over a given liquidity horizon. New shortfall optimal portfolios are now identified as more efficient for decumulation. It is no surprise that portfolios that are efficient for wealth accumulation are not efficient for wealth decumulation, because the two investment problems are significantly different.

Figure 14.7 shows optimal *static* asset allocations for the portfolio. However, are static portfolios truly optimal for the decumulation problem?

The answer is no because movements in the markets have a major impact on the amount of shortfall risk present in the portfolio over time. It makes sense, then, to alter the asset allocation over time to manage this risk. A 10 percent decline in value may increase shortfall risk substantially, perhaps necessitating a more conservative portfolio to reduce the risk level. A 10 percent increase in value may reduce shortfall risk, allowing for a more aggressive portfolio to serve the objective of growing wealth.

When little cash-flow risk is present, the objective function begins to act like the wealth-based mean-variance model. On the other hand, when substantial cash-flow risk is present, the objective function begins to take on more of the characteristics of a cash-flow matching model. A dynamic

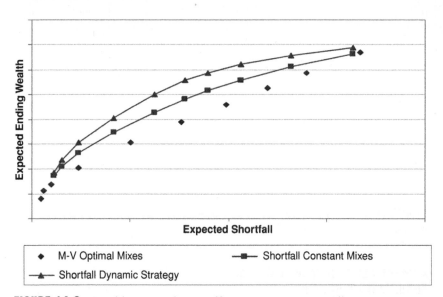

FIGURE 14.8 Wealth Decumulation Efficient Frontier (Static Allocations versus Dynamic Strategy)

allocation strategy makes these adjustments when necessary. Because the optimal (utility maximizing) asset allocation is dependent on the value of the portfolio at any time, any static investment strategy will necessarily suffer lost utility due to its inability to respond to real world changes.

Given any current level of wealth, time horizon, series of cash flows, cash-flow risk aversion, future wealth goal, wealth risk aversion, and capital-market expectations, the goal is to find dynamic strategies that provide wealth/risk combinations that are superior to the optimal static strategy, shifting the efficient frontier up as shown in Figure 14.8. It makes no sense to take unrewarded risk, so dynamic strategies are compelling for retirees exposed and averse to cash-flow risk (this excludes those so wealthy or so frugal that they don't need to worry about outliving their money).

The illustrations shown here assume annual rebalancing of the static portfolios and annual resetting of the dynamic portfolio. However, because the current level of wealth changes daily, shortfall risk also changes daily and, thus, the optimal allocation changes daily. Consequently, the more frequently the allocation is reset, the greater is the benefit offered by a dynamic strategy. In the ideal world, it would be reset daily, but any resetting should take place only when the benefit exceeds transaction costs. In the real world, resetting the allocation would occur less frequently than daily and more frequently than annually.

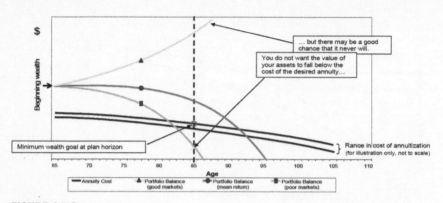

FIGURE 14.9   Use of an Annuitization Hurdle (Cost of Desired Lifetime Income Annuity Relative to Portfolio Value)

A Practical Approach: Using an Annuitization Hurdle

Of course, dynamic strategies may be burdensome for some financial planners and advisors to implement, in which case they may outsource the portfolio management function to investment managers better equipped to the task. Regardless of the investment methodology, the framework still provides an intuitive and simple way for planners and advisors to assist their clients in retirement while avoiding the undesirable task of selecting a drop-dead date.

Figure 14.9 illustrates how the amount needed for continuing lifetime income can be viewed as an annuitization hurdle. Here, inflation-adjusted withdrawals are taken from a portfolio, and potential paths for the portfolio value are displayed. Overlaid on these paths is the cost to annuitize a desired lifetime income stream if this annuity were to be purchased in any subsequent year. In other words, the first-year cost is for an annuity purchased at retirement, whereas the fifth-year cost is for an annuity purchased in the fifth year of retirement. Because life expectancy decreases with age, the cost to annuitize generally also decreases with age.

Investing in the capital markets involves risk and, as John Maynard Keynes might have put it, the markets may underperform your expectations longer than you can remain solvent. Many financial planning approaches use a portfolio value of *zero* as the threshold for plan success or failure (*X* percent chance your portfolio will last for *Y* years). This method considers *failure* to mean "financial ruin."

In contrast, the portfolio decumulation framework uses the *cost to annuitize* as the threshold for success or failure (*X* percent chance your portfolio will last for *Y* years and still retain enough value to annuitize a guaranteed

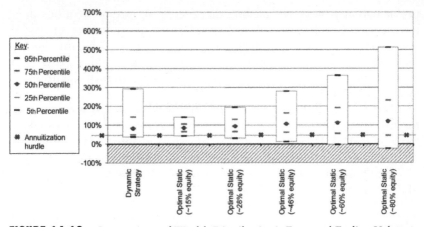

FIGURE 14.10 Comparison of Wealth Distributions. Expected Ending Value as Percent of Initial Value (Year 20)

lifetime income). This method considers *failure* to mean, "having to annuitize your assets before you really hoped to." For most retirees, this is a more comforting threshold to use than financial ruin. In Figure 14.9, shortfall occurs when the portfolio value drops below the cost to annuitize.

Combining the annuitization hurdle with a dynamic investment strategy relative to that hurdle tells a compelling story to the client. Figure 14.10 shows a range in possible outcomes after 20 years for a dynamic portfolio as well as optimal static portfolios of varying risk levels. The investment objectives in this hypothetical example include a 5 percent initial withdrawal rate in the first year that is subsequently adjusted for inflation. The lifetime annuitization hurdle is a projected range of values. Portfolio values below zero represent financial ruin, whereas values below the annuitization hurdle represent an inability to fund the desired annuity.

Dynamic strategies adjust the composition of the portfolio over time based on the current portfolio value, remaining cash flows, and annuitization-hurdle amount. Figure 14.10 shows that the dynamic strategy works to meet the cash flow *and* the wealth (annuitization-hurdle) objectives regardless of market performance, thereby actively managing longevity risk. It compresses the set of potential outcomes at the lower end of the range to stay above the hurdle, while preserving as much upside as possible.

CONCLUSION

The investment problems of accumulation and decumulation are significantly different and, therefore the investment model best suited for them must necessarily be different. Decumulation is a much more complex problem to manage. Logic dictates that retirement income solutions should leverage the best features of both investments and insurance. Given the many competing goals and the complex nature of the risks, the timing of the invest-or-annuitize decision is important to the overall success of any retiree's financial plan. The use of annuitization hurdles helps frame the problem in simple terms.

Traditional accumulation-based investment portfolios are suboptimal for this problem. Redefining the investment objectives and risks in the client's terms is critical. Dynamic strategies appear well suited to the problem of decumulating portfolios that must provide for lifetime income.

(Further technical references are provided in the Bibliography at the end of this chapter.)

APPENDIX 14A OBJECTIVE FUNCTION FOR LIFETIME PORTFOLIO DECUMULATION

We can describe the objective function in terms of expected utility. Utility is a measure of the expected satisfaction gained from investing, subject to the investor's relative risk aversion. Relative risk aversion is a measure of the marginal reward required for taking on additional risk.

For decumulators, the utility function is a complex combination of wealth goals, cash-flow goals, and the risk tolerance toward each. The decumulator seeks to maximize:

$$E[W_T] - \sum_{t=1}^{T} (\lambda_t \times \text{Crisk}_t) - \lambda_T \times \text{Wrisk}$$

where
T = period of investor's death (if a couple, the last to die)
W_T = ending (terminal) wealth
λ_t = risk aversion parameter of the cash-flow desired in period T
Crisk_t = risk of not obtaining the cash-flow desired in period T
λ_T = risk aversion parameter of wealth
Wrisk = risk that the desired level of wealth may not be accomplished

Translating, the goal is to maximize wealth subject to achieving the desired cash flows to fund consumption goals during the remaining lifetime, and subject to achieving the desired bequest and other wealth goals. This maximization is also subject to the investor's tolerance for risk in each of these goals.

This multiperiod model addresses, not only the periodicity of the cash flow goals, but also the investor's risk tolerance toward them. Depending on the investor's preference, the goals may be specified in either nominal or real terms. The fact that the variable T is not known with certainty is problematic to developing a closed-form equation that may be optimized. This can be resolved by use of a liquidity horizon and annuitization hurdle as described earlier. The decumulator views risk in terms of shortfall, meaning the portfolio may fall short of delivering the required cash flows and achieving or retaining the desired level of wealth. A number of methods are available for computing shortfall risk, but the shortfall penalty functions described in Bouchey, Cariño, and Fan (1999) are particularly useful because they explicitly link the investor's tolerance for risk to both the probability and magnitude of bad outcomes. Recall our earlier equation:

Total Risk = Probability × Magnitude
In the context of our utility function,
Shortfall Risk = Probability of Shortfall × Magnitude of Potential Shortfall

To accommodate the investor's relative aversion to shortfall risk, a penalty is applied to the magnitude of any potential shortfall (for example, by squaring it). For determining the optimal portfolio, asset allocations with larger potential shortfalls are increasingly penalized.

APPENDIX 14B COST TO ANNUITIZE AN INCOME STREAM

Because the previous equations are written in discrete-time form, that convention is continued here. The cost of a \$1 per year lifetime annuity is shown below. If inflation adjustments are desired, then the discount rate may be based on real interest rates; otherwise it may be based on nominal interest rates.

$$a_{(x+T)} = \left[\sum_{t=1}^{\infty} \frac{{}_t p_{(x+T)}}{(1 + r_t)^t} \right] (1 + L)$$

where: $x =$ the investor's age today
$T =$ time in years until annuitization
$a_{(x+T)} =$ cost to annuitize \$1 at the age the investor will be T years from now
$r =$ discount rate (based on the forecasted yield curve at time T)
${}_t p_{(x+T)} =$ probability that an individual of age $(x + T)$ survives for another T years

$L =$ the insurer's expense load as a percentage of the pure annuity cost

This annuity factor is then multiplied by the investor's lifetime annual income goal, which becomes the end-of-horizon wealth goal.

$$A_T = a_{(x+T)} \times C^M$$

where: $A_T =$ wealth required at time T to annuitize the required lifetime income
$C^M =$ required minimum annual lifetime income

As illustrated in Figure 14.5, the value A_T comprises the "continuing–lifetime-income" portion of the ending wealth goal at the liquidity horizon. Recall that we are pricing this annuity in the future. As a result, a stochastic approach should be used based on forecasts for the yield curve over the liquidity horizon.

Example

Although a detailed explanation of forecasting methods is beyond the scope of this chapter, the following example shows how the methodology may be implemented. We must determine the variables for age (x), liquidity horizon (T), annuity expense load (L), a set of mortality factors [the $_tp_{(x+T)}$'s], and a set of discount rates (the r_t's).

Consider a single male, age 65 at retirement with a 20-year liquidity horizon. Expense loads are assumed to be 5 percent. Thus, $x = 65$, $T = 20$, $x + T = 85$, and $L = .05$.

For the mortality factors, we can obtain a mortality table from an organization such as the Society of Actuaries. The table should be based on individual annuitant mortality and ideally would also factor in expected future mortality improvement. The Male Individual Annuity 2000 Basic table is partially represented in the first two columns of Table 14B.1, which shows by age the probability of dying that year (q_x).

For the discount rates, yield-curve forecasting models may be available from investment companies, insurance firms, pension actuaries, and other sources. The term structure of the yield curve specifies the discount rate (r_t) for each period. Here, I use a simplified model with a flat yield curve, so the discount rate is the same in each period.

Say you believe that nominal bond yields are normally distributed, with a long-run equilibrium mean of 6 percent and standard deviation of 1.5 percent, and that you wish to use a 90 percent confidence level in your estimation of the future interest rate. Further, you believe that the long-run equilibrium inflation rate is 3 percent.

A 90 percent confidence level means that we seek the value that is approximately 1.282 standard deviations from the mean. In Excel, this can be calculated using the function NORMSINV(0.90). Because annuity prices increase as interest rates decline, we are concerned with the left-hand side of the distribution and thus seek the interest rate that is -1.282 standard deviations from the mean.

The nominal rate we seek is $.06 - 1.282(.015) = 4.077$ percent. Our retiree prefers to maintain his standard of living over time, so we subtract the long-run inflation rate from the nominal yield to obtain a real yield of 1.077 percent as our discount rate. Table 14B.1 shows the remaining calculations.

For each period t, $q_{x(t)}$ is obtained by looking up a value in the mortality table

$$p_{x(t)} = 1 - q_{x(t)}$$

$$_t p_{x(t)} = {}_t P_{x(t-1)} \times P_{x(t)}$$

$$DF_t = (1 + r_t) - t$$

Note that $_t p_{x(0)}$ is, by definition, equal to 1 because we assume the retiree to be alive at the time of the annuity purchase. Each r in this example is the same due to the assumption of a flat yield curve.

The annuitization factor before expense loading for this male single-life inflation-adjusted annuity is the sum of the discounted probabilities of survival in each period:

$$\sum_{t=1}^{\infty} DF_t \times {}_t p_x = \$6.30, \text{ rounded to the nearest cent.}$$

The expense-loaded annuitization factor is then computed as

$$a_{(x+T)} = \$6.30 \times (1 + .05) = \$6.61 \text{ per real dollar of annual income.}$$

Finally, assume that our retiree's required minimum annual lifetime income (C^M) in real terms is \$25,000. At an inflation rate of 3 percent, its future value at the time of annuitization is:

$$C^M = \$25,000 \times (1 + .03)^{20} = \$45,152.78$$

TABLE 14B.1 Annuitization Factor Worksheet

Age	Probability of Dying within Year (q_x)	Probability of Living through Year (p_x)	Period (t)	Probability to Survive t Years ($_tp_x$)	Discount Factor (DF_t)	Discounted Probability ($DF_t \times {}_tp_x$)
85	0.081326	0.918674	1	0.918674000	0.989344757	0.908885305
86	0.088863	0.911137	2	0.837037872	0.978803048	0.819295221
87	0.096958	0.903042	3	0.755880354	0.968373664	0.731974628
88	0.105631	0.894369	4	0.676035957	0.958055407	0.647679904
89	0.114858	0.885142	5	0.598387819	0.947847094	0.567180155
90	0.124612	0.875388	6	0.523821516	0.937747553	0.491212345
91	0.134861	0.865139	7	0.453178422	0.927755625	0.420438830
92	0.145575	0.854425	8	0.387206974	0.917870163	0.355405728
93	0.156727	0.843273	9	0.326521186	0.908090033	0.296510635
94	0.168290	0.831710	10	0.271570936	0.898414113	0.243983161
95	0.180245	0.819755	11	0.222621632	0.888841293	0.197875300
96	0.192565	0.807435	12	0.179752498	0.879370473	0.158069039
97	0.205229	0.794771	13	0.142862072	0.870000566	0.124290084
98	0.218683	0.781317	14	0.111620566	0.860730499	0.096075225
99	0.233371	0.766629	15	0.085571563	0.851559206	0.072869252

Age			Age			
100	0.249741	0.750259	16	0.064200835	0.842485636	0.054088281
101	0.268237	0.731763	17	0.046979796	0.833508747	0.039158071
102	0.289305	0.710695	18	0.033388306	0.824627509	0.027532916
103	0.313391	0.686609	19	0.022924711	0.815840902	0.018702917
104	0.340940	0.659060	20	0.015108760	0.807147919	0.012195004
105	0.372398	0.627602	21	0.009482288	0.798547562	0.007572058
106	0.408210	0.591790	22	0.005611523	0.790038843	0.004433321
107	0.448823	0.551177	23	0.003092943	0.781620788	0.002417508
108	0.494681	0.505319	24	0.001562923	0.773292428	0.001208596
109	0.546231	0.453769	25	0.000709206	0.765052809	0.000542580
110	0.603917	0.396083	26	0.000280904	0.756900986	0.000212617
111	0.668186	0.331814	27	9.3208E-05	0.748836022	6.97975E-05
112	0.739483	0.260517	28	2.42823E-05	0.740856992	1.79897E-05
113	0.818254	0.181746	29	4.41321E-06	0.732962981	3.23472E-06
114	0.904945	0.095055	30	4.19497E-07	0.725153082	3.042E-07
115	1	0	31	0	0.717426400	0
Totals				6.694207885		6.299900008

Male age $(x + T) = 85$.
Discount rate $(r_t) = 1.077\%$.

Therefore, the end-of-horizon wealth goal (annuitization hurdle) in nominal terms is

$$a_{(x+T)} \times C^M = \$6.61 \times \$45{,}152.78 = \$298{,}459.88$$

Or, in real terms,

$$\$298{,}459.88 \times (1 + .03)^{-20} = \$165{,}250.00$$

Our retiree may be interested to know that, should he reach age 85, his life expectancy would then be just over $6^{1}/_{2}$ years (found in Table 14B.1 as the sum of the $_tp_x$ terms).

Implementation with More Sophisticated Economic Models

By obtaining a properly calibrated economic model for inflation and interest rates from a trusted source, the simplifying assumptions in this example may be relaxed. A Monte Carlo simulation could then model numerous possible economic conditions in each period. If 5,000 simulations of inflation and the (presumably nonflat) yield curve are modeled for each period, then 5,000 possible annuity factors result after plugging in the simulated values of r_t. A 90 percent confidence value would be determined by selecting the 5,000 $\times$ 0.90 = 4,500th largest one. Regardless of the number of scenarios modeled, the formula is applied in exactly the same way.

ACKNOWLEDGMENTS

Richard Fullmer thanks Don Ezra, Yuan-An Fan, Grant Gardner, and Randy Lert, along with the paper's anonymous referees, for their comments and insights.

BIBLIOGRAPHY

Bodie, Z. "On the Risk of Stocks in the Long Run," *Financial Analysts Journal* (May–June 1995).

Bouchey, P., D. Carño, and Y. Fan. "The Behavior of Shortfall Functions in Asset Allocation." Russell Research Commentary (August 1999).

Fan, Y., R. Fullmer, and G. Gardner. "Successful Investment Strategies for Funding Retirement Spending." Russell Investment Group working paper (March 2006).

Harlow, W.V. "Asset Allocation in a Downside Risk Framework." *Financial Analysts Journal* (September–October 1991).

Horneff, W., R. Maurer, O. Mitchell, and I. Dus. "Optimizing the Retirement Income Portfolio: Asset Allocation, Annuitization, and Risk Aversion." Pension Research Council working paper (July 2006). The Wharton School, University of Pennsylvania.

Markowitz, H. *Portfolio Selection: Efficient Diversification of Investments* (New York: John Wiley and Sons, 1959).

Rom, B. and K. Ferguson. "Post-Modern Portfolio Theory Comes of Age." *Journal of Investing* (Winter, 1993).

Sortino, F. and R. van der Meer. "Downside Risk: Capturing What's at Stake." *Journal of Portfolio Management* (Summer, 1991).

NOTE

1. M. Milevsky and V. Young, "Optimal Asset Allocation and The Real Option to Delay Annuitization: It's Not Now-or-Never," Working paper (April 2002).

Lessons Learned from Retirement Income Research

R ussell Investments conducted three major focus group studies on retirement income: the first two in 2007 and the third in 2009. Mathew Greenwald and Associates led these research projects. This report provides:

- Description of the sources of information for this summary.
- Retiree viewpoints on the production of income.
- Advisor viewpoints on the production of income for retirees.

Editor's note: All references to investment products offered by Russell Investments have been removed from this summary report.

SOURCES OF INFORMATION

In September 2007, Russell conducted focus groups with financial advisors: two with wealth managers, one with small-account managers and one with money managers. Three groups with retirees were also conducted. The groups were held in Phoenix and San Diego. All the financial advisors had at least three years of experience, at least $10 million of assets under management (AUM), at least 50 percent of their assets from individual investors, at least 25 percent of their retail assets in mutual funds, and at least 15 percent of their business from retirees. The retirees were ages 55 to 70, had investable assets of at least $250,000, and had less than a third of their income from defined benefit plans.

In December 2007, five groups were held with financial advisors: three with wealth managers and two with investment advisors. The advisors had the same requirements as the aforementioned groups. These groups were held in Los Angeles and Seattle.

In 2009, four focus groups were held with retirees and one with preretirees (in Deerfield, Illinois; Minneapolis; Atlanta; and Scottsdale, Arizona). Two retiree groups had anxious retirees who were ages 68 to 75, had investable assets of $400,000 to $1 million, were not regular savers, and were scared by the economic developments of that time. The other two groups of retirees were premiers who were ages 60 to 67, had investable assets of $1 million to $3 million, were regular savers, and did not feel that impacted by the economic events of the time. The preretirees were 57 to 59 years old, expected to retiree within five years and use a financial advisor.

At that same time, seven groups were held with financial advisors (four with wealth managers and three with investment advisors). All the advisors had at least three years of experience and at least $10 million in AUM. At least half of their AUM was from retail clients and at least a quarter of their retail assets were in mutual funds. Also, all the advisors had a minimum of 20 percent retired retail clients and at least 20 percent of those retail clients currently withdrawing money from their investments.

The highlights from these three sets of groups will be the basis for this summary.

Retiree Viewpoints on the Production of Income

Retirees have two important concerns about their financial security. First, there is considerable concern about running out of money. Second, there is awareness that there can be large expenses at the older ages because of health problems and the possibility of needing long-term care. These concerns lead retirees to want to preserve a significant amount of capital. Indeed, many retirees try to live mainly off defined benefit income and Social Security. Income from real estate is an important source for some. Those that need additional income most often seek to at least preserve their asset levels and take out only dividends, interest, and capital gains. Some try to increase their asset levels to keep up with inflation. This strategy does not take into account inflation's impact of reducing the value of the asset levels. When equities fall in value, there is a tendency for people to reduce spending.

Importantly, although they are often concerned about running out of money, most retirees do not have sophisticated strategies for preserving their assets or ideas about how to most efficiently invest. Also, most do not consider leaving an estate to be important. They are more concerned about not being a burden on their kids.

Many retirees do not have formal budgets, but most are quite aware of their level of monthly expenses and try to live within their means. However, there are often events, such as vacations, capital expenditures (for such things as a new car or major home repair) or unexpected costs (such as an adult child losing a job and needing support) that require large outlays.

In the face of these concerns, the retirees appear fairly conservative. They use a range of asset allocations, but many appear to have about half of their assets in fixed investments.

Advisor Viewpoints on the Production of Income for Retirees

The advisors in the focus groups held in 2009 agreed with six statements presented to them about the problems faced by retirees:

1. It can be hard to determine how much regular income is needed in retirement; circumstances can change.
2. No one knows how long they will live in retirement. Investors need confidence that they can pay bills for a potentially long period of time.
3. Health care costs are a major concern of retirees.
4. Defined benefit plans and Social Security do not meet the lifestyle expectations of many retirees.
5. Many retirees find that their nest eggs decline in their later years and can also encounter unexpected costs. They need to protect income and have opportunities to grow.
6. Fixed investments are safe, but often return too little, whereas aggressive equity investing can bring losses. Balance is essential.

The advisors verify a good deal of the observations made by retirees. They report that many of their retired clients try to live on defined benefit income, Social Security, and dividends. Most advisors state that only a small proportion of their clients need a significant amount of regular income from their accumulations. However, most of the advisors expect that the proportion of their retired clients who will need regular income will grow strongly.

When withdrawals are made, most advisors think that the amount taken out each year should be between 4 percent and 6 percent of the assets clients have at the start of retirement. Many say they have gotten more conservative on that point than they were several years ago.

In terms of strategies for providing income, the most commonly used approaches are bond laddering and systematic withdrawal. In a few of the focus groups, the moderator probed reactions to the assertion that asset allocation should be different during the income stage than during the accumulation stage because during the accumulation stage, market downturns are actually beneficial—investors can buy low, but they are quite different during the income stage, because investors taking income must sell low. There is widespread acceptance of this assertion. However, financial advisors do not seem to have developed asset allocation strategies for those drawing income that reflects those different dynamics. Generally, asset allocations for those drawing income are similar to those for accumulators, except that, with age, there is a tendency for advisors to think that more allocation should be given to fixed investments. That, however, does not seem to be universally implemented.

The advisors report that retired clients require more of their time than working clients. Also, those who take income require more of the advisor's time, because strategies for taking income tend not to be highly automated. Some produce income each month, when needed, by harvesting capital gains and taking dividends and interest. Some rebalance; others do not. Some use annuities for this purpose. Some take a major amount of money out at the start of the year and put it in cash. They then withdraw from this cash account to produce income. This means that the large sum taken to provide income for the year gains hardly any return.

The New Language of Retirement

In 2009 and 2010, maslansky luntz + partners (Maslansky) conducted research on behalf of Russell Investments. In part, the purpose of the research was to assist Russell in developing effective language for use with financial advisors and end investors on the topic of retirement income. Maslansky talked with both end investors and advisors.

The investors participated in one of three instant response dial sessions in San Francisco, Chicago, and Fort Lauderdale. The sessions lasted three hours each. The investors ranged in age from 50 to 69, half were preretiree and half were retirees. If retired, they had at least $500,000 in investable assets. If working, they had at least $250,000 in investable assets. All investors in the study were working with a financial advisor.

The advisors participated in one of 12 instant response sessions over the phone, using web-based instant response software. The sessions lasted 45 to 60 minutes each. Each advisor had at least 100 clients, 5 percent of whom were retirees. All advisors focused on a mix of financial planning and investment selection for their clients. Each advisor had at least $10 million of assets under management, the majority of which was from individual investors and at least 25 percent from retirees.

We've condensed the findings, so what appears in this summary are suggestions for financial advisors when talking with an end investor about retirement.

OVERVIEW OF FINDINGS

- Your story must make you stand out from the competition and resonate with your target audience.
- Your language must anticipate the end investor's perspective, not just your own.
- Your language needs to be *relevant*, *real*, and *responsive*.

- *Relevant* means planning for a lifestyle, not just retirement. Solutions need to be personalized. Use language that end investors understand, not industry jargon. Do not use analogies.
- *Real* means addressing tough questions head on and finding answers based on the evidence (meaning the investor's personal situation).
- *Responsive* means you can make a plan for actively navigating the right course as their lives and needs change; supporting them through, not just to, retirement.

What to Say

- I want to help you get real about retirement. I can help you do a retirement reality check.
- I think it's important to ask the tough questions now, not later, to get you back on track to meet your goals.
- I want to help you with lifestyle planning, not just retirement planning, because your needs are based on the life you want to live after retirement.
- I can help you navigate your retirement, by making adjustments along the way, responding to changes in your life and the markets when necessary.
- I use a flexible strategy that protects you from getting locked into anything, and from a volatile market.

What Not to Say

Sometimes knowing what not to say is as important as knowing what to say. Saying the wrong thing can cause your audience to shut down and stop listening.

- Avoid the negative sell. Criticizing other strategies, other companies, common practices, or even the general industry makes investors defensive.
- Avoid insider jargon. Using unfamiliar or industry acronyms or terms alienates and confuses investors.
- Avoid metaphors. Talking about their money in any terms but their money makes them think you are not taking this seriously.
- Avoid overpromising. No one believes the market is a sure thing, so claims to insure or ensure come off as hollow and deceptive.

Be Relevant

In the age of iPods, Facebook, and TiVo, things that aren't personalized aren't relevant. Personalization is the cost of entry to even be considered by the investor. *Tailor* your process to the individual. Investors' concerns are bigger than just retirement. It's about their personal lifestyle. No one believes they are like the rest of the baby-boomers. They are going to retire their way, not the way their parents did.

But … personalized isn't differentiating; lifestyle planning is.

Lifestyle planning is the foundation of a financial plan. A client's lifestyle is *the* element an advisor can use to personalize their client's plan. It's a more relevant kind of planning.

Lifestyle planning works because it's an audience-defined concept. They all have different thoughts about what they want to do, and will imagine the lifestyle they want when they hear the word.

Language to USE—"There is no right answer to what retirement should be, there's only your answer. And that's why I like to look at this not as creating a retirement plan but as creating a lifestyle plan."

Avoid jargon. It's easy to fall into using insider language because you live and breathe it, but investors don't understand it.

Be Realistic

Get real about retirement. Without being negative, the phrase acknowledges investors are disenchanted by the financial industry. Advisors know it's their job to keep investors grounded. "Get real" sums up what investors know they need most going into retirement, namely, transparent advice.

Language to USE—"I think it's important to get real about retirement. I have the tools I need to help you paint a realistic picture of your financial future, to tell you the truth about where you stand and the things we need to do to keep your retirement on track."

Be the one that asks the tough questions. End investors have their guard up against being sold to or manipulated. Tough implies direction, discipline, and objectivity.

End investors would much rather hear the news (good or bad) now than later. They're ready to start working toward their retirement goals. They want to hear it straight. However, this doesn't mean the conversation should be painful, so be careful not to push too far.

Advisors find tough questions truly differentiating, and they see having those tough conversations now as essential for averting crisis later. However, they are also cautious. They've got a lot at stake. They can lose business if they come off as impolite, insensitive, or alarmist. If they push too hard, investors might stop listening.

Language to USE—"We have distilled the retirement process, not over-simplified it. We've developed a framework that allows us to ask the tough questions. First, how much do you need for your standard of living during retirement? Second, will you run out of money? Third, what do you need to do to keep on track?"

Give evidence-based answers. It implies objectivity, research, and no bias. Evidence should also reference the specifics of their financial situation. This makes your answers both real and personalized.

Language to USE—"I will work with you step-by-step to set realistic goals, and then I will provide transparent, straightforward solutions. I am not asking you to go on faith. We work only with evidence. So we will get the answers right from the start."

Don't oversimplify. Investors know financing retirement is complicated and difficult. That's why they go to advisors. Oversimplification of the process comes across as condescending and can sound suspicious.

Don't get fancy. Avoid analogies, similes, and anything else that compares money to something else. Even if they make sense, they sound reductive.

Don't use cutesy or colorful phrases. They raise red flags with investors across the board. There's nothing more serious to them than their money.

Be Responsive

Give investors something flexible that can change as they or their situation changes. Investors don't believe you can guarantee or insure retirement because there is no sure thing with investments. So you need to be able to change with the times.

Emphasize being active in all you do. Investors like hearing active management and active oversight.

Language to USE—"Our philosophy on your future is that you can retire from your job, but you should never retire from investing."

Navigate their retirement. Everyone is aware that the market goes up and down. Navigation is both active and reactive. Navigation is also real time. It incorporates themes of flexibility and personalization. Advisors can help end investors course-correct based on what has just happened, but don't beat the metaphor to death with hiking or nautical language.

Get them *through* not just *to* retirement. It shows you understand the need to manage beyond the day they retire. End investors know they're going to need even more help once they retire.

Language to USE—"I have a different philosophy. I want to get you not just to retirement, but through it. That means helping you before retirement to accumulate as much as you will need to maintain your standard of living. Once you're retired, I'll help you transition into receiving the money you've worked so hard for, and make it go as far as it can. This way, I will help you enjoy a safe, secure, and fully funded retirement."

Language to USE—"A retirement portfolio should be flexible. It should change as you do. Simply put, it needs to be flexible enough to meet your needs every step of the way."

SUGGESTED READING

Luntz, Frank. *Words That Work: It's Not What You Say, It's What People Hear.* New York: Hyperion, 2007.

Maslansky, Michael, with Scott West, Gary DeMoss, and David Saylor. *The Language of Trust: Selling Ideas in a World of Skeptics.* Upper Saddle River, NJ: Prentice Hall, 2010.

About the Authors

Timothy Noonan is managing director of capital markets insights for Russell Investments. Tim heads the group responsible for shaping and delivering client-service strategy, and delivering capital markets information to private client advisors. He is chairman of the Private Client Services Strategic Advice Committee.

In 2006, Tim was appointed head of product development and management for Russell's U.S. private client services business, at which time he formed the capital markets insights group. Its charter is to keep advisors informed of Russell's viewpoints on a broad range of investment research, economic and market environment, product and client service topics. In addition to those duties, he also frequently represents Russell at client and industry events and with the media. He came to Russell from the Lotus Development Corporation in 1991.

Matt Smith is a consultant and author of two other Wiley Finance books, *Managing Your Firm's 401(k) Plan: A Complete Roadmap to Managing Today's Retirement Plans* (2010), and *The Retirement Plan Solution: The Reinvention of Defined Contribution* (Ezra, Collie, Smith, 2009).

Matt was formerly senior vice president and defined contribution practice leader in the United States for Aon Consulting. Prior to Aon, Matt was managing director of retirement services for Russell Investments.

Matt has been involved with design, implementation, administration, consulting, and asset management of retirement plans for over 28 years. He has written and spoken widely on topics involving retirement plans during his career. Matt lives and works in the Seattle, Washington area.